Commonwealth and Independence in
Post-Soviet Eurasia

Of Related Interest

Companion volume:

CONFLICTING LOYALITIES AND THE STATE IN POST-SOVIET RUSSIA AND EURASIA
edited by Michael Waller, Bruno Coppieters and Alexei Malashenko

Contents: Introduction; 1. Form and Content in Soviet and Post-Soviet Nationality and Regional Policies *Bruno Coppieters*; 2. Ethnic Conflicts in Ukraine *Natalia Lakiza-Sachuk*; 3. Conflicting Loyalties in the Crimea *Natalia Belitser and Oleg Bodruk*; 4. The Kaliningrad Region of Russia in a New Geographical Setting *Yuri Zverev*; 5. Qualified Sovereignty: The Tatarstan Model for Resolving Conflicting Loyalties *Alexei Zverev*; 6. Tajikistan I: The Regional Dimension of Conflict *Aziz Niyazi*; 7. Tajikistan II: The Regional Conflict in Confessional and International Context *Said Akhmedov*; 8. Russian Nationalism and Islam *Alexei Malashenko*; 9. Soviet Religious Policies in Central Asia, 1918–30 *Mustafo Bazarov*; Conclusions: Conflicts of Loyalty in the Soviet Union and Its Successor States *Michael Waller and Alexei Malashenko*; Notes on Contributors; Index.

SOCIAL DEMOCRACY IN A POST-COMMUNIST EUROPE
edited by Michael Waller, Bruno Coppieters and Kris Deschouwer

THE SOVIET TRANSITION: FROM GORBACHEV TO YELTSIN
edited by Stephen White, Rita di Leo and Ottorino Cappelli

BEYOND STALINISM: COMMUNIST POLITICAL EVOLUTION
edited by Ronald J. Hill

PARTY POLITICS IN POST-COMMUNIST RUSSIA
edited by John Löwenhardt

POST-COMMUNISM AND THE MEDIA IN EASTERN EUROPE
edited by Patrick O'Neil

PARTIES, TRADE UNIONS AND SOCIETY IN EAST-CENTRAL EUROPE
edited by Michael Waller and Martin Myant

HUNGARY: THE POLITICS OF TRANSITION
edited by Terry Cox and Andy Furlong

HUNGARY 1956 – FORTY YEARS ON
edited by Terry Cox

Commonwealth and Independence in Post-Soviet Eurasia

edited by
BRUNO COPPIETERS,
ALEXEI ZVEREV and
DMITRI TRENIN

FRANK CASS
LONDON • PORTLAND, OR

First published in 1998 in Great Britain by
FRANK CASS PUBLISHERS
900 Eastern Avenue
London IG2 7HH

and in the United States of America by
FRANK CASS PUBLISHERS
c/o ISBS
5804 N.E. Hassalo Street
Portland, Oregon 97213-3644

Website: http://www.frankcass.com

British Library Cataloguing in Publication Data

Commonwealth and independence in post-Soviet Eurasia
1. Regionalism – Former Soviet republics 2. Former
Soviet republics – Politics and government 3. Former
republics – Foreign relations
I. Coppieters, Bruno II. Zverev, Alexei III. Trenin, Dmitri
320.9'47

ISBN 0-7146-4881-7 (cloth)
ISBN 0-7146-4480-3 (paper)

Library of Congress Cataloging-in-Publication Data

Commonwealth and Independence in post-Soviet Eurasia / Bruno
Coppieters, Alexei Zverev and Dmitri Trenin.
    p.   cm.
Includes bibliographical references and index.
ISBN 0-7146-4881-7 (cloth) ISBN 0-7146-4480-3 (paper)
    1. Former Soviet republics – Politics and government. 2. Former
Soviet republics – Ethnic relations. I. Coppieters, Bruno.
II. Zverev, Alekseĭ. III. Trenin, Dmitriĭ Vital'evich.
DK293.C656   1998
947.086–dc21   97-49408
                                                                      CIP

Printed in Great Britain by
Creative Print and Design (Wales), Ebbw Vale

Contents

A Note on Transliteration

Any work in English dealing with Central Asia encounters a major problem of transliteration. In the presentation of names we have adopted a number of principles which take consistency as the overriding consideration:

1. Since all the states and regions covered in the text were part of the Soviet Union and still all use the Cyrillic script, we have used one of the standard forms of transliteration from Cyrillic into English-language texts – that of the US Board of Geographic Place Names – whatever the cultural derivation of the name (Russian, Turkic or Arabic in the most prominent examples).
2. The text deviates from this rule in one respect, the letter *j* being used in preference to the conventional *dzh* (Tajikistan, Khojent).
3. Words current in Islamic usage and stemming in large part from Arabic or Iranian sources are italicized and presented in a standard transliteration from the Arabic.

This problem of transliteration is compounded by the process of change that has affected the entire post-Soviet territory, since linguistic and orthographic forms have been caught up in the assertion of new identities, and a work addressing conflicts of loyalty cannot ignore them. As regards the *forms of the names* themselves, therefore, we have tried to be as sensitive as possible to the spirit of change. In the Ukrainian case we have used the Ukrainian forms of place names, adding the Russian variant in parenthesis when this is judged to aid comprehension in view of past usage.

Introduction[1]

DMITRI TRENIN

As the cold war in Europe was drawing to a close, the idea of repairing the continent, so that it might become 'whole and free', assumed an enormous power of attraction. With the division of Europe about to be overcome, prospects for new co-operation seemed virtually boundless. A common European home, complete with a new security architecture, was being sketched. The coming together of West and East was thought to be the first step towards the eventual, and speedy, integration of the continent.

In 1990, Germany was reunified. 1992 saw the signing of the Maastricht Treaty, offering the prospect of a European Union with a broader political agenda as regards financial and monetary integration, and common defence and security policies. Within this new Europe, which had just shed the barbed-wire borders in its eastern half, new regions were emerging, such as Central Europe, the Baltics and the Black Sea coastal area. The new regional groupings of states were believed to be able both to add colour to Europe's political and cultural landscape and to improve its economic performance. In Europe's east – along the eastern borders of Central Europe – the situation was the opposite. Towards the end of the USSR, many of those who called themselves Russian democrats were given to repeating a line from Lenin, which read, 'In order to unite more closely, we must first separate'. Whereas the Bolshevik leader had been concerned about the purity and cohesion of his party, the latter-day reformers were busy dismantling what the Tsars had founded and the Communists had preserved – that is, the Russian empire, alias the Soviet Union. Its dissolution, however, was not seen as an end in itself. True, to some the formula was quite simple or even simplistic: the USSR minus the Russian Federation equalled the end of Communism and the beginning of democracy, at least for Russia. The disintegration of the old superstructure would open the way towards a rearrangement of its constituent parts, which would ensure a healthier, and thus more lasting, form of integration.

The Russian democrats' genuine willingness to rid themselves of the Soviet Union was not to be explained, to be sure, simply by the idealistic expectations of 'a more perfect union', or even by the more mundane calculations of the cost of subsidizing other Soviet republics through the common budget. Setting the Baltic states free, recognizing the independence of Ukraine and abandoning Transcaucasus and Central Asia to their own fate was to have prepared the stage for reaching the radical Democrats' ultimate goal: Russia's speedy integration into the community of what was referred to, at the time, as 'the civilized countries', otherwise known as the West. Much smaller than the Soviet Union, the Russian Federation was more Slavic, taken to mean more European, and more Orthodox, meaning Christian. Ending the rule of the Communist Party was compared by some to overpowering a gang of hijackers who had managed to hold a vast country hostage for more than 70 years. Others, apparently more self-critical, talked about the return of a prodigal son who had repented of his sins committed under a Communist spell and could now rejoin the family of nations to which he had always belonged. In the autumn of 1991 – when the situation inside Russia was chaotic, currency reserves were at an all-time low and the major urban centres survived largely on Western humanitarian aid – Moscow's new leaders were talking loudly about a strategic alliance with the United States, membership of NATO and integration into the European Union.

The elites of other former Soviet republics, in particular in the Baltic and the Transcaucasus regions, had equally high expectations. To them, leaving the USSR also meant 'entering the world of civilized nations', but in an even more physical sense than for the Russian Federation. Having been actually cut off, by means of an impenetrable Soviet border, from their immediate neighbours, and constrained to deal with the outside world only through Moscow, they saw independence as an unmitigated blessing. The end of Soviet/Russian rule would open the way to more advantageous co-operation with others in the West and the East. Feeling unappreciated and ruthlessly exploited by Moscow, the newly independent states believed that they could only benefit from becoming fully-fledged members of the international community.

Several years on, many of these early expectations for a new Europe have failed to materialize. Germany is incorporating its new eastern Länder, but slowly. The Maastricht process is continuing, but not without serious problems. Europe has not become 'whole and free'. New divisions are emerging, even as some of the old ones are being successfully stitched up. The new states in the Baltics and Central Asia are placing emphasis on regional co-operation, and all look to Brussels, which is pondering the costs and complexities of NATO and EU enlargements. Russia has discovered that it is not a Western country, but otherwise is still seeking its new identity. Moscow has thus changed the focus of its foreign policy, and since 1993 has paid increasingly more attention to the CIS. Integrationist rhetoric has been louder than integrationist practice, but the Russian elites are serious about eventually dominating much of the former USSR. Where the West is concerned, all talk of an alliance has ceased, and even the much more modest strategic partnership appears too ambitious a goal for the time being.

Russia can probably not be integrated into something which is larger than itself, while over time it may regain a capacity to integrate others. Within the Russian elites, the debate between the Westernizers and the Eurasians is as heated as ever. After a brief interlude, a decision was made in 1996 that Russia would start constructing a power centre of its own, keeping 'equidistant' from the other international constellations.[2] Yet no return to the Communist/cold war past is possible, and even a smaller-scale confrontation with the West is not inevitable. Russia's search for a new identity is by no means unique. Europeans in the west and the centre have been asking, 'What is Europe? How far to the east does it reach?' In the absence of clear-cut political and military divisions, some refer to the cultural fault lines. The eastern border of Western Christendom – running along the eastern borders of Norway, Finland, the three Baltic states and Poland, between western and eastern Ukraine, along the eastern and southern borders of Hungary, Croatia's eastern and southern borders and the north of Greece – was suggested by some as the line where Europe's progressive integrationist movement will achieve its logical limit. Others disagreed, and were willing to push the line still further, to the external borders of the CIS. Still others included Ukraine. No one seriously nominated Russia.

From a standard Western point of view, Russia is at best only partly European. The obvious fact that the Russian Federation stretches all the way to the Chinese border, the Sea of Japan and the Bering Strait is used to demonstrate that Russia has important interests thousands of miles away from Europe, and cannot see itself as wholly European. This is putting it politely. In reality, although Russia's heartland does lie on the eastern marches of geographical Europe, and the Russians have been taking an active part in the political, economic and cultural affairs of Europe for the last three hundred years, the West has always seen Russia as 'in' rather than 'of' Europe. This view rests on an assumption that 'Europe' is essentially a Western concept, and that a non-Western Europe simply does not exist. Many Russian Westernizers would challenge that, but to no avail. The concept may have to change only if, at some point in the future, an economically recovered Russia (should this ever exist) is seen as an essential resource to be tapped by an expanded European Union in the latter's intensifying competition with the world's other economic power constellations. Then, and only then, a Greater Europe, which would include Russia, may emerge.

Other post-Soviet states, able at last to rejoin the adjacent regions, have resumed a long-standing tradition of looking for outside patrons. The old 'centre', that is, the Kremlin, is gone; long live the new ones. The West in general, and the United States in particular, have been invited to be arbiters, benefactors and protectors. NATO and the EU have been offered vast opportunities for intervention, which they declined, much to the dismay of their petitioners. Those who, like Turkey and Romania, have toyed with imitating Russia's 'near abroad' approach by reaching over the ex-Soviet border to their own ethnic brethren, have done less well, mainly for lack of proper resources. Perhaps of all newly independent states, Georgia presents the most interesting example of a nation whose well-educated elite yearns to be 'Western' but has been unable to change the country's political geography. Dreaming of being recognized as part of the West but having to live in Russia's shadow and on Turkey's doorstep may become an intellectual and practical ordeal. Ghia Nodia carefully and candidly analyses this predicament. The Georgian elites are not the only ones who would like to leave their precarious environments, but cannot. While some would still move away from Russia at any cost, others bitterly conclude that there is no alternative to finding some sort of accommodation with Russia.

Moscow's policies, however, complicate its neighbours' problems. Hard-pressed Russia is currently practising integration on the cheap. It no longer rules or even controls other CIS states, but neither does it subsidize them as the Soviet Union used to.

An analysis of Western European policies towards the peripheral states is provided by Bruno Coppieters, who, too, uses Georgia for his case study. He frankly states that, where the ex-USSR is concerned, the West regards only the Balts – that is, Protestant Estonia and Latvia and Catholic Lithuania – as its own. These three nations can hope to become members of the European Union one day. On the other hand, no CIS state can be integrated into the EU in the foreseeable future. This is not to suggest that these states are about to be abandoned, or relegated to the Russian sphere of influence, but the amount of attention they are going to get from the West will be limited by the West's own interests, which are real, and sometimes important, but usually less than vital. Ukrainian geopolitics and Caspian Sea oil stand out as the most prominent.

After the failure of the early pro-Western model, Russia's problem has been to decide what sort of relationship with the West is both desirable and realistic. It has been suggested by many observers that Moscow's policies in the CIS, and the West's reaction to them, as well as the West's own objectives in these newly independent states, will turn them into a functional equivalent of post-Second World War Eastern Europe. In the opinion of Dmitri Trenin, this does not have to be so. Competition and occasional rivalry notwithstanding, Russia and the West, he argues, have no fundamental conflict of interest regarding the crises in the former USSR.

The instability ushered in by the end of the cold war, the collapse of Communism and the demise of the USSR has been felt most acutely in the territory of the ex-Soviet Union. The war in Chechnya claimed about 100,000 lives; the civil war in Tajikistan, at least 50,000. Although the conflicts in Nagorno-Karabakh, Ingushetia, North and South Ossetia, Abkhazia and the Dniester region of Moldova have been stopped, none is resolved. Just below the surface, tension exists in many other areas, including Crimea, northern Kazakstan and the Baltic states. Dealing with this instability has been a problem. Because of its obvious interest, but also by default, Russia has taken the lead, and has nearly monopolized peacemaking activities within the CIS. Moscow's policies, whether in war or in peace, however, evoke suspicions of its uneradicated neo-imperialistic ambitions. Domination? Use of force? Respect for Western values, such as human rights? Russia's actions certainly have important implications for Moscow's relations with the outside world, including the CIS, the West and the Muslim countries. They will also have a bearing on the nature of the political regime in Russia itself.

On the other hand, the various degrees of interest which the USA, Europe, China, Turkey and the Islamic states have started paying to the newly independent republics of the former USSR have aroused Russian suspicions. Fears are expressed about the possible use of Ukraine as a bulwark against a potentially resurgent Russia, and a counterweight to it within the CIS; about the Baltic states being included within the NATO defence perimeter, and turned into a Western point of pressure against Russia; about oil and gas exploration in the Caspian Sea basin being taken over, and Russia left out in the cold as regards transportation routes; about pan-Turkism and Islamic fundamentalism being used to undermine Russia's positions on the periphery of its borders and to threaten the unity and integrity of the Russian Federation itself.

In reality, while conflicts of interest between Russia and the West clearly do exist, they are not of a fundamental nature. Claims about the 'opposition from certain quarters in the West to integrationist processes in the territory of the CIS, in order to prevent the formation of a powerful centre in the new post-Cold War multipolar world'[3] must not be treated uncritically. There is no sign of a Great Game II in the offing. On the contrary, there is a fair amount of common ground when it comes to the need to stabilize and progressively resolve the conflicts which have already erupted, and to prevent those which are simmering beneath the surface. If Russia, the United States and Western Europe are careful enough not to create wrong impressions about each other's true objectives, the former Soviet Union will not become a latter-day equivalent of post-Second World War Eastern Europe.

It is more difficult to reach this level of understanding with the regional and local players. Ghia Nodia's analysis of Georgian attitudes towards Russian policies is very revealing in this respect. Elsewhere, too, both Moscow's peacemaking and its integrationist policies are often dubbed imperialistic. The Caucasus is a prime example. Western lack of interest and Russia's self-serving interventionism have helped to revive the old idea of co-operation across the region, known as the Caucasian Home. A region so small but so diverse should be treated as one whole, otherwise none of its problems can be resolved. This is a widely shared belief. Reference is usually made to the Mountain Republic in the Northern Caucasus (1918–20), stretching from the Black Sea to the Caspian, and the Transcaucasian Socialist Federative Soviet Republic which existed from 1922 to 1936. Hrant Avetisian, however, cautions that in an area traditionally coveted by powerful neighbours, even the idea of regional co-operation could become a screen for great-power ambitions. That the Caucasus is a buffer is a given. The question is, whose buffer? When Russia was weak in the aftermath of the Bolshevik revolution and the resulting civil war, Turkey attempted to act as a patron *vis-à-vis* the nominally independent states to the north-east of its borders. Does the dissolution of the USSR now present it with a similar opportunity? Pan-Turkic pronouncements by the late President Turgut Ozal in the early 1990s and the arrival of the Islamist Welfare Party to power in Turkey in 1996 have favoured the integration of Armenia with Russia on defence matters.

A different view of the Caucasian Home is presented by Rafig Aliev, who concentrates on the Northern Caucasus. An overarching structure bringing together both the territorial entities and the many ethnic and religious communities of the region, represented by their nominal and traditional leaders, appears to be the best forum for dealing with the prevention and resolution of disputes. Indeed, the Confederation of the Mountain Peoples of the Caucasus (KGNK) repeatedly offered itself as a vehicle for solving the conflict in Chechnya. The Russian government is known to have toyed with the idea of turning Pyatigorsk, a famous spa in the area, into a 'Caucasian Geneva' for untying the region's many knots. A regional summit was held in June 1996. The results, so far, have been meagre. In reality, Moscow's approach is characterized by very traditional geopolitics, of which Chechnya is the crudest example. Memories of both the Caucasus war of the nineteenth century and the Soviet Union's Afghan war are easily evoked.

The two examples of federations notwithstanding, the other states in the region show little willingness to co-operate more closely. There is no real tradition of this. The Transcaucasian Federal Soviet Socialist Republic was a communist creation which was to have smoothed the process of the integration of Armenia, Azerbaijan and Georgia into the USSR. The way the Karabakh and Abkhazian issues were dealt with in the 1920s and 1930s prove clearly that the federation was a prime means of control for Moscow, and little else. The existence of the Mountain Republic, in the midst of civil war and foreign intervention, was extremely ephemeral. There was little intra-regional interaction in the Soviet years. Each local elite had a separate, and competitive, relationship with the centre, which had learned to use these rivalries as a means of control. With the conflict just beneath the surface, but never publicly discussed (it is a widely known fact that the Armenian and Azeri Communist party secretaries did not talk to each other at national party gatherings in Moscow), the Soviet Union had no tools at its disposal for addressing the nationalities crisis when it erupted and overwhelmed it. As for the local elites, instead of preventive measures, they often used the ethnic issue in the struggle for getting or preserving power.

Can this change? Despite all the professions of Caucasian unity, it does not appear likely, for the time being. The three states in Transcaucasus tend to use their available levers (oil for Baku, the personal connections of president Eduard Shevardnadze for Tbilisi and diaspora connections for Yerevan) to mobilize foreign support. Whether the conflicts in the Caucasus can best be settled by those immediately affected is an open question. In this respect, the role of the nearer neighbours is often emphasized. Dagestan and Ingushetia, in the case of Chechnya. Georgia, in the case of the Karabakh conflict.

Alexander Kukhianidze poses the broader question of the foreign policy strategy for a country jammed between a Russian-led and a Turkish-dominated alliance. Georgia, in his view, occupies a pivotal position at one of the world's most difficult geopolitical crossroads. This raises the general problem of countries claiming to serve as 'bridges'.

The Caucasus, to be sure, is not the only area where intraregional co-operation would be welcome. Central Asia is another obvious candidate. The Baltic states, which have been competing for the attention of the Western countries and institutions, are learning to do business together in such fields as economic, security and defence co-operation. To all of them, however, near neighbours, rather than a source of stability or investment, remain secondary or at best supplementary partners. This phenomenon may also be observed elsewhere in Europe. The Visegrad Group, despite all the free advice from the outside, consciously rejected the idea of forming a Central European Union and opted for the fastest possible integration into Western structures such as NATO and the European Union. The idea of a Baltic–Black Sea association, initially advanced by Ukraine, found no takers. The countries of South-Eastern Europe, such as Bulgaria, Serbia/Montenegro and Macedonia, which are all unlikely to become members of either NATO or the EU for many years, if ever, prefer to deal more with Brussels than with their immediate neighbours.

The grand design of some politicians and geopolitical philosophers, of uniting the vast area to the east of the line dividing eastern and western Christianity, appears doomed from the start. The only regional associations which were set up in Europe after the double collapse of Communism and the USSR, that is, the Council of the Baltic Sea States and the Black Sea Economic Co-operation Council, may owe their limited success to the participation of Western states (which in the latter case means Greece and Turkey).

Last but not least, there is the question of the prospects for the CIS. In the recent past, some have feared that it was heading for a Soviet Union Mark II. Many Russian officials have talked about an EU model for post-Soviet integration, while a number of experts dismiss this idea by saying that the most it can be is a messier version of the British Commonwealth or the French Communauté. In short, most observers tend to blame the CIS for something it was clearly unable to accomplish, while failing to appreciate its very real contribution to the relative smoothness, so far, of the still to be completed process of dismantling the USSR. The CIS has been and remains, above all, a form of transition from the unitary Soviet super-state to national statehood. In 1991, none of the republics, not even Russia, was ready for independence or complete separation. Only the three small Baltic states, thanks to their history of sovereignty and the very real assistance which they were getting from the West, had some head start. The others, despite all their pro-independence rhetoric, needed the CIS as a necessary support on the road to independence.

The most visible aspect of the CIS is the regular summit meetings of the leaders of the new states. The existence of this top-level 'club', especially in the situation where normal diplomatic contacts were slow in developing, was instrumental in keeping the lines of communication open and preventing crises – for example, between Russia and Ukraine – which might otherwise have occurred. While for the leaders the CIS has become practically reduced to the conference hall in the President Hotel in the centre of Moscow, which since 1994 has served as the venue for their meetings, their publics appreciate visa-free travel within the Commonwealth and the remaining ex-USSR infrastructure. To the vast majority of former Soviet citizens, the arrival of the CIS has substantially softened the blow which they suffered with the sudden collapse of the USSR.

Thus the CIS is to be commended for the remarkably civilized way in which the 'divorce proceedings' among the Soviet successor states have worked out. Not one of the twelve states of the Commonwealth has lost its newly-acquired independence, or succumbed in a domestic conflict, although Georgia came close to that in 1992–93, and Tajikistan is not yet out of the danger zone. In contrast to that, the CIS as a means for post-Soviet integration has been a spectacular failure. This is not for any want of trying. There is no shortage of solemn decisions aimed at promoting closer interaction within the CIS. Kazakstan's President Nursultan Nazarbaev even proposed, in 1994, a plan to create a fully-fledged Eurasian Union. It took about four years, however, to realize that integration at twelve was unrealistic to expect, at least in the foreseeable future. Russia opted for creating a 'nucleus' within the Commonwealth, consisting of itself, Belarus, Kazakstan and Kyrgyzstan. A treaty establishing a customs and payments union of these states was signed in 1996. An even closer union was envisaged, in 1996 and 1997, between Russia and Belarus.

Russia, of course, is viewed as the driving force behind this integration. However, Moscow's capacity for paying the inevitable costs of integration remains extremely limited. Even for the least controversial case of Belarus, the immediately available resources fall short of requirements. Concentration on Belarus as a prospective partner in a new confederacy with Russia has led to less attention being paid by Moscow to Almaty and Bishkek. The latter two have little option but to move closer together, to parallel in a way the Russo-Belarussian union. Needless to say, the Central Asian integrationists experience an even greater lack of resources than their Eastern European partners.

In 1991, the last hope of re-forming the USSR as a federation was destroyed by the Ukrainian independence referendum. At the same time, it was long considered essential for any real integration in the post-Soviet space to include an element of free co-operation between Ukraine and Russia. This issue is taken up by Sergei Vlasov. Relations between the two Slavic countries have not been faring too successfully since the break-up of the USSR, even if the possibility of an open conflict has been avoided. There is little prospect of a fundamental improvement in their relations until Kyiv feels confident enough that Ukrainian independence has been firmly established, and Moscow fully internalizes the fact that 'old Russia' is finally gone.

Meanwhile, bottom-up economic co-operation can create strong and natural ties between Russia and Ukraine, adding to stability in the new Eastern Europe, but it is unlikely to lead to a political merger of the two countries, as in the case of Belarus. Across the former USSR, the real integrators will mostly be the likes of Russia's Gazprom and LUKoil, rather than the governments. Eventually, this may pave the way for a common economic space embracing Russia, Belarus, probably Kazakstan and possibly Ukraine. Of these, only Belarus, however, can join Russia in a confederacy of some sort.

There is thus considerable potential for interaction involving the post-Soviet states in all the main areas: (a) towards an expanded Western Europe, and an eventual Greater Europe; (b) new Euroregionalism; and (c) between Russia and her neighbours. At the same time, because of the real problems and serious limitations existing at all three levels, this potential cannot be realized until well into the next century.

NOTES

1. This study is one of two volumes that have resulted from a collective research project financed by INTAS (International Association for the Promotion of Cooperation with Scientists from the Independent States of the Former Soviet Union). The editors would like to thank Veronica Kelly, Alexei Zverev and Rachel Clogg for the translation of the contributions and the language corrections of the contributions. The companion volume is entitled *Conflicting Loyalties and the State in Post-Soviet Russia and Eurasia*, and is edited by Michael Waller, Bruno Coppieters and Alexei Malashenko (London: Frank Cass, 1998).

2. See, for example, *The National Security Policy of the Russian Federation (1996–2000)*, approved by presidential decree in June 1996.

3. See, for example, the speech by Russian foreign minister Yevgeni Primakov to the Russian ambassadors in the CIS states: *Segodnya*, 30 July 1996.

1

The Georgian Perception of the West

GHIA NODIA

Georgian political developments during the years of the fight for independence from the then Soviet Union (1988–91), and its struggle to build up new state institutions and maintain its independence *vis-à-vis* the neo-imperial cravings of Russia, are difficult to understand without a rather vague concept which has always been in Georgian minds: 'the West'. Once independent political movements began to emerge, thanks to the liberalization of the political regime under Gorbachev, new political elites began to conceptualize Georgia's position in the modern world and the policy choices open to it. This work of understanding took place in an imagined space constituted by two dimensions: Russia and the West. It was assumed that the question of 'political orientation' could be reduced to a simple choice: Russia or the West. The division of parties and politicians into 'pro-Western' and 'pro-Russian' continued to override all other principles in defining political agendas.

I said 'imagined space', although both Russia and the West are quite real and each of them (especially the former), and their interactions, have played an important role in determining post-communist political developments in Georgia. Nevertheless, the following chapter will deal predominantly with perceptions, inasmuch as they guided the behaviour of players on the Georgian political scene. By definition, perceptions differ from reality, but in the Georgian case, given that the new political elites had very limited knowledge of the real West and real mechanisms of international politics, the distance between the two was even greater than usual.

The following analysis distinguishes between two major paradigms upon which the perception of 'the West' has been based throughout this period. One is that of identity; another, closely related to it, is the idea of a 'patron'. One has to do with answering the question 'who are we?' or 'where do we belong?'; the other concerns political strategy in the modern world. It goes without saying that the two aspects were closely intertwined. Political choices relating to internal life, whether political or economic, were considered to be derivatives of this more 'fundamental' issue.

Origins of Georgia's 'Pro-Western Orientation'

In recent centuries, the identity of Georgia (as represented by the cultural and partly political elite) has been determined by the idea 'we do not belong here'. This has meant that, although throughout the medieval period Georgia had been politically involved in the Muslim – and in particular Arab, Persian and Turkish – worlds, and became part of the Russian empire in 1801, all this was considered to be happening against its will and, no less importantly, against its deep sense of identity. Georgia was just unlucky enough to have the wrong neighbours. Hence there had to be some cultural and/or geographical reference point, a 'centre of goodness and hope', against which the wrongness of the bad neighbours could be highlighted. In 'reality', Georgia 'belonged' to this centre of goodness; so only when it had established proper links with this centre would it be able to be its true self. For the Georgian elite since the nineteenth century, this centre of goodness and true self has been represented by the West, or Europe (these two terms – 'the West' and 'Europe' – have for the most part been used interchangeably in Georgia, with distinctions between the European and American models of 'westernness' dismissed as a minor detail). This implied that the basic Georgian project was to build bridges to the West, and to become westernized itself – which at the same time was seen as returning to its true self.

This identity paradigm was, however, linked to another, more practical one: the search for a proper patron. Georgia did not just happen to have the wrong neighbours: its neighbours were much more powerful, and at the same time expansionist. In the eleventh and twelfth centuries, the Georgian kingdom controlled the territory between the Black and Caspian Seas, and could be defined in today's terms as a respected regional power (and a small empire, which included modern-day Armenia, Azerbaijan and part of Turkey). After Georgia was crushed by the Mongols at the beginning of the thirteenth century, however, its history up to nineteenth century was one long struggle for survival, in which Georgia was alone in facing Turkey and Iran's determination to dominate it. Its strategy in this struggle was to play one expansionist neighbour off against the other. The country was reasonably successful in this. It maintained its identity (which was then marked primarily by Christianity, but also by its language), and was for the most part ruled by Georgian kings (although these were dispersed between several princedoms, whose rulers had to make their own arrangements with the Ottoman and Persian empires). The price of this relative success, however, included the permanent strain of warfare, periodical devastating invasions, and being doomed to 'backwardness' (that is, isolation from the trends of modernity). This is why an alternative strategy, that of looking for a proper patron, emerged over time.

The choice of a patron naturally had to be legitimized by the definition of identity. Of course, Georgia's identity was Christianity, and its function or mission was soon to be conceptualized as being an 'outpost of Christianity' commissioned by Providence to maintain it in the region (the Caucasus) in the fight against the Muslims who wanted exactly the opposite: to wipe out Christianity by islamizing the region. This uneven struggle could not last forever. Sooner or later, the 'big' Christian world was supposed to come to Georgia's rescue. In practice, however, a particular power, not 'Christianity' in general, would have to come forward as a saviour. Throughout the late medieval period, the Georgians considered Russia, their northern neighbour, to be the most natural candidate for this role: it was close, and it was not only Christian in general, but fellow-Orthodox. There is a history of the attempts which the Georgian kings undertook to establish links with Russia in order to find protection in their struggle against their all-too-strong Muslim neighbours. Until the end of the 18th century, however, Russia was not interested, since its empire had yet to reach the region, and its more urgent priorities lay elsewhere. Not until the late eighteenth century had it expanded enough to put the Caucasus on its immediate agenda. In 1783, a treaty was signed between Russia and Georgia (or, more precisely, Eastern Georgia), following which Georgia conceded its sovereignty in international relations to Russia in exchange for protection from Iran. The throne, the centrepiece of Georgian political identity, had to be maintained. The Russian vision of its patronage, however, differed dramatically from what Georgia had been expecting. In 1795, Russia did nothing to protect the country from the most devastating invasion by Iran, which had in fact been provoked by the above treaty. Ever since, Georgians have had a bitter suspicion that Russia did this intentionally in order to weaken Georgia even further and make it easier to do what it did later, in 1801: simply annex Georgia unilaterally, adding another province to its empire.

So the patron came, but the manner of its doing so was a great disappointment. Russia did bring peace, and it did guarantee the maintenance of Georgia's Christian identity. It also unified the dispersed Georgian princedoms under its umbrella, and with the milder policies of some of its namestniks (local governors appointed by the Tsar) it even promoted the Georgian culture.[1] But it deceived Georgia by taking away its political identity, and ultimately threatening its cultural identity too, through policies of Russification. As a result, the Georgian elites have developed a deeply ambivalent attitude to Russia, which has survived to the present day. On the one hand, the Georgians appreciated Russia's role in ensuring the 'physical survival' of the nation (which was believed to be endangered by continuous devastating warfare), in helping it escape the influence of the Muslim world (which was regarded as not just culturally alien, but also 'backward'), and in bringing the country closer to modernity. On the other hand, they saw in Russia an enemy to their freedom and a threat to their identity. An anti-Russian conspiracy in 1832 by a group of young Georgian nobles (who were arrested before they had had a chance to act) was the first expression of this protest.

Until the nineteenth century, the idea of the West had played only a peripheral role in Georgian political discourse. Strategic thinking moved within the Russia–Iran–Ottoman Empire triangle. In geographical terms, the issue of fundamental orientation would be more adequately represented in the North–South dimension: Christian North, Islamic South. There was, however, an episode in Georgia's history in the early eighteenth century which is quite reminiscent of the 'pro-Western orientation' of recent years. Then, a Georgian writer and lexicographer, Sulkhan-Saba Orbeliani, led the movement to convert Georgia to Catholicism in the hope that Western countries would provide better protection for a Catholic Georgia. He even paid a visit to Louis XIV, though without success.

At home, Orbeliani was ostracized by the Orthodox clergy. A couple of Catholic villages in southern Georgia remain, however, as a reminder of the possibility of Georgia's confessional westernization. Later, Sulkhan-Saba kept his place as one of the heroes in the national pantheon, despite the fact that his idea failed to gain many followers. In this century, in the 1960s, poet Mukhran Machavariani (later an active supporter of the first Georgian president, Zviad Gamsakhurdia) turned the story of Orbeliani's visit to the indifferent French king into a popular ballad, symbolizing how the West neglects Georgia's appeals for protection.

Once new generations of Georgian intellectuals were exposed to modern Western political thought through their studies in Russian universities, they shared the general preference of the Russian intelligentsia for liberal ideas. The path of Western liberalism, however, was eventually to fork in two. A larger part of the Georgian elite followed the evolution of Russian liberals to different versions of socialism, establishing their own contacts with the Western left and gaining positions of influence in all-Russian socialist movements. Niko Nikoladze, the first figure of prominence within this trend, had meetings with Karl Marx himself. But there was another option too, which never developed in Russia proper: that of Western liberal nationalism. Georgians began to acquire the modern Western paradigm of nationhood, taking Western nationalist movements as role models. Ilya Chavchavadze, a prominent public figure, writer and banker, became the spiritual leader of the Georgian national revival. Before the Russian revolution of 1917, however, Chavchavadze's liberal nationalism failed to dominate political discourse. Nationalists, who formed a minority among educated Georgians, were still too few and too timid to put forward slogans demanding full independence. Their agenda was centred on the preservation of their cultural identity; only at the beginning of the twentieth century did they begin to advance claims for autonomy within the borders of the Russian Empire.

Thus, despite the rise of cultural nationalism, most Georgian intellectuals did not differ much from their Russian counterparts in showing preference for socialist ideas. There was no separate Georgian socialist party, and most socialists did not initially support any nationalist ideas. One can say – as many Georgians do – that, by choosing the socialist ideology, Georgian intellectuals followed their Russian counterparts; but they only joined the pro-Western trend within the Russian intelligentsia. Being pro-Western did not imply moving away from Russia, and vice versa. Unlike in Russia, there was no nativist anti-Western backlash like the 'Slavophile' movement.

The Bolshevik revolution brought a rift. Bolshevism was a Russian heresy opposed to the mainstream of Western social democracy. Whether or not this potential was detected in the beginning, the Bolsheviks eventually built on this heresy the stronghold of a new anti-Western civilization. By refusing to accept the Bolshevik coup and choosing loyalty to the classic Western version of social democracy, the Georgian social democrats in practice opted to follow the West against Russia. Paradoxically, it was they (so often reproached by the nationalists for neglecting the 'national question' – that is, not putting national independence on the agenda) who were destined not only to lead the first independent Georgian republic, but also to create the modern paradigm of the country's political orientation. After declaring independence in May 1918, they also looked for guarantors of this independence in the West (Germany, Great Britain). In the end, Georgia made a choice in favour of Germany rather than Britain, because Germany took more interest in Georgia and seemed to be winning the war. This proved to be a miscalculation; but more importantly, a new paradigm was born: by the logic of its internal development, Georgia tended to flee from the totalitarian Russia and strove to become part of the democratic West. The latter was to provide security guarantees for its independence and democracy against the imperial yearnings of Russia. Georgia's struggle to obtain membership of the League of Nations was a major part of its effort to obtain these guarantees. In 1921, when Red Russia regained Georgia by military force, the West failed to help. However, it had been expected to do so, and – although the Georgians were not entirely confident about it – this expectation became a constant element in Georgian political thinking.

It was at this period that the ideology of Georgian cultural psychological 'westernness', as opposed to the Asiatic-despotic nature of Russia, began to gain ground. According to this view, Georgian individualism and love of freedom was something which contrasted sharply with Russian collectivism, egalitarianism and traditions of slavery, thus making Georgia's political subordination to Russia conflict with the Georgian national personality.[2] Under communism, Georgians – understandably – had no great opportunities for taking political action or building bridges to the West. The idea that Georgia intrinsically belongs to the West, while Russia does not, continued to develop. Clearly, it could not openly dominate public discourse, and Georgia did not have a dissident movement strong enough to make much impact on the wider public. But the milder repression of independent thought in the post-Stalin period allowed the idea of intrinsic Georgian westernness to become quite influential among intellectuals and – as became evident later – it was this idea that provided the ideological foundation for at least one strong trend in the anti-communist opposition movement.

The thesis of Georgia's intrinsic westernness found its basis in research by Georgian historians, such as Ivane Javakhishvili, Niko Berdzenishvili and Simon Janashia, later developed by newer generations of historians.[3] These described the socio-economic evolution of Georgian society in the medieval period, or the period of Georgian feudalism, which in their interpretation continued from the first century well into the nineteenth. Writing under Stalin, these scholars were unable to show parallels with Western research or draw conclusions about an affinity between the Georgian and Western medieval societies. These parallels were drawn by their disciples working in the post-Stalin period. The latter claimed that, until the Georgian Golden Age in the eleventh and twelfth centuries, the evolution of Georgian society betrayed striking similarities to the 'classic feudalism' of central and eastern France. This was called 'parallel evolution', with the Georgian developments even preceding those in the West by one or two centuries. The features in question comprised private ownership of land (unknown in eastern despotisms), social structure, the existence of large feudal seigneuries with immunity, and so on.

After the twelfth century, however, the parallel lines went astray. In the West, the medieval system of serfdom began to deteriorate with the development of cities, trade, representative institutions, etc. In Georgia, some stirrings in the same direction at the end of twelfth century, which had been its Golden Age, caused a crisis in relations between the monarchy and the nobility, and it was in the middle of this crisis that the country failed to repel its first (and still not very powerful) invasion of Mongols. From then onwards, Georgian history went awry, with the country finding itself in a vicious circle: incessant invasions by Mongols, Persians and Turks left no chance for internal development, while the lack of this left the country backward and unable successfully to withstand the attacks. In the terminology of Berdzenishvili, the country found itself in periods of impasse (thirteenth to fifteenth centuries) and stagnation (sixteenth to seventeenth centuries). However, it was the old traces of 'westernness' – the Christianity and private ownership of land – that helped the country to succeed in keeping its separate identity even under this terrible pressure.

However familiar – or otherwise – intellectuals outside a narrow circle of medieval historians may have been with these theories, their very existence added validity to the 'pro-Western orientation', since history was believed to be the major source of awareness of identity. These theories did not necessarily imply a contrast between Georgian and Russian feudalism, but a number of Georgian intellectuals made the point that, while Georgia had a feudal system typologically close to the European one, the medieval system of social and economic relations in Russia was more despotic. The theory of a 'Georgian Renaissance' put forward by another Western-educated Georgian academic, Shalva Nutsubidze, who claimed that Renaissance ideas had developed in medieval Georgia even earlier than in Italy, was another notable expression of the same trend. This latter concept, however, was much less widely shared.

It is beyond the scope of this chapter (and beyond the field of expertise of this author) to evaluate the soundness of this or that historical hypothesis. They may be well based in historical reality, or represent wishful thinking. But in either case these studies provided a definite theoretical basis for the 'pro-Western orientation'. The particular importance of medieval studies for this propensity to present Georgia as intrinsically Western may be explained by the fact that, under communism, more open and modernity-oriented pro-Western forms of expression would have been punishable. But it also showed that more recent history provided less evidence to support the claim of Georgian westernness.

After Communism: The West as Dutiful Saviour

The 1918–21 period of independence did not appear to be enough to change dramatically the way Georgians perceived their political identity on the mass scale as well as on the elite level – unlike what

20 years of independence did to the Baltic nations. Georgians had no time to get used to living in an independent state, and there was no generation for which self-awareness as a citizen of Georgia was something natural. However, when the Georgian political mentality began to defrost after decades of communism, the paradigms acquired during the glimpse of political sovereignty came to dominate Georgian political discourse. The basic system of reference points remained unchanged: there was totalitarian Russia which had enslaved Georgia by sheer force and which wanted to maintain its deadly grip, again through force and conspiracy; and there was 'the West', the embodiment of freedom and fairness, which had to come to the rescue. It seemed that this new attitude represented merely a new version of the older paradigm. As in medieval times, Georgia was facing a force which wanted to dominate it, and was not strong enough to defend itself on its own. It still needed an ally, which really meant a patron. Russia had replaced the Muslim world in the role of hostile force keen to dominate Georgia, while the West took over the role that the same Russia had once played, that of a natural ally-cum-patron.

While Georgia's choices in the 'West versus Russia' dimension can be traced back to the situation that followed the Bolshevik revolution, the deeper and more paradigmatic conviction that Georgia had to be rescued from the cruel neighbour by a powerful and benign patron was definitely of medieval origin. Since the theory of the intrinsic westernness of Georgia was also, for the most part, based on medieval studies, this combination in the current policy of a declared 'pro-Western orientation' with an essentially medieval vision of international relations became a peculiar feature of Georgian political thinking for several years.

One inference of this conviction widely shared by the Georgian national movement, especially in its early stages, was that the West was morally obliged to help Georgia. First, the West should care about Georgia because the latter intrinsically belongs to the former; by caring about Georgia, the West cares about itself. Second, since in contrast to Russia the West was seen as an embodiment of fairness, by definition it was obliged to support just causes, and Georgia's claim to independence was clearly just. The West was seen as a fair arbiter powerful enough to impose its own judgment. If it failed to help Georgia, this was because certain (Western) leaders were bad, or because the West had to make temporary compromises with Russia, or it had its hands full with other problems. But the basic moral obligation was there, and the West was certainly expected at least to have sympathy with the Georgian causes – that is, independence and, later, territorial integrity.

This naive reliance on the West expressed itself in the fetishization of 'international law'. From its very beginning, the Georgian movement for national independence became dominated by the wing which called itself the 'irreconcilable' or 'radical' opposition. Being 'radical' did not mean legitimizing violent means of struggle (the radicals did indeed lead Georgia to years of turmoil and violence, but this violence was never really directed against the force considered to be the major enemy: imperial Russia). It implied the conviction that, since Georgia had been incorporated into the Soviet Union against its will, all the existing state institutions represented 'occupying powers', hence no co-operation with them (for instance, participation in officially held elections) was morally or politically acceptable, and no Soviet laws could be recognized as binding in any way. The independent Georgian republic of 1918–21, which had been recognized at the time by a number of great powers, was still considered to be a legally valid entity from the point of view of 'international law'. The strategy was, therefore, to build everything on this symbolically existing independence. Hence the first commandment in the philosophy of the radicals: not to do anything which would put this pure idea of 'independence recognized by international law' in doubt. The strategy of the popular fronts in the Baltic states – to come to power through 'Soviet elections' and then to promote the agenda of independence through institutions the legitimacy of which Moscow would not be able to deny – was for them despicable 'collaborationism', undermining the above sacrosanct principle.[4]

It is easy enough to criticize this position from the standpoint of political realism. Indeed, the 'irreconcilable' leaders hated to be asked: 'How do you really think you can gain independence?' For them, this question itself smacked of 'collaborationism'. Like many other radicals, they did not really mean to fight for particular political ends – in reality theirs was merely an infantile protest against the existing order. However, if the strategy of following exclusively 'international law' made any sense at all, it meant seeking help in the West. The radical movement was born out of Soviet dissident practices, in which the main point was to make your protest action seen by a Western reporter and to have it publicized in the Western media, and especially radios broadcasting to the Soviet Union (VOA, Radio Liberty, BBC, etc.) Since the Soviet authorities really did not like this kind of publicity, these tactics worked to a certain extent. Radical nationalists, by saying: 'We follow only international law, not Soviet law', were sending a double message to the West: not only 'We share the same values as you', but also 'You are obliged to support us', because what is the West about, if it does not try to enforce 'international law'? Actions of civil disobedience – the only legitimate means of struggle accepted by the radical opposition – were intended to undermine communist rule and, at least on the esoteric level of the 'irreconcilable' strategists, also represented moral pressure on the West: if we are resolute and ready for sacrifice, it is morally unacceptable of you not to intervene.

A round-the-clock peaceful mass rally at the beginning of April 1989, with radical pro-independence and anti-communist slogans, was the high point of the 'radicals'' crusade. The massacre perpetrated on 9 April by Soviet troops – who left 20 people, most of them women, dead – became a great moral victory for the 'irreconcilable' leaders and a turning-point in Georgia's fight for independence. It was here that the communist regime in Georgia lost its nerve and all the residues of its legitimacy, thus de facto handing over power to nationalist radicals. It also contributed towards delegitimizing the Soviet communist dictatorship in general: the public outcry after the Tbilisi massacre created what was later called the 'Tbilisi syndrome', that is, fear of using force against anti-communist and anti-Soviet movements. Initially, however, the organizers of the rally had only a vague idea of what they were going to do, or how long the rally should last. It was quite clear that what later became known as a 'velvet revolution' could not happen in Georgia as long as it was part of the Soviet Union, and even radical leaders of the demonstration had no illusions about that. Although the wave of pro-independence enthusiasm was dominating the city, many people expressed their doubts about whether the strategy behind the action had been sufficiently well thought through. Against this kind of criticism, there was the 'esoteric' rationale which was talked about among those initiated: shortly before the rally began, it had become known to the radical leaders that US senators Helms and Wilson had initiated hearings on the Georgian question, with a possibility of questioning the legitimacy of Georgia's incorporation into the USSR in 1921. The rally in Tbilisi was intended to support this cause, sending a message to American politicians that Georgians really felt occupied and forcibly annexed by communist Russia, and that in this regard their country was no different from the Baltic states.

Seeking and expecting protection from the West was not the only expression of Georgia's 'pro-Western orientation'. Georgia was supposed to borrow its basic models of state-building exclusively from the West, and the only model available appeared to be the democratic nation-state. It was taken for granted, that (1) Georgia had to be an independent country, since Georgians were a separate nation (if France or Romania, were independent, why not Georgia?) and (2) independent Georgia would be a free country with market economy (being intrinsically 'Western', it would become like other Western countries as soon as it got an opportunity to develop on its own). Neither issue ever became the subject of any serious public discussion. This does not mean that nobody entertained any doubts about the prospects for Georgian independence, or that the Georgian public was so deeply committed to democratic values. It was simply that there was no other language with which to express political values and aspirations. Once communism was rejected (in a general ideological sense, at least), there was no other reference point left except the modern West.

Gamsakhurdia: The First Disappointment

After independence, the general disposition of Georgian public opinion in favour of 'Western' democracy and a market economy was soon put to a rather severe test. 'Pro-Western' nationalists succeeded in setting the agenda, but real developments as they unfolded did not quite correspond to their vision of Western ideals. Major challenges came not from the communist/imperial 'centre', which appeared to be collapsing on its own, but from internal political dynamics, and in particular from the reaction of certain ethnic minorities (namely, the Abkhaz and the Ossetes) to the Georgian demand for independence, and from emerging rifts between different nationalist factions. The new elite tried to explain away both sets of problems by reducing them to Soviet-Russian provocation.

This claim was far from groundless, since the centre had a direct interest in encouraging internal conflicts in independence-minded republics, and the ability to do so. But, whether orchestrated from outside or home-bred (and there were elements of both), the challenges were there, and the Georgian elite failed to meet them. Soon, Georgia became an arena of continuous ethnic-territorial wars and civil unrest. This not only made life much worse for the citizens of an emergent new state and undermined the credibility of the national independence movement, but also ruined Georgia's international reputation. Not only did the West fail to meet its supposed obligation to offer support for the Georgian cause – it actually rejected this cause. It was not simply that Western politicians did not want to undermine Gorbachev by supporting nationalists: that applied to all independence-minded Soviet republics. Georgia received the most discrediting media coverage. Most Western publications (often reprinted in Georgia) described Georgian developments as bizarre, and the new political elite as something between insane and fascist. This was a real shock to Georgians, who felt bitterly misunderstood. At least for a while, they thought they were just failing to get their message through to the West, putting all the blame on the same Russia – or, at most, blaming their own lack of experience in waging a 'war of information'.[5]

The reign of Zviad Gamsakhurdia, the country's first post-communist president, became especially notorious. Although he was not a particularly consistent person in either ideas or behaviour, his sources of political ideas may definitely be described as 'Western'. In the 1970s, he had founded a Georgian Helsinki Group, a human rights organization. After becoming a president, he loved to be compared to General de Gaulle (as a strong democratic leader who unified the nation) and Václav Havel (as a dissident turned head of state). He had never questioned the principles of democracy and presented himself as their staunch supporter. On 6 January 1992, however, he had to flee the parliament building, which was being bombarded by rebels who were calling him a dictator and claimed to be democratic and pro-Western themselves. How committed to democracy the latter really were is another question, but most observers agreed that Gamsakhurdia's record as a democrat had been rather questionable.

His ethnic policies attracted especially harsh criticism abroad. A former human rights activist, he was well aware that citizenship rights in a democratic country must not depend on ethnic origin, and (contrary to some accusations) he never made 'Georgia for (ethnic) Georgians' a statement of his programme. He himself accused ethnic Abkhaz and Ossete separatists of 'apartheid' policies (and with good reason). His own political practice, however, smacked of exactly that. His real fervour expressed itself most strongly in general rhetoric against 'disloyal' minorities. The very existence of the ethnically-based autonomous units of Abkhazia and South Ossetia was indeed an explosive issue, but Gamsakhurdia's aggressive rhetoric and uncompromising stance contributed greatly to stirring it up. He displayed the same inconsistency in dealing with his political opposition: one day he would admit that the existence of the opposition in a democratic society was perfectly legitimate, only to say later (in an interview with CBS TV's '60 minutes' programme) that, since he was a democratically elected president (with 87% of the vote), the opposition had no right to criticize him. Anyone who actually opposed him he would brand a 'traitor to the nation' and 'agent of the Kremlin'.

Peculiar and bizarre personality that he was, Gamsakhurdia still accurately represented the general contradiction described above, between the general (and in a way sincere) admission of Western democratic principles and a very un-Western style of political behaviour. The period of the national independence movement which culminated in Gamsakhurdia's unfortunate rule exposed a deep gap between the nation's ideal self-image, which had developed when Georgia was denied any possibility of real action, and the modes of political behaviour real Georgians turned out to be capable or incapable of. Even those political skills which the nation had displayed in 1918–21 appeared to have been lost. Political thinking found itself in the realm of mythology rather than reality. The language in which newly emerging politicians tried to express themselves was a bizarre mixture of nineteenth-century nationalism and pidgin Soviet Marxism.

The collapse of the naive vision of Georgia's westernness and the ensuing identity crisis could lead different ways: either to a reconsideration of Georgia's identity through the development of a non-Western or anti-Western, nativist concept of Georgianness; or to an attempt at self-correction, a second effort to build bridges to the West. In the last phase of Gamsakhurdia's rule, when he felt finally abandoned by the West, some of his supporters did in fact begin to look in the nativist and fundamentalist directions. On the one hand, with Chechen separatist Dudaev becoming Gamsakhurdia's sole international friend, the idea of 'Iberian-Caucasian solidarity' ('Iberia' being an ancient name for Georgia) became the centrepiece of the ideology. This was based on the hypothesis of a tribal and linguistic kinship between the Georgians and a number of peoples from the Northern Caucasus (including Chechens, Abkhaz, Circassians and others, but excluding Turkic-speaking peoples and Ossetes, as well as Georgia's South Caucasian neighbours, the Armenians and Azeris). This idea, typologically reminiscent of nineteenth-century pan-Germanic or pan-Slavic movements, provided a certain alternative to Georgians' westernizing aspirations. It did not necessarily imply clear-cut anti-Western sentiment, but, with its cult of archaic tribal traditions, emotionally and psychologically it ran contrary to the Western liberal trends of the intellectual elite.

The second group which emerged within Gamsakhurdia's camp tried to anchor its ideology to a fundamentalist version of Eastern Orthodox Christianity, with most quotations coming from the vehemently anti-Western brand of Russian theologians at the beginning of the century. In their paranoid obsession with a worldwide Masonic conspiracy, they became little different from the nationalist Russians. They fell short of making declarations of direct solidarity with the latter – paradoxically, Russia continued to be an enemy for them too – but the focus of their resentment was the Russian westernizers who were actually in power, namely Gorbachev and Yeltsin. Their allegedly only ostensible rivalry was seen as part of the anti-Georgian conspiracy, supposedly masterminded by Eduard Shevardnadze, and including such figures as Bush, Baker and Genscher.

Both these trends undoubtedly bore a great potential for anti-Western sentiment. However, Gamsakhurdia and his followers were not consistent in that either. The above views have not died out to this day, but nor did they develop into any coherent anti-Western doctrine or movement. They provided a kind of emotional background, but never the basis of mainstream doctrine. Gamsakhurdia and his supporters always based their claims on the democratic legitimacy of the popularly elected president and government. Particular actions by Western governments, not Western principles, were the target of criticism. For instance, the US government was often criticized for applying double standards to Haiti and Georgia, two countries where popularly elected presidents were deposed by military insurgents. 'Masonic conspiracy' was understood quite narrowly, so the defeat of the hated Bush initially gave rise to hopes of the 'non-Masonic' Clinton, who would behave as a democratic American president should – that is, reject Shevardnadze's 'junta' and help the legitimate government to restore justice.[6] Even after the new administration failed to do this, the 'Zviadists' did not turn anti-Western. With the Zviadists still an influential force, if anti-Western sentiment is ever to increase in Georgia, their milieu might be quite susceptible to that trend. So far, however, one can only speak of trends, not of a doctrine or movement with any coherence or power.

Shevardnadze: The West as Failed Saviour

It is not easy to describe the ideology or political orientation of those who came to power in Georgia by overthrowing its controversial but legitimate leader. The coalition was probably kept together by nothing more than opposition to Gamsakhurdia and a shared belief that extreme methods were acceptable in getting rid of him. This sentiment united liberal intellectuals, pro-independence nationalists, the restoration-minded nomenklatura and romanticist criminals. Whatever interests and sentiments each of these various groups might have had, however, like all insurgents they needed a claim to legitimacy. In this case, the claim was based on the idea of democracy. The insurgence described itself as a popular rebellion for democracy against 'dictatorship' or, as Gamsakhurdia's regime was later labelled, 'parochial fascism'.

Once the domain of ideological slogans and name-calling has been relinquished, however, one has to remember that Gamsakhurdia was primarily undermined because of a split in his own camp. It was his former lieutenants who attacked him in the first place; they may have had different personal motives for defecting, but one of the most important political ones was that they saw him as a failure who had alienated the West, the only potential friend on whose support Georgia had pinned all its hopes of independence. Although the insurgence was directly led by Tengiz Kitovani, an artist turned military commander, all the other major defectors had dealt with foreign policy in one way or another: the prime minister, the foreign minister, the chairman of the parliamentary foreign affairs committee. These were the people who had first-hand knowledge of how Georgia was rejected by the West. And they thought, with good reason, that a country with a visiting card like Gamsakhurdia had no chance of ever being internationally accepted.

This explains why the insurgents chose to invite Eduard Shevardnadze, former communist leader of Georgia and foreign minister of the USSR, to take the position of leadership. Many former communist leaders were reinstated as leaders in post-communist countries, and Shevardnadze may be regarded as just another case (actually, one of the first) in this general trend. Benefiting from the feeling of popular nostalgia for the relatively orderly and affluent past, they brought with them an image of experienced leadership and stability after years of sweeping changes and, in some cases, turmoil. Gamsakhurdia described Shevard-nadze's comeback as a communist counter-revolution, and there was an element of truth in this: the communist nomenklatura welcomed this as at least a partial restoration of its legitimacy, while for a substantial part of the population he was a symbol of past (and hope of future) order and stability.

But with Shevardnadze it would be an oversimplification to reduce the rationale of his comeback to this element. Shevardnadze did not receive his power from the (nostalgic) people; he was invited, welcomed, or at least accepted by various political forces with an anti-communist and pro-Western stance. He was given less credit for being an experienced communist leader than for his contribution to destroying the communist regime. And the main reason why Shevardnadze was quite widely accepted as a leader of independent and non-communist Georgia was that he was believed to be the sole leader capable of successfully yoking Georgia to the West. This was not someone who would allow himself to be treated as Sulkhan-Saba Orbeliani had been by Louis XIV: modern democratic monarchs would not keep him waiting in their power parlours.

In Shevardnadze, the age-old hope of Western patronage found its near-perfect embodiment. This was a person who was not only widely known; he was somebody to whom the West must surely feel indebted for destroying its greatest enemy. The 'moral obligation' on the West to promote Georgian independence as a just cause was augmented by an obligation the West was under to Georgia's leader personally. In a political culture where the understanding of political alliances was based on a medieval vision of personal friendships between princes on the one hand and the communist experience of clientelist networks on the other,

Shevardnadze's international profile and reported personal friendship with Western leaders could not help but raise enormous – and unrealistic – expectations. In the words of one of his supporters, he was the only person in the whole of the Caucasus who could pick up the phone and call the American president in his office. One could not think of a more potent image of personal power. Thanks to Shevardnadze, Georgia was now a couple of phone calls away from freedom and prosperity.

The degree of naivety might vary from one Shevardnadze supporter to another, but his image as sole deliverer of Western recognition and assistance was the cornerstone of his otherwise shallow legitimacy. Without this, military leaders like Kitovani and Ioseliani would never have shared their power voluntarily with the shrewd schemer, the virtuoso of bureaucratic intrigues they knew him to be. But they felt it would be much, much easier to make the West accept their rule with Shevardnadze at the top, and they intended to keep him as the nominal leader of the country, in charge of foreign policy only. They understood that somebody like Shevardnadze would not readily agree to be simply their puppet, but they hoped that their control over the 'fighters for democracy' (that is, paramilitary groups now with official status) would be enough to keep his ambitions in check. And of course they would never have imagined that his ingratitude would one day go so far as to put both of them in jail. As frequently happens with followers of the Realpolitik school of thought, they tragically underestimated the legitimacy factor.

As soon as Shevardnadze came, he appeared to begin delivering on his promises. International luminaries like James Baker and Hans-Dietrich Genscher showed up, Western embassies began to open, Georgia became a member of the UN, Western humanitarian assistance started to flow in. If the priority was to build bridges to the West, Georgia was definitely lucky to have Shevardnadze. Indeed, the level of humanitarian assistance Georgia received from the West – especially the USA, Germany and the European Union – was quite high, and it was absolutely indispensable in enabling Georgia to live through tough times of anarchy and war. Shevardnadze's supporters could make a point of saying that, were it not for him, the level of help would be much lower (in any case, nobody could check this without removing him). However, this was not all that was expected. Humanitarian assistance was all very well, but what the West – the powerful and benevolent patron – was primarily supposed to do was to safeguard and guarantee the country's security *vis-à-vis* the major challenger – Russia.

To these expectations, the West – and Shevardnadze completely failed to live up. Georgian independence and integrity were indeed challenged by Russia – not directly, but through its almost open support for the separatist forces first in South Ossetia, then in Abkhazia. The war in Abkhazia, which began in August 1992 and ended in September 1993 with a crushing defeat for Shevardnadze's central government, was the most dramatic development in modern Georgian history. Georgia lost a sizeable part of its territory, hundreds of thousands of people became refugees, and it had to concede to pressure from Russia by joining the CIS and, later, legitimizing Russian military bases on Georgian territory – which was seen by many as effectively losing the country's sovereignty. The West did not help at all. Personified by United Nations observers, all it really did was to observe, leaving Georgia to cope with its problems alone.

What was the reason for this? Why did the West fail to help? Two schools of thought emerged, dominating Georgian political discourse in the period 1992–95: pro-Shevardnadze forces on the one hand and his nationalist, anti-Russian opposition on the other. From the perspective of the latter, the division was between 'pro-Western' and 'pro-Russian'. Shevardnadze was accused of being plainly pro-Russian and hence anti-Western. He had never finally buried his communist past (when he became famous for saying that, for Georgia, the sun rose in the North) – that is, he had never truly believed in Georgian independence. The West did not help Shevardnadze because he did not try hard enough to obtain its help. He never showed the West that he was unequivocally pro-Western, he never said that in fact it was Russia who was fighting Georgia in Abkhazia, and never asked the West to help Georgia against Russia. Shevardnadze's message to the West was never clear – that was why the West failed to grasp it or to react adequately.

Shevardnadze and his supporters, however, never agreed to being labelled pro-Russian. From their perspective, the real difference was between pragmatic realists (that is, themselves) and an irresponsible, incompetent and/or populist opposition. The West would not help because a new division of the world between super-powers had taken place, with the West informally regarding Georgia as being within the Russian zone of influence. It was on the recognition of this unfortunate reality that Georgia had to base its policies. The only thing that Georgia could do was to discriminate between two Russias: one good (that is, democratic, pro-Western) and one bad (reactionary, red-brown, communist). Georgia's only hope was that the 'good' Russia would prevail and that Georgians would succeed in befriending it. At the same time, it was privately recognized that, in practice, in their approach to Georgia the 'two Russias' did not differ greatly. But ostensibly at least, Georgia had to make a sharp distinction between them because this would play into the hands of the West. It was the West that, scared as it was of the increasingly popular red-brown reactionaries, supported Yeltsin no matter what. With the formula of the two Russias, Georgia pursued two aims: it tried to win the benevolence of the acting Russian government, and it sent a message of loyalty to the West saying: 'We are willing to join in your political game.'

In this sense, what appeared from the opposition's perspective to be a pro-Russian policy could, in fact, be presented as a basically pro-Western strategy. The policy of compliance with or appeasement of Russia had nothing to do with abandoning Western models of state-building or economic reform. In this, Russia could not be the alternative to the West, as it was keeping to the same guidelines in struggling to reform itself. Following suit to Russia was relatively acceptable insofar as Russia was democratic and pro-Western. In its relations with its northern neighbour, Georgia merely had to follow Western policies, and it was the West which was indeed pro-Russian: not undermining Russian democracy was the absolute priority for the West in its approach to the whole of the post-communist world, especially the Newly Independent States, and if this involved turning a blind eye to Russian expansionism in the Caucasus, thereby allowing neo-imperialists to let off some steam, then so be it. Shevardnadze's concessions to Russia, which included avoiding being too pro-Western, did nothing to undermine his stand with Western leaders.

Being 'Pro-Russian': An Aspect of Self-Denigration

However, to portray the 'pro-Russian' trend in Georgian politics as a purely pragmatic policy choice which did not really call into question the general pro-Western mood would be only partly accurate. The 'back to Russia' trend had a much deeper and more sincere aspect as well, and in this section I will try to analyse its roots and meaning. The difference between the 'pragmatic' and the 'sincere', however important, is more analytical. It was never articulated enough to lead to distinct political divisions, and it is not easy to distinguish clearly between the proponents of a pragmatic 'lesser evil' approach and those who had a genuine belief that 'we cannot make it without Russia'. The line was there, but it more often crossed individual souls, not just parties and groupings.

The real 'pro-Russian' (and potentially anti-Western) sentiment was based on the feeling of self-denigration. Several years of bitter divisions, chaos, evident political immaturity, images of moral degradation and the extremely sharp decline in the economic situation fostered serious doubts among Georgians concerning their own political and economic viability. Shevardnadze himself was clearly not immune from this sentiment. In September 1993, the worst nightmare period of post-communist Georgian statehood – when Shevardnadze faced the simultaneous escalation of the separatist war in Abkhazia, the insurgence by Gamsakhurdia's supporters in Western Georgia and the possible defection of Jaba Ioseliani with his Mkhedrioni, his major military support at the time – he said to a crowd of his followers that 'now he understood why Erekle wanted to sign a treaty with the Russians'. A couple of weeks after that, humiliated remnants of what was known as the 'Georgian army' had to flee Abkhazia together with the whole ethnic Georgian population, losing most of its arms to the pro-Gamsakhurdia militia (the 'Zviadists'), which controlled the territory between Abkhazia and the rest of Georgia. The Zviadists did not appear to be strong enough to gain final victory either. They were too much hated by too large a part of the population, and had tainted themselves by covert co-operation with the Abkhaz separatists in order to undermine Shevardnadze. The country was visibly falling apart.

Under the circumstances, Shevardnadze had to swallow his pride and accept Russia's help against Gamsakhurdia, just days after Russian-backed separatists had forced Georgians out of Abkhazia. Joining the CIS and further compliance with Russia's geopolitical aspirations was the price to be paid. After that, everything changed miraculously. The Russians did not even have to fight: the mere knowledge that they were now backing Shevardnadze, the sight of the tanks (passed on to the Georgian army, but reportedly driven by Russians) and especially the Russian Black Sea Fleet warships which came to the harbour at Poti, were enough to demoralize the Zviadists, thus ensuring swift, easy and final victory to the government troops. It might seem difficult to comprehend this effect today, now that the war in Chechnya has revealed the real capabilities of the Russian military. But at the time, the myth of the Russian army was still very much alive in Georgia and was able to make the decisive difference.

This proved to be a turning-point in post-communist Georgian history and, from today's perspective, it was definitely the start of the recovery. Yes, Abkhazia was gone (possibly for good), with over 200,000 embittered refugees to be accommodated and pacified. But the war was over, and with it the power of the shattered paramilitary formations started to diminish. Shevardnadze began consolidating his authority, relying for the most part on the police and using the fight against crime as a popular (and indeed timely) slogan. The process was completed after a failed attempt on Shevardnadze's life in August 1995, which he made use of to gaol his last armed adversaries. Thus he succeeded in fulfilling the first and minimal requirement which makes a state a state: establishing a monopoly over the legitimate use of force.

But in the autumn of 1993, things felt very different. It felt like, and was, a humiliating defeat. But it was not just like losing the war to a stronger power (as I have said, everybody in Georgia considered that a war in Abkhazia was a war against Russia). It was perceived as the final collapse of the national project. Despite the ostensible projection of all the blame onto Russia, faith in Georgia's viability as a nation had already been diminishing during the periods of chaos and disorder. 'Es vin vqopilvart – you see who [how bad] we turned out to be' became the catchphrase of the national mood. The statement that Georgia was 'ultimately' a Western nation, which only Russia had prevented from really becoming part of the West and being embraced by NATO and the European Union, would be met with deep scepticism by everybody except a bunch of die-hard 'radical' nationalists. Joining the CIS – which a sober observer would see as basically a symbolic act which by no means necessarily entailed the loss of the country's independence – was perceived across the political spectrum as the beginning of the end, as giving in to Russia, after which the concession of all the other elements of Georgian independence would automatically follow. Joining the CIS was compared to losing her virginity for a woman: if she gave in to illegitimate advances once, she was bound to become a whore.

But giving up was also a relief from tension. Georgia no longer had to fight. Moreover, once Russia regained possession of Georgia, it would also take care of it. Roads would be repaired, salaries would be brought into line with those in Russia (quite low by Western standards, but much higher than in Georgia), and echelons loaded with butter and sugar would start to pour in. This is not an intellectual projection by this author: this is what some pro-CIS politicians preached from the television, with a substantial part of the public appearing to believe them.

From this perspective, the 'pro-Western' orientation had been just part of the naivety of immature and irresponsible nationalists – those who henceforth had to take the blame for all Georgian disasters. What West? Do you not see that they have sold out on us to the Russians? And, after all, what do we have in common with those tidy but cold-hearted westerners? Shevardnadze did so much for them, and then how did they respond to his pathetic appeals? And can you imagine us Georgians ever becoming as orderly and law-abiding as they are? We are destined to be with (OK, maybe under) the Russians, and we have to admit it. And they are not really so bad if you are nice to them. They give you lots of things if you wine and dine them, and their women have always been willing to have sex with us. They punished us cruelly, but we deserved it. Who would not, in their shoes? And who are these much-cherished Americans and Germans after all, but well-fed Russians?

This mood, defeatist at its roots, was by no means aggressively anti-Western. It was shared to some degree by many representatives of the cultural elite who were quite pro-Western in their values, but did not believe in Georgia's ability to 'make it'; for them, being pro-Russian was just an extension of their elitist scepticism about their 'backward' or 'Asiatic' people. They felt more comfortable with the westernized Russian intelligentsia than with their own 'mob'.

Those whose views may be described as pro-Russian usually took no interest whatsoever in the Slavophile (now 'Eurasianist') historiosophy which preaches an exceptional role for Russia. Being 'pro-Russian' did not imply any positive value preferences, any belief that the 'Russian idea' or 'Russian route' was intrinsically better in any way, so that it would be more appropriate for Georgia to opt for them. It simply meant giving up one's political personality, believing that Georgia does not really have options and is not supposed to make choices – it should just follow its destiny, which is to be under Russia. This did not, however, imply giving up ethnic Georgian features: the focus of 'Georgianness' should move from politics to the preservation of cultural traditions, especially those represented in the rituals of wine-drinking ('Ra dagvrchenia – what else is there left for us?' being the catchphrase).

But, as I said, potentially, if developed into a coherent ideology, the 'pro-Russian' approach could become anti-Western as well. Despite incidental deviations within the Zviadist community, being pro-independence and pro-Western had always been parts of a single ideological package in Georgia. A 'pro-Russian' mood and nostalgia for communism comprised the alternative package. On a mass scale, being 'pro-Russian' meant being restorationist. It was simply an aspect of nostalgia for a stable and secure past, a generic feature of post-communist regimes, understandably stronger in countries where the transition from communism had been more troubled. The most outspoken advocates of the pro-Russian approach were the old-style enterprise managers, who saw a panacea for overcoming the economic crisis in 'restoring economic contacts with Russia', with entering the rouble zone as the first step. Of this, they seemed to have convinced Shevardnadze as well, at least for a period. But they did not display any understanding of the change which had occurred in the Russian economy since these contacts had been severed by 'irresponsible nationalists'. They – and their listeners – imagined that those links were again as they had been before, that is, based on bribing the right officials in Gossnab and Gosplan (centres for planning and distribution in the Soviet economic system). 'Restoring the links' could only imply the 'restoration' of all the underlying political and economic system, otherwise it did not make sense.

In short, the 'pro-Russian' sentiment could only become a coherent doctrine inasmuch as it developed into neo-communism. Despite all the opposition's allegations to the contrary, it was not Shevardnadze who went the whole way in this direction. Eventually, Shevardnadze appeared to betray the expectations of the pro-Russian neo-communists by falling for IMF-World Bank lures and continuing a game of geopolitical balancing even under new circumstances (between Russia and the West). The real neo-communist alternative, however, did develop, and by election time in the autumn of 1995 it became the major alternative open to Shevardnadze. The neo-communists united behind the candidacy of Jumber Patiashvili, the last leader of the orderly communist Georgia, whose previous career had ended disgracefully with the massacre of 9 April 1989. He got only about 19 per cent of the vote to Shevardnadze's 74 per cent, but without enormous pressure on the voters from local officials, and possible fraud, the ratio might have been different[6] (though most commentators believe it would still have been in favour of Shevardnadze). Patiashvili, however, was altogether too uninspiring for an alternative leader. A greater hope for the neo-communists might have been embodied in the figure of Igor Giorgadze, the young and ambitious head of the Security Service, who allegedly decided to take a shortcut to power for himself and the pro-Russian party by masterminding a coup attempt against Shevardnadze in August 1995. After Shevardnadze survived the assassination attempt, he had to flee to the country to which he had wanted to lead the whole of Georgia.

Neo-communism is definitely the most formidable alternative to Georgia's pro-Western orientation. But although it is anti-Western in the political, ideological and geopolitical senses, emotionally it is not, unlike its Russian counterpart. There is no ingredient of the resentment of a downgraded super-power; for the Georgians, neo-communism is really about communism, that is, about a recollection of the peace, security and relative well-being they enjoyed under the communist regime, and about their difficulty in accommodating to market reforms.

Largely because neo-communist sentiment lacks this identity ingredient, it remains a predominantly anti- or non-elitist phenomenon. During the election campaign, the neo-communists had a real problem in finding articulate speakers to make their points. Sleeker and younger representatives of the former party and intelligentsia nomenklatura, who would also like to capitalize on popular feelings of nostalgia, prefer to portray themselves as Western-type social democrats and condescendingly sneer at pro-Russian neo-communists.

One could only speculate about what the impact of a return to power by communists in Russia might have been. It was expected that this would stir up neo-communists in Georgia and boost their hopes and confidence – but ultimately it could also have alienated Georgia from Russia even further. Georgians may have some appreciation of what Russia has done in certain periods of history to help the country to modernize (that is, westernize) itself. But Georgian elites appear much less willing to follow Russia in the opposite direction.

They Came at Last: The IMF and the Oil Pipeline

However divisive different attitudes to Russia had been, one thing was clear: Russia did not deliver on the expectations – whether positive or negative – that supporters or opponents of joining the CIS had had at the moment of taking this step. Helping Shevardnadze against Zviadist insurgents remained the only time when Russia had done something visibly important. Economic links were not 'restored', and neither was there any increase in new economic contacts to speak of. Russians were almost absent from the Georgian market, which was dominated by Turkish, Iranian, Chinese, Bulgarian, Greek and other commodities. Nor did anything come in the form of assistance. Talk of joining the rouble zone died down. If Russia really wanted to dominate Georgia and the rest of the CIS, it would have to restore the rouble zone, and many post-Soviet countries seemed ready to join; but it did not do so, and with good reason – because it did not want to ruin its own economy. The Russians got Shevardnadze to sign treaties on guarding the 'CIS border' with Turkey, and on having military bases in Georgia, but in doing so they were only legitimizing what was already there. In return, the Russians were supposed to hand over one who was believed by the Georgians to be their puppet, the Abkhaz separatist leader Ardzinba, and give back Abkhazia.

In effect, they only preserved the *status quo*, that is, Abkhazia being under separatist control and without (ethnic) Georgians. In Georgia proper, life improved, for the most part because the police overcame the paramilitaries; but this was done without any Russian assistance. If Russia could take some credit, it was for not undermining Georgia any more (or not as much). Actually, this was quite a reasonable benefit which Georgia got for its concessions. But it was not what the pro-Russian party had expected (and urged the population to expect). Russia punished Georgia like a jealous paterfamilias (or mafia godfather) who felt abandoned and not properly appreciated; but, after the return of the prodigal son, it failed to do the job of a benevolent patron.

However sincerely Shevardnadze had believed in the ability and willingness of the appeased Russia to solve Georgian problems, soon he received another offer he could not refuse: credits from the IMF and the World Bank, though made conditional on drastic changes in economic policy. From the spring of 1994, Georgian economic policy was gradually taken over by the IMF and the

World Bank. Instead of 'entering the rouble zone' and 'restoring economic ties', stabilizing the national currency through necessary financial austerity, privatization and the like became the talk of the town. The new policy became a showcase for how successful IMF guidance could be: hyperinflation was cut; the new national currency, the Lari, which had been introduced in the fall of 1995, ousted the Russian rouble (which had hitherto dominated the Georgian market) in a matter of a week, and has displayed a miraculous stability ever since; economic life began to look more animated; hopes of investments became more realistic and some investments (although still quite few) actually started to come. Compared to the total and seemingly hopeless disaster of 1992-93, this looked like a miraculous turnaround.

Although the activities of these international institutions (which of course were always understood as another embodiment of the West) were for the most part restricted to issues of fiscal and macroeconomic policy, otherwise they happened to fit perfectly the archetypal image of the benevolent (Western) patron, and this is important for an understanding of their success. Nobody doubted how powerful these organizations were – their assets looked inexhaustible indeed compared to the ridiculous budget of the Georgian Republic; they were strict and required obedience to certain rules, but this strictness supposedly served the ultimate interest of the client. In short, they were strict and powerful, as a real patron, who cares about ultimate well-being of his clients, is supposed to be.

It is all too evident why the new policies had to be embraced by the pro-Western democrats. However, there were not so many of these involved. Changing policy, Shevardnadze did not bother much to change policy-makers: save for a number of people who were not powerful, and reportedly not Shevardnadze's favourites, the Cabinet was dominated by the same apparatchiks and managers of the communist breed, who had only recently been so vocal in promoting the 'restoration of ties' agenda. They were politically more acceptable to Shevardnadze than the nationalist opposition that was calling for an open and visible change of orientation from Russia to the West. If some theorists of democratic transitions speak about 'democracy without democrats', this was a case of free market reforms without free marketeers – or at least, almost without them. However, these apparatchiks and directors, who had never really believed in a free market and could not like what the

IMF and the World Bank were enforcing upon them, still did not actually try to stand up to the pressure from the latter, at least in the beginning. They could not, because structurally the IMF factor fully fitted the image of economic management they were used to. Having been taught to follow guidelines coming from a Higher Authority, they never thought of designing any economic policy of their own. For them, the IMF became the new Gosplan. Of course they knew that the Authorities have to be cheated when they are not looking, they have to be approached with bribes, but economic policy had to be structured according to those guidelines (in Russian, it used to be called 'direktivy', with the IMF and the World Bank, it is 'recommendations' – but what do words matter …). The country's budget was again effectively drafted elsewhere, and this felt so familiar and comfortable. It was a pity that they did not speak the same language as these people and did not know how to deal with them, but so many things had changed, and they recognized that they had to adapt.

The stabilization of the economy under the IMF made it possible for the other dream to come true – or at least become less of a dream: involving Georgia in the international network of oil pipelines. Once Shevardnadze came to Georgia, he began talking about making it a country of international transit between East and West, Europe and Asia. In particular, Georgia was an obvious candidate for routing through its territory a pipeline which would take to the West oil from the Caspian oil-fields controlled by Azerbaijan. Georgia could perhaps also become a candidate for the transit of oil from the Tengiz oil-fields in Kazakstan. As long as the country appeared to be no more than a space in incessant turmoil, nobody took its bid seriously. With stabilization in Georgia and, on the contrary, the unleashing of a civil war in Chechnya, which lay on the competing oil-pipeline route in the Northern Caucasus area of Russia, the Georgian option began to look increasingly attractive. In October 1995, the solution the international consortium in charge of Caspian oil opted for was a political compromise: to use both the Russian and Georgian routes, giving some priority in time to the Russian one, which needed much less initial investment. In March 1996, Aliev and Shevardnadze, the Azerbaijani and Georgian presidents, signed an agreement on actually building a pipeline from the Caspian oil-fields to the village of Supsa on the Georgian Black Sea coast (in part making use of the old existing one, which had ended up in Batumi, to the south of

Supsa). In December 1995, Georgia was visited by the president of Chevron, which was a sign that transporting Kazakstani oil through Georgia might also come on to an agenda.

Whatever direction this develops in, Georgia's success in convincing the West (this time represented by oil companies) that it is stable and reliable enough for transporting something as precious as oil has been regarded as the single most important event providing hopes of future economic prosperity. But, apart from the purely economic aspect, the reason the pipeline issue was so popular was because of its geopolitical implications. It implies competition between Russia and the West. Russia strongly resents routing a pipeline through Georgia, not primarily because of losing revenue, but because it views this as the end of its domination over the Transcaucasus, which in this case becomes the Southern Caucasus. If the pipelines materialize, it will mean that the West has come to the Caucasus at last, and is hitched to this place by something more up-to-date than just a shared Christian heritage. What Sulkhan-Saba Orbeliani wanted will have been achieved without the need to convert to Catholicism.

This explains why the prospect of pipelines has caused nothing but enthusiasm in Georgia, in sharp contrast to a Soviet-era project to build a trans-Caucasus railway from Russia to Iran through Georgia, which caused a public outrage in 1987 and actually became the first episode of the pro-independence movement. It is not just that an oil pipeline is more lucrative than a railway (nobody made calculations about that), or that Georgians have at last acquired a greater sense of economic rationality (although they did). The railway was supposed to link Georgia to Russia even more, while the oil pipeline would connect it to the West. A new railway linking Georgia to Russia would cause fewer protests in 1996 than it did in 1987, but there would still be a considerable outcry.

With pipelines, nobody (except the anti-Shevardnadze communists) seems to have any objection. Even the environmentalists, who led the protest movement in 1987, have now become leaders of the mainstream pro-Shevardnadze party and promote pipeline decisions as the greatest policy success. The major negative emotion about it is the fear that it is too good to be true, and Russia is not going to allow it anyway.

The West May Have Come. But What Is It?

The Western presence is felt in Georgia as never before in its history (save for a very brief period after the First World War when British troops were stationed here). The IMF is in charge of ongoing economic reform, while the prospects of future prosperity are linked to oil pipelines and other possible Western investments. Western retail chains are visibly coming. On the still scarce jobs market, Western embassies, international organizations and NGOs are the most attractive employers, and it is hoped they will be followed by Western companies on a much greater scale. Despite all decisions on Russian military bases, young Georgians are keen to learn English, not Russian, as their career language.

But as the Western presence becomes a reality, the myth of the West is bound to be shattered. The belief in an intrinsic Georgian 'westernness' that automatically comes with the country's Christian heritage or inborn individualism had already been called into question. Now the image of the West as duty-bound and benevolent patron also has few chances of survival. More direct encounters with the West are bound to expose the major contradiction between Georgia's notional pro-Western orientation and the quite un-Western attitudes which lie at its roots. The idea of the West in its modern form has gone beyond its medieval progenitor, the idea of Christendom, the Christian world – although the link is still alive in civilizational interpretations of 'westernhood'. The modern idea and image of the West are very much rooted in the ideal of the free, autonomous, self-sufficient human individual. The Georgian 'pro-Western orientation', on the contrary, was based on a very un-Western idea of dependence.

Enthusiasm over the oil pipeline project implies – and may reinforce – a vision of parasitic well-being under magnanimous patronage, with Georgia living off the transit charges without taking too much strain itself. Given the traditions of a bureaucratic and corrupt state, a substantial amount of steady revenue (if it comes), which the government receives without any interaction with its own people, may indeed become a crucial impediment to social and political development in the direction of real westernization, as the example of a number of oil-rich states has shown. If the state succeeds in deriving substantial revenues from its pipeline business, it will have a better chance of preserving the quite un-Western paternalistic view of itself as protector and provider for its still infantile citizens.

The understanding that 'pro-Western orientation' means primarily acquiring the Western values of self-sufficiency, initiative, being law-abiding, being disciplined at work, and so on, rather than just seeking Western protection and benefits in exchange for loyalty, is only starting to make its way into Georgian minds. Actually, the experience of surviving the complete breakdown of the communist state may have contributed even more to this understanding (if not always articulated into clear-cut ideological formulas) than the policies of austerity enforced by the IMF, although no credit should be denied to this particular influence. Georgia re-emerged from several years of nightmare politically and economically more viable, relatively democratic, and in fact more independent than one could have imagined a couple of years ago. It has learned its tough lesson, and now its 'pro-Western orientation' has a chance of emerging from the realm of mythology and day-dreaming.

This process is not going be easy. Naturally, some forms of anti-Western reaction may be part of it. At this point, one can only guess what particular shape this reaction will take – or shapes, as there will probably be several. Predictably, one might expect a reinforcement of the above-mentioned trends which have been there already without being very strong: cultural/religious nativism on the one hand and neo-communist reaction on the other. In this case, the controversy will also largely revolve around the 'elite'/'masses' dichotomy (especially when it comes to the neo-communist reaction). There is not much evidence that this kind of reaction is going to be popular on the elite level; this also means that, if there are no major upheavals, the elites are unlikely to allow either openly pro-Russian neo-communism or anti-Western type nativist nationalism too much influence in defining the political agenda. Of late, some new voices have been heard calling for unity with Russia on the basis of their common Orthodox heritage (targetting, naturally, the onslaught of the IMF, Turkish capital and other 'satanic forces'). According to Huntington's model of a 'clash of civilizations',[7] they would presumably determine Georgia's ideological orientation. So far, however, no influential figures have emerged among supporters of this trend.

On the other hand, there are signs that the resentment against the image of the 'soulless capitalist West' which is represented at this point by the IMF and World Bank – that is, the type of economic policies promoted by them (and which may possibly be reinforced in the future by the presence of oil or other kinds of Western corporations) may take the shape of liberal and leftist ideologies characteristic of the (post-) modern West itself. This may include mainstream social democracy as well as more peripheral movements. In this case, role-models for shaping anti-Western sentiment will come from the West itself, which will thus make it perfectly acceptable for the elite not to appear to be anti-Western in the ethnic cultural sense. I would thus expect the more elitist and 'progressive' Georgian anti-westerners to be such in terms of the Western 'adversary culture' only – which would only be another aspect of Georgia's joining the West.

NOTES

1. Anthony L. H. Rhinelander, *Prince Michael Vorontsov: Viceroy to the Tsar* (Montreal: McGill–Queens University Press, 1990).
2. This is what a French-educated Georgian essayist wrote at the time: 'Our intense subjectivism is unknown to the Russians. The historians say that ancient Slavs beheaded their victorious military commanders: they could not tolerate individuality which went above the average level. This inclination to sameness and tediousness has stuck to Russians ever since ... We will never cope with this peculiar egalitarianism and centralism. Nor will our neighbours tolerate our subjectivism. That is why we will always remain spiritually alien to one another.' Geronti Kikodze, *Erovnuli Energia* (Tbilisi: Gr. Tskhakaya Publishers, 1919), pp.161–2.
3. For my better understanding of this issue I owe much to my discussions with Dr David Ninidze of Tbilisi State University.
4. See more in Ghia Nodia, 'Georgia's Identity Crisis', *Journal of Democracy*, No.1 (1995) pp.104–16.
5. A few days before Clinton's inauguration, Gamsakhurdia said to the 'Kartuli Azri' newspaper: 'There are forces in Europe and America that may help us in our fight to restore legitimacy and justice in Georgia. Up to now they were paralysed under pressure from the Bush administration' – *Tskhra interviu sakartvelos respublikis prezident zviad gamsakhurdiastan* (Tbilisi, 1995).
6. *Parliamentary and Presidential Elections in Georgia, November 1995: Report from Election Monitoring Program* (Tbilisi: Meridian Publishers, 1996).
7. Samuel P. Huntington, 'Clash of Civilizations?', *Foreign Affairs*, No.72 (1993) pp.22–49.

2

Georgia in Europe: The Idea of a Periphery in International Relations

BRUNO COPPIETERS

An analysis of Western European policies on Georgia is a peripheral question for the study of European foreign policies. Ethnic conflicts and political instability in Georgia have never constituted a threat to Western European security. Georgian politics are of no concern to public opinion in Western Europe. This does not mean that Georgia is of no interest for European studies. The very concept of a periphery is in fact central to an analysis of the European integration process.

This chapter[1] analyses five different meanings of the concept of a periphery in international relations studies and in political discourse on Europe. A periphery has, first of all, a positive and practical sense in the core/periphery model of European integration. A second meaning of the term can be found in Johan Galtung's centre/periphery model. This meaning is negative in so far as the periphery is seen as being dominated and exploited by the centre. Third, a periphery may be seen as a location delimiting the territories of conflicting states, regions or civilizations. Fourth, a state used as a bridgehead by other powers in order to influence a particular regional security complex may also be described as their periphery. Fifth, the term periphery may be used in the description of specific forms of indifference in the policies of major world powers in relation to small nations. The following contribution assesses to what extent these different meanings of the term are appropriate to a description of Western European policies on Georgia. An analysis of some particular Western European or

Western policies on Georgia may be helpful for such an assessment. These include the Western European attitude towards both the Georgian independence movement and the ethnic and civil wars in Georgia, and the European Union's technical and humanitarian assistance programmes in Georgia.

The Core/Periphery Model of European Integration

The term periphery does not necessarily carry a negative meaning. It is an essential element in the idea of European integration. The unification of Europe has traditionally been conceived according to a core/periphery model. This model was intended to resolve the basic contradiction between the real process of European integration, encompassing only a minority of European nations, and the ideal of a European unification which included the entire continent. According to the core/periphery model, the construction of Europe should be conceived as the result of a process which started from a core and is gradually encompassing large peripheries of the European continent. The core refers to the given actors in the European integration process and the periphery to its future players.[2] The periphery of Europe should gradually become part of its core and take part in the common decision-making process. The core/periphery model is part of the discourse on a European identity, as it presupposes that all European countries will sooner or later join the community of countries defending European values and common security interests. The idea of a European identity underpins the institutional unification process in Europe and runs counter to the sacrosanct idea of national sovereignty.[3]

The unification process was started by some Western European countries in the 1950s. Since then, the core of Europe has successfully incorporated a large part of the continent's southern and northern periphery, and it is at present engaged in a process which will encompass parts of Eastern Central Europe in the near future. The fact that the practical and ideological validity of the core/periphery model has been confirmed by the successes of the integration process in Europe does not mean that the future unification of Europe will therefore continue to proceed in accordance with the original ideological content of this model. The possibility of an enlargement of the European Union to some countries of Southern and Eastern Central Europe does not imply that all the other parts of the European periphery will, at some stage, necessarily take part in the future unification process. The basic contradiction between the European Union's claim to represent the destiny of Europe and the fact that it represents exclusively its more affluent part is not likely to be solved in the future.

In 1992, European Community documents were using the following differentiations in post-Soviet Europe:[4] first, the European core with the EC and the European Economic Area; second, the PHARE region (Poland, Hungary, Bulgaria, Czechoslovakia, Albania, Romania, Estonia, Latvia, Lithuania and Slovenia) and the Mediterranean; third, the region of the newly constituted CIS republics in Eurasia. In 1996, when it was not yet possible to assess which of the Eastern Central European countries would be integrated into the core of the European Community, an information leaflet on PHARE regarded the core/periphery model as being still valid for Central and Eastern Europe:

> From 1945 until 1989, the countries of central and eastern Europe were cut off from the mainstream of European development, locked into a system of centralised political and economic control. They now desire to resume their central place in Europe's culture and civilization and rejoin the economies and societies of Europe. They face the challenge of re-building their economies to catch up with the changes which have taken place in western Europe in the last half century.[5]

No similar statement is to be found in the EU leaflets on the TACIS Programme, devoted to the transfer of know-how to promote economic transformation and the development of democracy in the CIS countries (the 'Newly Independent States' as they are called in EU documents) and Mongolia.[6] The European Union's foreign policy does not make any distinction in principle between the countries of the Transcaucasus which consider themselves European and the countries of Central Asia. Georgia's chance of being fully integrated into the European Union may be regarded as nil. The meaning of a periphery as used in the core/periphery model of European integration is not applicable to Georgia's position in Europe.

Johan Galtung's Centre/Periphery Model

The first meaning of a periphery can be characterized as positive, practical and ideological. The meaning of 'periphery' in Johan Galtung's[7] centre/periphery model is negative and theoretical. Galtung's model belonged to the numerous attempts in the 1960s and 1970s to conceptualize the dependence of the Third World on Western Europe and the US. Unlike the Marxist approach, Galtung's does not consider imperialism to be a specific historic stage of capitalism. He presents his concept of centre/periphery relations as a 'structural theory of imperialism'. The centre/periphery model should, as an ideal type, have a heuristic function in an understanding of the basic structure of all empires throughout history.

Galtung states that the world consisted and consists of Centre and Periphery nations, and that every nation in turn has a centre and a periphery. Imperialism is to be conceived of as a special type of domination in which the centre of the Periphery is used by the centre of the Centre as a bridgehead in order to establish a harmony of interests between both, whereas there is a disharmony of interests between the periphery of the Centre nation and the periphery of the Periphery nation. This disharmony of interests (interests are generally defined as material and non-material living conditions) is greater within the Periphery than within the Centre. The centre of the Periphery nation serves, for instance, as a transmission belt for the procurement of raw materials for the Centre, whereas the subsidiary economic effect of the extraction of raw materials for the development of the Periphery is – in the worst case – not much more than the digging of a hole in the ground.

The unequal exchange of value does not only take place in the economic field. Unlike the Leninist and other economic definitions of imperialism, Johan Galtung distinguishes between different types: imperialism may be economic, political, military, communication or cultural. In the political type, the Centre nation provides decision-making models – and in the cultural type cultural models – to the Periphery. A division of labour in which the Periphery produces events that the Centre turns into news is seen as an example of communications imperialism. In all types, the Centre establishes a monopoly position in its vertical relationship with the Periphery nations, impeding interaction between them.

As relations between empires are competitive, Periphery nations may try to protract a conflict between different Centres in order to bargain for an optimum gain. Galtung does not think that such a strategy can change the basic structure of imperialism. It may lead to some modifications in the vertical interaction structure, but without any changes in the fundamental feudal relationship. Galtung provides better strategies for structurally changing the international dominance system. He considers that the horizontalization of Centre/Periphery relations – that is, a division of labour and exchange of products on more equal terms, a reduction of the vertical interaction and more self-reliance in defining the preferences of the Periphery nations – constitutes an initial strategy for structurally changing the international dominance system. A second strategy would be provided by a defeudalization of international relations, including the development of viable organizations of Periphery countries.

The intention of this brief synthesis of Galtung's concept of imperialism is not to assess its value as a systematic theory, but merely to see how far the statement 'Georgia is at the periphery of Europe' may be understood in the light of Galtung's centre/ periphery model. At first sight, Western Europe's relationship with Georgia could easily be defined, in different respects, as a dependency relationship characteristic of an imperialist centre/ periphery structure. Where the political and cultural types of imperialism are concerned – in which models from the centre are implemented on the periphery – Georgia could easily be seen as a good example of a periphery in Galtung's sense of the term. And indeed, the idealization of European democracy and culture has a long-standing history in Georgia, even though the 1995 Georgian constitution demonstrates an even greater attraction to the presidential model of the US.

At the same time, however, it would not be difficult to consider such a characterization of Georgia's peripheral position as being rather superficial, neglecting important aspects of the country's dependence on Europe. First, Western Europe has produced a universalist approach to politics and cultures that transcends each individual centre/periphery relationship. The Western European centre regards its own model of civilization as being emancipatory for its periphery. This positive view of a centre/periphery relationship – in opposition to Galtung's and all other theories of imperialism – has, for instance, been dominating discussions on the accession of Georgia and other former Soviet republics to the Council of Europe.

Secondly, Galtung's approach to centre/periphery relations disregards the idea of a free choice, replacing it with the concept of self-reliance. Galtung pleads for a structural theory, as players cannot always be considered to be aware of their own real interests. The alternative between a voluntary and a non-voluntary adoption of political and cultural models should, however, be considered more fundamental than Galtung's alternative between a dependence on foreign models and the self-reliant production of autochthonous models by the Periphery itself. If we compare, for instance, the relations between Georgia and Russia/the Soviet Union on the one hand and the relations between Georgia and Western Europe on the other, Galtung would characterize them both as political and cultural types of imperialism, stressing the similarities between both forms of dependence on a foreign model. There is, however, a basic difference between the imposition of a model by Russia/the Soviet Union and the choice made by a large majority of Georgian public opinion, which opted for a Western political model. This choice may itself be explained as a reaction against dependence. The idealization of Western Europe by the Georgian intelligentsia in the nineteenth and twentieth centuries is, to a large extent, a consequence of its rejection of the Russian and Soviet 'imperial' political and cultural models.

The notion of a free political choice is far too important to be neglected in an analysis of the dependency relationships existing in the post-Soviet world. This does not mean that the conscious rationality of social players should be overestimated, or that the social consequences of this choice are in line with political intentions. The Georgian independence movement wanted to sever all ties with the Soviet Union in order to facilitate its integration into Europe. Since independence, ethnic strife and the rupture of economic ties with Russia have led to the breakdown of economic life. It is unclear to what extent the new links between Georgia and the world market may lead to the country's economic revival. From the economic point of view, Georgia has no strategic importance for Western Europe as a supplier of raw materials or as a consumer market. It has, however, a strategic location on the Black Sea, as it may provide one of the pipeline routes from the Caspian Sea. With 40 billion barrels of oil reserves found and 100 to 200 billion barrels of suspected oil reserves, the Caspian Sea and its surrounding region is considered to be one of the largest future energy suppliers for Western Europe (Kuwait has proven oil reserves of 97 billion barrels).[8] The possibility of transporting oil from the huge Tengiz field in Kazakstan through Azerbaijan and Georgia is taken into account in negotiations with oil companies. According to an initial project involving Chevron, Georgia is unlikely to earn any substantial income from transit fees until early next century, as the oil company is asking for sharply reduced concessionary tariffs for 30 years in return for financing this pipeline.[9] In the long run, positive spin-offs for the whole Georgian economy are expected. It is too early yet to assess how helpful Georgia's strategic location may be in establishing a harmony of economic interests between Georgia and Western Europe. Whether their relationship can be characterized as an economic type of imperialism according to Galtung's theory remains an open question.

Other consequences of Georgia's choosing independence and a market economy are easier to assess, for instance, in the field of education. Before independence, its economy was far below Western European levels as regards per capita GDP and other economic indicators, but Georgia enjoyed a relatively high standard of education. Curricula and equipment were often obsolete, and corruption was widespread in the education system, but some indicators – for instance, number of years' schooling and adult literacy – were comparable with those in Western Europe.[10] Since independence, the education system has been in a state of disarray, primarily because of the insufficiency of allocated funds. In regions of civil strife, schools have been destroyed or are used for the accommodation of displaced persons. Many teachers have resigned because of low pay. Schools have to close in winter because of lack of heating. Teaching materials are scarce, or unaffordable for parents. In recent years, only the newly emerging private schools, and the few state schools that receive help from a Western partner, have been able to provide quality teaching.[11] It is highly improbable that the Georgian government will mobilize sufficient resources to keep education at the level it had attained under Soviet rule, and private initiatives in education seem incapable of reversing this trend. Fees are generally too high for a population hard hit by the economic breakdown. This means that Soviet Georgia, despite its anti-Western orientation, apparently managed to develop an education system which certain indicators showed to be comparable with the Western European system, whereas the new regime, despite its Western orientation, has widened the educational gap between Georgia and Western Europe.

Galtung stresses the monopoly position of the centre in its vertical interaction with periphery nations and the lack of interaction between periphery nations themselves, seeing this as a basic structural characteristic of imperialism. This type of unilateral relation for Periphery nations has indeed been characteristic of many colonial and neo-colonial regimes. Under Soviet rule, all Union republics in the Transcaucasus were closely tied to Moscow, whereas their links with neighbouring states in the region were entirely neglected. Soviet policies did not aim at the economic integration of the Caucasus as a region in its own right. Economic links between Georgia, Turkey and Iran were severed throughout the Soviet period, despite the geographical proximity of these countries. It will be many years before Georgia can manage to overcome the consequences of these Soviet policies.

The Shevardnadze government took important initiatives in order to re-establish trade relations with neighbouring countries. In 1994, Turkey had already replaced Russia as Georgia's main trading partner, accounting for 25 per cent of all foreign trade that year, while Russia accounted for only 16 per cent. In 1995, trade with Turkey had risen to 32 per cent, whereas the figure for Russia had dropped to nine per cent.[12] Georgia's membership of the Economic Cooperation Organization (ECO) would be a further step in the normalization of its economic relations with neighbouring countries. Neither Russia nor Western states belong to this regional organization, of which Iran, Pakistan, Turkey, the five Central Asian States and Azerbaijan are members. The accession of Georgia and Armenia to the ECO (Armenia's membership would probably necessitate a settlement of the Nagorno-Karabakh conflict) could be considered an important step in the light of the strategy, favoured by Galtung, of building organizations of 'Periphery' nations. The idea of a Caucasian Home (which has been invested with a contradictory political content by various groupings in the region throughout the entire twentieth century) could – if it does not exclude any Caucasian country or nationality from its project for regional integration – fit in with the same strategy.

France and the US have established intensive diplomatic links with Armenia, Germany has preferential links with Georgia[13] and the United Kingdom with Azerbaijan. Despite the varying degrees of diplomatic presence in the different Transcaucasian capitals, no Western governments or institutions aim to have exclusive links or to hamper the mutual integration of the three states. Such an imperialist policy would be contrary to the Western interest in creating safe routes for energy transport westwards from the Caspian Sea. In its political and economic approaches to the region, the European Union favours integration projects between Azerbaijan, Georgia and Armenia. The development of the transit route between the Black and Caspian Sea, Central Asia and the Caucasian countries, to achieve an optimum utilization of transport facilities, considered a priority for the 1992 TACIS programme. The European Union regards a more active dialogue between the Transcaucasian states, with neighbouring countries and with the ECO as one of the main means of accelerating the reconstruction process.

Can Georgia's peripheral position in Europe be understood according to the meaning given to the concept of a periphery in Galtung's structural theory of imperialism? This theory, despite its claim to be ahistorical, is based on an analysis of the capitalist system during the cold war period and seems inappropriate for analysing the new dependencies created by the demise of the Soviet system. The application of Galtung's centre/periphery model to present-day Georgia fails to ascertain the significance of universal norms and models, of the deliberate choice made by the Georgian people to be part of the Western world, or of the deliberate integrative approach to the Caucasus region taken by Western governments. This does not mean that the peripheral position of Georgia should not be analysed as a position of dependence, or that its choice in favour of Europe leads to a harmony of interests between Centre and Periphery. Galtung's analysis was one of the most systematic and conceptually refined theories of imperialism discussed in the 1970s. A similar theoretical discussion on the value of the term imperialism (today exclusively used in the West as an ideological concept for condemning Russian policies and used in Russia to condemn Western policies) is hardly needed in order to analyse the new centre/periphery relations in Europe since the demise of the Soviet Union.

The Periphery as a Place of Exclusion and Confrontation

A periphery may be understood as a place of exclusion and confrontation between different countries, alliances or civilizations. In this sense, a state's border, delimiting the territory on which it exercises its sovereignty, is an element of its identity. The border of a country may even be regarded by its population as sacred. According to the just war theory, defence of a border is a ground for the use of force.

The analogy between the borders of a national state and those of a region is used explicitly in the legitimation of the Russian concept of a 'Near Abroad'. The Soviet-era borders between the Union republics were administrative lines, without strategic military significance. After the dissolution of the USSR, Russia stressed its legitimate right to defend specific and exclusive security interests in the former Union republics. The involvement of other powers in 'near abroad' areas was seen as a security threat. Moscow has negotiated the stationing of border guards at the former Soviet external borders in Kazakstan, Kyrgyzstan, Turkmenistan, Georgia and Armenia. From the Russian point of view, Georgia is at the periphery of its security zone – the term periphery referring to the line where other powers are excluded.

This meaning of a periphery as a place of confrontation may be used in relation to European borders, to the extent that Europe is seen as constituting a particular civilizational entity. Samuel Huntington predicted that 'the most important conflicts of the future will occur along the cultural fault lines separating ... civilizations from one another'.[14] Civilizations are regarded by Huntington as the broadest level of cultural identity, defined in a particularistic way 'both by common objective elements, such as language, history, religion, customs, institutions, and by the subjective self-identification of people.'[15] He considers the violent eruptions between Ingush and Ossetians and between Azeris and Armenians, and the deployment of Russian troops in the Caucasus in order to secure southern Russian borders against a Turkish threat, as different forms of the current clashes between civilizations.[16]

Dan Diner defends a similar thesis, when he states that the self-image of civilizations is constituted at their periphery through their opposition to other civilizations. The Oriental Question of the nineteenth century, which was raised when the decay of the Ottoman empire gave other world powers the opportunity to readjust the balance of power to their advantage, reflected such a conflict between Western Christianity, Eastern Christianity and Islam. The present conflicts in the Caucasus and the Balkans are, likewise, viewed as reconstituting cultural identities.[17]

The fate of Europe and the idea of a European identity have been

felt to be at stake in the Balkans. But Western European discussions
on the need for military intervention have used the concept of a
civilization with a very different meaning from that of Huntington
or Diner. In contrast to their historic and particularistic definition
of a civilization, public opinion in Europe has regarded the
universalistic idea of human rights as constituting the basis of
European civilization. The acts of war and ethnic cleansing in the
former Yugoslavia have not been interpreted as clashes between
particular civilizations, but perceived as an expression of a clash
between civilization and barbarism. The French writers Bernard
Henry-Lévy and André Glucksmann have stressed the need for
Western European powers to intervene militarily in order to oppose
a flagrant violation of human rights in a conflict taking place not at
the periphery but in the heart of Europe. André Glucksmann drew
up an electoral list for the June 1994 French elections to the
European Parliament in order to draw the attention of the French
public to the war in the former Yugoslavia. The list was called
'Europe starts in Sarajevo'. Sarajevo was not at the periphery of
Europe.

Huntington and Diner present the conflicts in the Caucasus
between Azeris and Armenians and between Ossetians and Ingush
– involving ethnic groups with different religious and cultural
backgrounds – as a confirmation of their thesis that a clash of
civilizations is taking place at the periphery of Europe. Can Western
policies on Georgia be interpreted within the framework of a clash
between civilizations, in which civilizational values are at stake? In
fact both Zviad Gamsakhurdia and his successor, Eduard
Shevardnadze, repeatedly claimed Western support by asserting
that the fate of Western civilization was at stake in the Caucasus.
They were able to base this interpretation on the traditional self-
image of the Georgian intelligentsia. The Georgian elite has always
stressed that Georgian national culture belongs to European
civilization. Georgia, together with Armenia, was the first
European state in which Christianity was introduced as a state
religion. In so far as Christian values are considered to be a
necessary component of a European identity, Georgia could be said
to have made a significant contribution to Western civilization.[18]
Contrary to an archaeological definition, the idea of a civilization as
it was used by the Georgian intelligentsia had far-reaching
normative and political consequences. The argument that European
identity had its primary roots in a distant past and in common

religious origins did not, however, find much suppport among European public opinion. It made the granting of special guest status to Georgia in the Council of Europe possible in May 1996, but does not have important consequences for Western European policies on Georgia.

The ethnic conflicts in Georgia were not seen as a civilizational issue in Western Europe. Unlike the civil war in the former Yugoslavia, the Georgian wars were not a major item in news coverage by Western agencies. Newspaper commentaries stressed the inability of the governments of both Gamsakhurdia and Shevardnadze to reach compromises with the ethnic minorities. The takeover of Sukhumi by the Abkhaz secessionist forces, the thousands of civilian casualties and the fleeing of more than two hundred thousand refugees were depicted in the media as a tragic consequence of both Shevardnadze's failure to control radical Georgian paramilitary troops and Russian meddling in Georgian affairs. The interview with the Georgian general Karkarashvili, who said that he was personally ready to send 100,000 soldiers to their death in order to kill 80,000 Abkhazians (in other words, virtually the entire Abkhazian population), was widely broadcast in the Western media.[19] Western governments condemned the violation of the territorial integrity of the Georgian state, but such official statements had no effect on public opinion. Unlike in the former Yugoslavia, Europe had no moral stance to defend in the Caucasus.

European civilization was an issue in the discussions on the accession of Georgia, with special guest status, to the Council of Europe, but not in the way Huntington's theory would have predicted. From the geographical standpoint, none of the Transcaucasian states belongs to Europe. But as both Georgia and Armenia were accepted as belonging to and representing European civilization, Azerbaijan's application to this organization for guest status could not be refused, if new civilizational fault lines in the Transcaucasus were to be avoided. The Council of Europe was of the opinion that – in view of their cultural affinities with Europe – Armenia, Azerbaijan and Georgia should all be able to apply for membership, on condition that they clearly showed a desire to be considered part of Europe and to share its basic values.[20] In May 1996, Georgia was granted 'special guest' status in the Council of Europe and it sent a formal request for membership on 14 July 1996.[21]

The Periphery as a Bridgehead

The function of a bridgehead for Western interests in a particular region, during and after the cold war, has traditionally been attributed to Israel and Turkey. Turkey's membership of NATO was legitimized by its role as a bulwark against communist expansion. After the demise of the Soviet Union, the Turkish government presented itself both as the centre of a Turkic civilization stretching from the Mediterranean to the Chinese border and as a bridgehead for Western economic and political interests wishing to penetrate the Transcaucasus and Central Asia. After independence, Armenia was perceived – and feared – by other regional powers as a possible bridgehead for Western interests in the region, in much the same way as Israel was in the Middle East. This fear was not realized, however, since Armenia has kept a careful balance between Russia, the West and even Iran. Georgia failed to keep such a balance. It had hoped to consolidate its economic and even military links with the West – Shevardnadze tried in 1992–93 to persuade his Western partners to create a belt of 'democratic countries' around Russia – but when these hopes were not fulfilled, it had to accept Russia as the dominant power in the region. Neither from the economic nor the military point of view can the peripheral position of Georgia in Europe be understood as representing a bridgehead for Western interests.

Benevolent Indifference

One of the first accounts of Western indifference towards the conflicts in the Caucasus is to be found in John le Carré's novel *Our Game*. Russia and the West are supposed to have agreed, for the sake of security, that they will not stop the massacres on the periphery of the former Soviet Union:

> Question from Thatcherchild Marcia: Why did the West refuse recognition to Gamsakhurdia after he was fairly elected? Then, as soon as Shevardnadze was put in as Moscow's puppet, not only recognize the little twerp, but turn a blind eye to his genocide of the Abkhaz, the Mingrelians, the you-name-them? Answer, dear Thatcherchild Marcia … , it's the Good Old Boys getting together on both sides of the Atlantic and agreeing that minority rights can seriously threaten world health … .[22]

Le Carré's novel tells of the search by retired British cold war spy Larry for a new battleground in the post-Soviet world and his support for the struggle by the Ingush of the Northern Caucasus against their oppressors, the Ossetes and the Russians. Larry's battleground is a moral battleground, a moral protest against the indifference of the West and its complicity with the other 'Good Old Boy'. For him, the fate of the Ingush exemplifies all the other lost causes of our post-cold war world. Larry's anger is also an expression of his indignation at Western hypocrisy and the betrayal of all its cold war values, for which he has been fighting (spying):

> It happens to be the Ingush because they exemplify everything most shabby about our post-cold war world. All through the cold war it was our Western boast that we defended the underdog against the bully. The boast was a bloody lie. Again and again during the cold war and after it the West made common cause with the bully in favour of what we call stability, to the despair of the very people we claimed to be protecting.[23]

John le Carré's concept of indifference is defined only negatively. The West is indifferent to the fate of minorities to the extent that post-cold war arrangements and its search for stability with the Soviet Union, and later Russia, are not based on moral principles. The 'good old boys' have a cynical attitude towards world events. In the following pages, Western indifference towards Georgia will be analysed differently. Western policies did not and do not preclude goodwill. Contrary to the convictions of John le Carré's spy Larry, the international order is based not on moral but on political and legal principles. Western indifference may be regarded as being positive, since it is based not on a negative criterion – the absence of a moral standard – but rather on political and legal criteria.

A positive form of indifference is basic to the liberal attitude of Western Europe in world politics. Every nation is seen as bearing full responsibility for its own fate, and a paternalistic attitude can only hamper its free development. The world community, however, may provide every nation with a stable international legal framework which can preserve its means for attaining wealth and well-being. Western indifference does not, for instance, preclude the possibility of providing some states with political and legal guarantees for security – as is the case with NATO enlargement plans – or supplying them with humanitarian, technical or other aid.

Where the fate of minorities in particular states is concerned, the international community will only intervene when the major world powers consider it politically opportune, and may only do so if this is legally possible under international law. Neither the political nor the legal preconditions were met in the case of most of the ethnic conflicts taking place on the territory of the former Soviet Union. Contrary to Larry's morals, the Ingush-Ossetian conflict of 1992 was regarded as an internal Russian affair. Western Europe is interested in a settlement of the conflicts in the Caucasus but – in contrast to the interpretation of spy Larry – does not 'claim to be protecting' the Ingush or the many other Caucasian nationalities.

Georgia has marginal significance for Western Europe, and this is reflected in policies that may be described as demonstrating a benevolent indifference. Two case-studies illustrate this. The first involves Western European policies on Georgia's struggle for independence and civil wars, until Georgia's defeat in Abkhazia and its compromise with Russia. As has so often been stated by historians and philosophers throughout history, war is the main demonstration of a state's power. In the war against the Abkhazian secessionists, Georgia had to mobilize all its domestic and foreign resources. The total disorganization of the state and the total dependence of the Shevardnadze government on paramilitary and other quasi-criminal groupings showed that it lacked internal sovereignty. Georgia's government also failed to mobilize foreign support to oppose the Russian and Abkhazian forces. The war proved that – contrary to some official statements that had been made in previous years – Western Europe had only a marginal interest in the country.

Georgia declared its independence in March 1991.[24] In May, Zviad Gamsakhurdia was elected president with 87 per cent of the votes. His nationalist ideology had a European flavour. Independence meant independence from the Soviet Union. The idea of Europe gave the Georgian national liberation movement an international perspective. The West did not give any substantial help, however, to the independence movements in the Soviet republics. The Baltic states could count on some declarations of support from Western governments but, where the other states were concerned, Western Europe and the US showed more confidence in Gorbachev's plans for federal reforms than in the nationalist movements. In the summer of 1991, President

In a television statement in October 1995, Eduard Shevardnadze reflected on the radical shift in foreign policy his government had made two years before. He declared that he had had no alternative but to find a compromise with Russia, as the US had withheld assistance, offering merely a few uniforms and medical equipment 'through our compatriot John Shalikashvili' (the Chairman of the US Joint Chiefs of Staff). In its attempt to recover its territorial integrity, Georgia could 'expect serious aid from no one but Russia'.[42] This did not prevent Shevardnadze from forging new links with the West. He opposed the idea of creating a Russian-led bloc to counter an expanded NATO, and military co-operation programmes were planned within the framework of NATO's Partnership for Peace. When German Foreign Minister Klaus Kinkel came to Tbilisi in January 1996 with new promises of aid, as 'an acknowledgement of Shevardnadze's role in bringing about German unification', Shevardnadze asked him to arrange for Germany to mediate in the ongoing conflicts between the central government and the breakaway regions of Abkhazia and South Ossetia. Kinkel declined the request.[43]

A second illustration of Georgia's marginal importance for Western European policies is provided by the European Union programmes for the Transcaucasus. The EU has no specifically 'European' considerations where Georgia is concerned: mutual co-operation policies are derived from considerations involving the region as a whole. Georgia's self-assessment as a country belonging to Europe through its culture and history is not taken into account when priorities in the Transcaucasus are defined. A European Commission document describes the whole of the region as a bridge between Europe and Asia. The European Union's policies on Georgia and the two other Transcaucasian states[44] are no different in principle from those pursued in Central Asia:

- to promote stability, democratization and the defence of human rights – seen as intrinsically linked to economic reform;
- to defend the interests of the European companies involved in the oil contracts: in the future, the European Union will be a major consumer of Caspian oil and gas reserves;
- to promote environmental security (for instance, concerning the nuclear plant of Medzamor NPP in Armenia) and the drilling for Caspian Sea oil in line with environmental standards.

In the economic field, the EU is potentially the region's main

Western trading partner and source of investment capital. The EU remains the major humanitarian donor in the region. In 1994, in the Transcaucasus, it implemented one of the largest food assistance programmes the Community has ever carried out. In 1993, it funded a $200-million support programme for Georgia, although at the beginning of 1994 it announced a decrease in this aid to 70 million dollars for that year.[45]

The European Union's low political profile in the region in the first few years after the demise of the Soviet Union was due not only to its concern not to provoke Russian fears of Western involvement at its borders, but also to the Western European governments' inability to formulate a common political policy on the Transcaucasus and, finally, to the lack of financial resources for funding major EU diplomatic representations in all three capitals. European economic interests may, however, now be favouring a higher political profile for the EU. European companies have to mobilize political support from their governments in their competition with American firms. An EU failure to influence decisions on the routing of pipelines could be a handicap for European companies in establishing themselves in the region.

Partnership and Cooperation Agreements (PCAs) are one of the EU's main instruments in attaining its objectives. PCAs with all three Transcaucasian republics were signed in April 1996, with the Heads of State agreeing to come together to meet in Luxembourg for the official signature. The PCA with Georgia described the development of political and trade relations between the parties and EU support for Georgia's effort to consolidate its democracy as among the main objectives of the partnership. The establishment of a political dialogue would foster co-operation on matters pertaining to the strengthening of stability and security in Europe.

In the general Western European strategy on the Transcaucasus, Azerbaijan's energy assets are of the utmost importance. Georgia may provide transport facilities. It has better communications with Western Europe than Azerbaijan or Armenia. It is directly adjacent to Turkey, whose importance has increased since it signed a Customs Union with the European Union. In the early years of independence, Georgia's economic decline (estimated by the European Commission at 80 per cent of GNP between 1990 and 1994) and lack of law and order were worse than in both the other Transcaucasian states. However, with the crackdown on para-military and other criminal groupings in 1994 and 1995, the introduction of a new constitution in August 1995 and a radical monetary reform in October 1995, the Georgian leadership managed to create basic conditions for economic reforms and foreign investment.

The European Community has provided TACIS funding for all Newly Independent States, including for advice on policy, the development of legal frameworks, and pilot and partnership projects. The budget for all former Soviet republics (excluding the Baltic republics) in the period 1991–94 was ECU 1,757 million, of which ECU 591 million was spent on multi-country programmes.[46] Georgia received ECU 28 million, less than the Central Asian republics of Kazakstan (ECU 56 million) and Uzbekistan (ECU 35 million). These figures are helpful in illustrating both Western Europe's goodwill and its indifference to Georgia's image of itself as a European state.

Conclusions

Different meanings of the concept of periphery have been analysed in this contribution. Most of them are not suitable for describing Georgia's place at the periphery of Europe. The concept of a periphery is to be found, for instance, in the core/periphery model of European integration, where the European periphery is assumed to be progressively integrated into the core. Georgia borders on the Customs Union between Turkey and the European Union but has no chance of being one day part of the European core. On the contrary, the European Union does not regard Georgia as belonging to Europe, but rather as part of a region bridging Europe and Asia. The European Union pursues neither specific Georgian policies nor a policy which acknowledges Georgia's image of itself as a European nation, but defends specific European economic interests and general ('universal') Western values throughout the Transcaucasus region. In this respect, its approach in the region is basically no different from that of the US when it supports specific economic interests and universal Western values. The whole problem of a European identity, which has been so decisive both for the process of European integration before the fall of the Berlin Wall and for Georgia's policies of independence, is absent from the European Union's strategic approach to Georgia. Western European policies on Georgia can best be described as an attitude of benevolent indifference.

NOTES

1. I am grateful to Jérôme Cassiers, Tamara Dragadze, Kakha Gogolashvili, Theo Jans, David Blackman, Alexander von Lingen, Veronica Kelly, Gerd Tebbe, Slava Chirikba Dmitri Trenin, Michael Waller and Alexei Zverev for their comments on the first draft of this analysis.
2. European integration literature makes a distinction between core and periphery members of the European Union. The use of the term periphery for EU member states such as Spain, Portugal and Greece indicates that formal membership of the common decision-making structures is not sufficient to eliminate basic differences between the participants in the integration process.
3. Anthony D. Smith, 'National Identity and the Idea of European Identity', *International Affairs*, Vol.68, No.1 (1992), pp.55–76; on the core/periphery model by 'the myth-makers of the European idea' ibid., p.74.
4. See Josef Janning and Cornelius Ochmann, 'Beyond Europhoria. Political and Economic Relations between the East and the West in Europe', in Hans-Georg Ehrhart, Anna Kreikemeyer and Andrei V. Zagorski (eds.), *The Former Soviet Union and European Security: Between Integration and Re-Nationalization* (Baden-Baden: Nomos Verlags-gesellschaft, 1993), p.159; Barbara Lippert, 'Questions and Scenarios on EC-CIS Republics' Relations – An Outline on the Political Dimension', in ibid., p.138. The 'Poland and Hungary Action for Restructuring of the Economy' (PHARE) became operational in January 1990 for Poland and Hungary, and was extended thereafter.
5. European Commission. Phare Information Office, *What is Phare? A European Union Inititiative for Economic Integration with Central and Eastern European Countries* (Brussels, 1996), p. 1.
6. See for instance: European Commission, *Tacis Annual Report 1994* (Brussels, 1995).
7. Johan Galtung, 'A Structural Theory of Imperialism', *Journal of Peace Research*, 1971/2, pp.81–117.
8. *The Economist*, 4 May 1996.
9. *Tehran Times*, 20 Jan. 1996.
10. Wolf Scott and George Tarkhan-Mouravi, Government of the Republic of Georgia/United Nations Development Programme, *Human Development Report. Georgia 1995*, (Tbilisi, 1995), pp.10 and 27.
11. Ibid., p.30.
12. See the contribution by Alexander Kukhianidze on Armenian-Azeri relations in this volume.
13. For Germany, the acknowledgement of Shevardnadze's role in the reunification process seems to be more important than basic economic calculations on energy resources. Christian Schmidt-Häuer, a journalist with *Die Zeit*, criticized the contrast between the exaggerated importance accorded by the German government to the embassy in Tbilisi and the lack of diplomatic staff at the German representation in Baku, despite the latter's greater economic importance. Christian Schmidt-Häuer, 'Alter Reichtum, neues Wunder', *Die Zeit*, 26 May 1995, p.10.
14. Samuel P. Huntington, 'The Clash of Civilizations? , *Foreign Affairs* (Summer 1993), p.25.
15. Ibid., p.24.
16. Ibid., p.33.
17. Dan Diner, 'Die Wiederkehr der Orientalischen Frage, *Die Zeit*, 1 Sept. 1995, p.54.
18. Grand Duke Giorgi Shervashidze, the last successor to the Abkhazian throne, once declared that Georgia's tragedy was that it had not been able to remain ahead of European civilization: 'Wenn uns das Schicksal nicht so heimgesucht hätte, wären wir heute weiter als Europa. Denn als der Apostel Andreas uns hier die Lehre Christus predigte, hüllten sich in Europa die Duken in Felle und gingen mit Spiessen in der Hand auf die Jagd.' Quoted in: Naira Gelaschwili, *Georgien. Ein Paradies in Trümmern* (Berlin: Aufbau Verlag, 1993), p.66.
19. Ibid., p.164.
20. Daniel Tarschys, 'The Council of Europe: the Challenge of Enlargement', *The World*

Today, April 1995, p. 62. According to an information paper published on 29 February 1996 by the Office of the Clerk of the Assembly, special guest status with the Parliamentary Assembly of the Council of Europe had been granted to Armenia and requested by Azerbaijan and Georgia. As the next step, those countries may request full membership of the Council of Europe.

21. *OMRI Daily Digest* I, No.135, 15 July 1996.
22. John le Carré, *Our Game* (Knopf: London, 1995), p.209.
23. Ibid., p.212.
24. On the following see Aleksej Zverev, Bruno Coppieters, 'Verloren evenwicht. Georgië tussen Rusland en het Westen, *Oost-Europa Verkenningen*, No.134, (Aug. 1994), pp.38–47; Alexei Zverev, 'Ethnic Conflicts in the Caucasus', in Bruno Coppieters (ed.), *Contested Borders in the Caucasus* (Brussels: VUBPRESS, 1996), pp.13–71.
25. *Sakartvelos Respublika*, 9 Aug. 1991. An overview of the Georgian attitude towards the West in: Alexander Kukhianidze, 'The Georgian Media on Western Policies', 1994 (manuscript).
26. *Sakartvelos Respublika*, 14 April 1992. In his memoirs, Genscher does not refer to the numerous talks he had with Shevardnadze concerning possible Western help for war-torn Georgia. On Georgia see Hans-Dietrich Genscher, *Erinnerungen* (Berlin: Siedler Verlag, 1995), pp.996–8.
27. *Sakartvelos Respublika*, 14 April 1992. Translated by Alexander Kukhianidze.
28. *Droni*, 18 April 1992.
29. It is difficult to assess the extent to which the German and American governments have actually made firm promises to support Georgia's independence, or if such declarations were exclusively intended to back Shevardnadze's position for the benefit of Georgian public opinion. In interviews with the author in spring 1993, members of Shevardnadze's presidential staff said that the West had indeed made firm and far-reaching promises to support Georgia's independence. Western diplomats interviewed by the author confirmed that emphatic declarations like Genscher's were quite usual for foreign visitors, and they considered that Shevardnadze, as an experienced politician, should have known better than to take such words at face value. Whatever the real commitments of the different parties, Genscher's words strengthened the conviction among Georgians that a break with Russia was both necessary and realistic. It also made it more difficult for Shevardnadze to go against public opinion in order to reach a compromise with Russian interests in the region.
30. *Die Zeit*, 21 Aug. 1992.
31. *De Standaard*, 24 June 1993.
32. On this and the following, see *The Independent*, 23 Aug. 1993.
33. *Svobodnaia Gruzia*, 3 July 1993.
34. According to the Georgian TV programme *Time Out*, 1 Aug. 1993.
35. *International Herald Tribune*, 22 Oct. 1993.
36. *Le Monde*, 1 Oct. 1993.
37. Personal friendships between Shevardnadze and Western governments did not alter Georgia's dependence on Russia but they did help in attracting humanitarian support and even investment projects. Former US Secretary of State James Baker was said to have gathered support for the project from international banks and oil companies in his home state of Texas. See *Monitor*, 12 Jan. 1996. After Genscher's departure as Foreign Minister, Germany continued to play a prominent role in supporting Georgia economically.
38. *Financial Times*, 20 Oct. 1993.
39. *Wall Street Journal* (European edition), 9 March 1994.
40. Resolution 937 (1994) 'welcomes the contribution made by the Russian Federation, and indications of further contributions from other members of the CIS, of a peacekeeping force, in response to the request of the parties (...) in coordination with UNOMiG on the basis of the arrangements described in the Secretary-General's report of 12 July 1994, and in accordance with the established principles and practices of the United Nations'. United Nations. Department of Public Information, *The United Nations and the Situation in Georgia*, Reference Paper, April 1995, p.32.
41. *De Standaard*, 3 Aug. 1994.

42. *Monitor*, 2 Oct. 1995.
43. *OMRI Daily Digest* I, No.18, 2, 25 Jan. 1996.
44. See Commission Communication, *Towards a European Union Strategy for Relations with the Transcaucasian Republics*, 1995.
45. *Frankfurter Allgemeine Zeitung*, 9 March 1994.
46. *Tacis Annual Report 1994*, op. cit.

3

The 'Caucasian Home' and Pan-Turkist Aspirations

HRANT AVETISIAN

The idea of creating a 'Caucasian Home', of the economic and political unity of the Caucasian peoples and the need to unify them (whether under a federation or a confederation), is nothing new. As far back as the Crimean War (1853–56), British Prime Minister Henry Palmerston put forward a programme to weaken Russia, narrowing its sphere of influence. The reasoning behind this was that the more entangled Russia became in the south, the less of a danger it would represent in the west. The role of main instrument in promoting such a policy was assigned to Turkey. At that time, Western politicians, especially French ones, did not understand the deterrent effect of the Caucasian barrier, that is, the existence of independent North Caucasian tribes which effectively blocked Russian expansion towards Central Asia and Asia Minor, and from there to the Mediterranean and the Persian Gulf. This was noted in a memorandum to the government of Austria-Hungary sent by political figures from the mountainous areas of the Northern Caucasus in July 1918.[1]

In the opinion of one of the founders of pan-Turkism, the Crimean Tatar Ismail Gasprinski (1851–1914), the Turkic-Tatar peoples inhabiting the vast expanses of Eurasia between the Christian West and the Buddhist East would be capable of 'opposing the Imperial policy of cultural levelling' only if they unified themselves. At the beginning of the 1880s, Gasprinski advanced the idea of a single body that might unify the Turkic-Tatar masses of the Ottoman Empire and Eurasia.[2]

Ismail Bey Gasprinski was active in the Crimea (Bakhchisaray). At the same time, the Ottoman idea of unifying Muslims from

Gibraltar to China was being developed in Istanbul. Standing in the way of that idea, however, were Western Armenia and the Armenians of the Caucasus. Muslims were therefore called upon to wage a religious war against the Armenians. That war was expected to be easily won, since the Armenians, as it was written at the time, 'have neither arms nor an army and no supporters'.[3] It was proposed to create a 'solid Muslim majority' in Anatolia (Western Armenia), that is, to exterminate the Armenians and settle Muslims on their lands. That idea was in fact supported by prominent German politicians and military, such as Paul Rohrbach and Field Marshal Colmar von der Goltz.[4]

Rohrbach was an active member and one of the main theoreticians of the Pan-German League (*Alldeutscher Verband*) (1891–1939), an organization which championed Germany's military and economic expansion, especially in the decades preceding the First World War. Among other things, he advocated the construction of the Berlin-Baghdad Railway in order to further German economic expansion in the Middle East, and for this an alliance with Turkey was indispensable. Von der Goltz, as head of the German military mission in Turkey in 1885–95, carried out a reorganization of the Turkish army on the German model; in 1909-12 he was Vice-President of Turkey's Supreme Military Council, and in the years of the First World War he commanded the Turkish armies at the various fronts.

To use the expression of the German Ambassador to Turkey, Hans von Wangenheim, Germany, Austria-Hungary and Turkey sought to build an indivisible triple unity that would not allow Russia to 'put pressure on Turkey, for Germany would never agree to sacrifice its interests in Anatolia'.[5] A Russian takeover of Western Armenia would signify the establishment of Russian domination over the whole of Asia Minor, and by the same token over the whole region from the Persian Gulf to the Mediterranean – the concentration in Russian hands of control over Transcaucasia, Northern Persia and Eastern Anatolia. 'If Turkey is to be preserved, then Armenia should also remain Turkish, and since it is necessary for us to support Turkey as long as possible, we cannot allow Armenia to pass into the hands of Russia', wrote the aforementioned Paul Rohrbach in his book *Der Krieg und die deutsche Politik.*[6]

First World War

In early August 1914, Germany formally pledged to compel Russia to 'modify the Eastern borders of the Ottoman Empire in such a way as to ensure direct contact between Turkey and the Muslim populations living in Russia'. That was the first point in the confidential letter of 6 August 1914 from Germany's ambassador to Turkey, von Wangenheim, to the Grand Vizier, Mehmed Seid Halim Pasha. The sixth point read: 'Germany shall use its influence to ensure that Turkey receives proper compensation for its losses'. Also important for Turkey was the third point: 'Germany will not conclude any peace without the evacuation of Ottoman territories which [at the time of the peace agreement] may happen to be occupied by enemy forces'.[7]

Point one, first and foremost, meant support from Germany for Turkey's claim on the three sanjaks (districts) – Kars, Ardahan and Batum – seized from it by Russia in 1878. In Kars there was a Russian fortress, a key to the defence of the whole Caucasus, while Batum was a terminal for the Baku-Batum railway, along which Baku oil was delivered, and an important port for its export shipments.

Nevertheless, the German–Turkish Treaty of Alliance signed in Constantinople on 2 August 1914, and the aforementioned confidential letter of 6 August the same year, did not signal agreement to a Turkish takeover of the Batum, Ardahan and Kars districts alone. For this would have meant the Turks establishing 'direct contact' with Russia's Georgians and Armenians, but it would not have given them direct access to Baku. The significance of the first point, as historian E. Ludshuveit rightly explained, lay elsewhere, i.e., 'in the recognition by Germany of Turkish claims to the seizure of territories beyond the three sanjaks', which would to some degree mean the implementation of the pan-Turkist programme.[8] A British historian, Wolfram Gottlieb, noted that the 'direct contact' referred to above signified the 'conquest of Russian Armenia'.[9]

With the outbreak of the First World War, the pan-Turanianist ideologists believed the time was propitious for the achievement of the 'national ideal', for which Turkey had entered the war in the first place. That ideal was spelled out by the Central Committee of the *Ittihat ve Terakki* (Unity and Progress) Party on 12 November 1914 in a circular letter to its local organizations: 'The national ideal of our people and our country requires from us the destruction of the Muscovite enemy, in order thereby to reach the *natural* borders that will enclose all our blood kinsmen. Our religious feeling impels us to free the world of Islam from the rule of the infidels'.[10]

The heralds of pan-Turanianism and the Turkish militarists dreamed not only of conquests at Russia's expense in the Caucasus, the Volga Region, the Crimea, Central Asia and Turkestan (Russian Central Asia), but also of the creation of 'the Great Turan' on an enormous territory stretching from Gibraltar to China. The pan-Turanianist movement, to use the definition of one of its activists, Ahmed Emin, 'strove for the unification of all the Turks of the world, and then for the brotherhood of all the races of Turanic origin, including the Hungarians, Finns and Bulgarians'.[11] Another noted figure, Tekin Alp (Levi Cohan), believed the objects of Turkish irredentism to include Siberia, the Caucasus, the Crimea and Afghanistan, as well as the banks of the rivers Volga and Kama in central Russia. The Caucasus stood out in this general chain. It was regarded as an integral part of the Ottoman Empire annexed by Russia.

Speaking about the war against the states of the Entente, a noted ideologist of pan-Turanianism, Omar Seifeddin, stated in November 1914:

> This is a war of the nation for an ideal and at the same time a religious war. Therefore we shall first save and accept within our political boundaries the Turks, our brothers in religion and language, who are now under the yoke of the Russians. We shall first take from the Russians the Caucasus and shall then advance steadily into Turkestan, which is our homeland and in which 50 million Turkic Muslims live.

With the takeover of the Caucasus, which it was planned to effect in the initial period of the war, the national might of the Ottoman Empire, in Seifeddin's opinion, would increase twofold while, after the incorporation of Central Asia, Turkestan, Southern Siberia and the Pamirs 'into the political boundaries' of the empire, the 'government of the western Turks will finally cease to be Ottoman, and a truly great government of Turks and Muslims – the state of Turan – will be established'.[12] It was the intention of all the Young Turks' leaders, including the War Minister, Enver Pasha, that the Caucasian Front should play the leading role in the achievement of the ideal of pan-Turkism. 'The Caucasus is the way to Turan', while

'Turan is in the Turkish heart',[13] concluded the main ideologist of pan-Turanianism, Zia Gökalp. 'Let us seize that Caucasus as soon as possible', appealed one of the leaders of the Young Turks, Bayaeddin Sakir, who assumed 'the main pioneering role in the promotion of the ideal of Turan'.[14] 'Azerbaijan must become a fortress, a part of the main, great motherland, the great and strong Turan',[15] the pan-Turkist ideologists kept reiterating.

On 31 October 1914 Turkey's War Minister, Enver Pasha, ordered the Commander of the Third Army, Izzet Pasha, to advance immediately with four cavalry divisions into the Russian Caucasus as far as Karabakh, Baku and Dagestan. In order to destroy Russia's war supply network and foment Muslim uprisings in its rear, he demanded that the troops 'raze everything to the ground, destroy railways and bridges, burn the railway stations and lift the population of the whole Caucasus to its feet'.[16] At the same time the Young Turks perpetrated genocide on the Armenians of the Ottoman Empire, deporting and destroying more than one and a half million people.[17]

'Independent Caucasus' in the Turkish Orbit

The idea of unifying the Caucasian Muslim peoples under the aegis of Turkey developed gradually. At the end of 1915, the Sublime Porte, as Ottoman Turkey was sometimes called, and a group of Caucasian Mohammedans in Istanbul put forward the idea of creating an 'Independent Caucasus'.[18] This idea was further developed in a book published in English by Georgian émigrés in Zurich in 1916 under the title *Georgia and the War*. The publication of the book was financed from secret German funds. The plan was to unify into a single federation the mountain peoples of the Caucasus – the Chechens, the Circassians, the Dagestanis and the Tatars (that is, the Azeris). The establishment of an autonomous Armenian administrative-cum-territorial unit was ruled out. Turkey was to annex part of the Erivan province and the Kars region as 'territories inhabited by the Turks'. The Armenians and the Tatars would be given the right to set up mixed Armenian-Tatar cantons. Northern Armenia was to become part of autonomous Georgia. The entire Caucasus was to come under the protection of Turkey, which in turn would declare its readiness to 'co-operate with the people for the creation of a neutral Caucasus'.[19]

The idea of unifying the Muslim peoples of the Caucasus was

proclaimed in October 1917 by a congress of the Musavat Party.[20] The programme it adopted was a 'call of blood' addressed to all Muslims – 'the hitherto noble people of Islam'. 'The idea of Turkism is not an encroachment on others, nor is it a renunciation of Islam', said Musavat leader Mamed-Emin Rasulzade: 'the Turks are one single nation'. Having accepted the idea of a federative arrangement of Muslim peoples embracing the Crimea, the Caucasus, Dagestan, Turkestan and Bashkiria (west of the Urals), the congress raised the question of whether to grant territorial autonomy to Azerbaijan, a name intended to cover the provinces of Baku, Elizavetpol (now known as Ganja) and Erivan (Yerevan) up to and including Kars and Ardahan, i.e., the whole Eastern and Southern Caucasus.[21] There was vigorous activity in setting up the Caucasian federation by the mountain peoples of the Northern Caucasus, notably the Central Executive Committee of the Union of Mountain Peoples of the Caucasus formed in Vladikavkaz. On 2 December 1917, this Union proclaimed the autonomy of the Northern Caucasus within Russia (the Mountain Republic, also known as the Terek Republic) and set up a government for Terek and Dagestan. Later, on 21 December 1917, the Union declared its separation from Russia. In March 1918 the Bolsheviks seized Vladikavkaz and deposed the government of Terek and Dagestan, some of whose members, fleeing to Tiflis (Tbilisi), were to proclaim the full independence of the Northern Caucasus on 11 May 1918. Refusing to recognize Bolshevik power, the Central Executive Committee of the Union of Mountain Peoples of the Caucasus sent a delegation to Tiflis in March 1918 with a view to working out a joint plan of action to set up a 'free and independent Caucasus' on a confederative basis.[22]

The Run-Up to Brest-Litovsk

The period from December 1917 until March 1918 saw painful negotiations between Bolshevik Russia and the Central Powers (Germany, Austria-Hungary, Turkey and Bulgaria, alias the Quadruple Alliance) on the conclusion of a peace treaty. This process culminated in the signing, on 3 March 1918, of the Treaty of Brest-Litovsk. As might be expected, in the diplomatic clashes with the Bolsheviks, the idea of the self-determination of nations was a welcome tool for the German bloc, especially since the nations in question had belonged to its erstwhile military adversary.

By supporting the independence of the Caucasian nations, Germany and Turkey legitimized separate treaties and the military occupation of the Caucasus. Conditions were gradually becoming ripe for a parting of the ways between the Caucasian peoples: in a few months, Georgia would seek German protection from the Turkish advance from the south (and would be occupied by Germany), Azerbaijan and the North Caucasian mountain peoples would opt for what seemed to them a natural alliance with Turkey, whose troops entered these regions; while Armenia, severely truncated by Turkey under the terms of the Treaty of Batum (4 June 1918), would be temporarily left without an ally.

In the run-up to Brest-Litovsk, the Sublime Porte had instructed its representatives at the Brest-Litovsk negotiations to demand not only an immediate return of 'the districts – Kars, Ardahan, Batum – previously handed over to Russia as a pledge to indemnify it for war losses', but also 'the recognition of an independent Caucasian state' and the renunciation of any interference in its internal affairs. 'Russia, in line with the principle of the right of peoples to self-determination proclaimed by its present government, must recognize that right also with regard to the Muslim peoples of the empire. This is meant to apply to Kazan [Tataria], Orenburg [a Russian city located at a point on the line of Cossack settlements between the Bashkirs and the Kazaks], Turkestan and Bukhara [in Central Asia]',[23] the German general von Seeckt informed Berlin in December 1917.

Practical steps to sever the Transcaucasus from Russia were taken by the Transcaucasian Diet set up on 10 February 1918 and by the government it formed. The Transcaucasus was to opt for a federative state arrangement. All the main Caucasian peoples would enjoy sovereignty in internal matters. *Vis-à-vis* foreign states, the Caucasus would represent a single political and economic entity. The Transcaucasian state was to comprise five provinces – Baku, Elizavetpol (Ganja), Erivan (Yerevan), Tiflis and Kuba (in north-eastern Azerbaijan); two regions – Batum and Kars; and two territories – Sukhum (Abkhazia) and Zakataly (a separate district in Tsarist Russia, in 1918–21 a part of Georgia, now in north-western Azerbaijan). The question of including Daghestan and the Black Sea province remained open, pending the election of delegates to the Transcaucasian Diet.

Buffer States in the Caucasus

Under the terms of the Treaty of Brest-Litovsk, Russia was forced to relinquish to Turkey not only the Turkish territories occupied during the First World War, but also Kars, Ardahan and Batum. This had an immediate sequel in the Trabzon peace conference (March-April 1918), held solely between Turkey and the delegation of the Transcaucasian Diet and government. This delegation was regarded by the Turks as representing, not a state, but peoples 'returned to the bosom of the Turkish Empire', peoples whom 'nothing separates' from Turkey. So went the statement made by the head of the Turkish delegation, Rear-Admiral Rauf Bey, at the opening session of the conference on 14 March 1918.

The Ottoman delegation expressed the wish that Transcaucasia should proclaim its independence and announce its form of government before the negotiations then under way were completed. The delegation expressed its regret at the experiences of the peoples of the Transcaucasus in the recent past, when the Turks had been prevented from fulfilling their historic duty to help the Caucasians. Having emphasized Turkey's special tasks in the Caucasus, Rauf Bey reassured the delegates that the bonds linking the Turks with the Caucasian peoples were 'not only historical and geographical but rather ones of blood, flowing from their common past'. According to the Turkish interpretation, the peoples of the Caucasus, restored to the bosom of Mother Turkey, had the same origins and the same religion. The Caucasians had been forcibly separated from the Turks and had languished in captivity for 200 years. Separating the Transcaucasus from Russia would remove the barrier between Turks and Caucasian Muslims and would 'consolidate the unity between kindred nations', Rauf Bey concluded.[24] Rauf Bey considered the defence of Transcaucasia from Russia by means of Turkish power to be the 'defence by Turkey of its rights', and the 'buffer state created' in Transcaucasia to be 'the best defender of its northern borders'.[25]

A. Pepinov, an advisor to the Transcaucasian delegation and a member of the Muslim National Council, suggested setting up – as a Turkish protectorate – a fourth, separate administrative unit consisting of the Muslim areas of the Batum and Kars regions. 'The bonds created by their similarities of race, religion, economy and everyday life are very strong and it will be very hard for them to exist without each other',[26] Pepinov argued in 'grounding' that wish.

Representatives of the Union of Mountain Peoples of the Caucasus, who had been invited to Trabzon, went on record as saying that an independent Caucasian state body could not exist without Daghestan and other North Caucasian territories.[27] With that aim in view, and having secured the sultan's consent, the delegation of the mountain peoples went from Trabzon to Constantinople and, in Batum on 11 May 1918, announced the secession of the Mountain Republic from Russia and the establishment of an independent state stretching from the Black Sea to the Caspian Sea, including the North Caucasian regions of Kuban, Stavropol, Terek and Dagestan.[28]

Believing that the solution to the Caucasian problem was entering a critical phase, as 'the Russian warrior was subdued for the moment but could still spring back to life', in a memorandum dated 5 July 1918 the leaders of the North Caucasian Mohammedans asked the government of Austria-Hungary 'to prohibit the resumption by Russia of its interrupted thrust into Mesopotamia and the Gulf of Alexandretta [Iskenderun on the Turkish Mediterranean]', which meant that Georgia had to be prevented from becoming part of Russia. To thwart Russia's activity in the area of Asia Minor and the Mediterranean, it was proposed to detach Georgia and Armenia from it and to liquidate the Cossack element – 'the blind instrument of Muscovite imperialism'.[29]

The mountain peoples of the Caucasus were supported by Caucasian expatriates living in Turkey. On 8 September 1918, in a memorandum to the Austro-Hungarian government, on behalf of 'one and a half million Caucasian refugees', the Turkish Caucasian Committee advised the Quadruple Alliance (the German bloc) to prevent the further expansion of Russia and the formation of a Slav confederation, to promote the secession of non-Slav peoples from Russia and to assist them in the formation of independent states. 'If it were possible to unify the peoples of the Caucasus in a joint federation from the start, the result would doubtless be magnificent. The federation would form a barrier to obstruct the Russian advance and prevent the small Transcaucasian states from becoming dependent on Russia.' The authors of the memorandum argued from the fact that 'the Russians opposed the creation of a single state in the Caucasus'. And furthermore: by virtue of its position, the Northern Caucasus commanded the East, obstructing further conquests by Russia and its extension towards the Persian Gulf. The conclusion was as follows: that, taking advantage of the

chaotic situation in Russia, a government that would act in close
liaison with Turkey and its allies should be set up in the Northern
Caucasus.[30]

The Turkish claims were further promoted at a conference held
in Constantinople in June–July 1918 and devoted to the discussion
of Caucasian problems. Taking part in the conference were the
newly-founded independent states of Armenia, Georgia and
Azerbaijan, with which Turkey had signed separate treaties on peace
and friendship on 4 June 1918 in Batum. Before that, on 22 April
1918, the Transcaucasian Federative Democratic Republic was
formed, only to break up on 26 May 1918, with Georgia, Azerbaijan
and Armenia all proclaiming independence on 26–28 May 1918. The
Young Turk leaders demanded that the delegation from the
Armenian National Council which arrived in Constantinople in the
middle of June 1918 should renounce its policy of neutrality and
conclude an *entente cordiale* on a confederation with Turkey. Until
'an *entente cordiale* or a confederation materializes, not a single
issue will be discussed with the Armenians', was the position of
Enver Pasha.[31] Turkey's resolve 'never, under any circumstances, to
have common borders with Russia', became even firmer. To achieve
that aim, Turkey strove to set up buffer states between the
Ottoman Empire and Russia. In an attempt to camouflage Turkey's
new aspirations, Talaat, the Grand Vizier of its government, sought
recognition by the allies – Germany, Austria-Hungary and Bulgaria
– of the independence of Armenia, Azerbaijan, Georgia and the
mountain peoples of the Northern Caucasus.

The Young Turks sought to transform the Black and Caspian
Seas into inner 'Turanic lakes'. The sultan's governor-general was to
administer the Crimea and Azerbaijan, while Turkey itself would
incorporate Armenia in the guise of a confederation, which in turn
would form a link in the chain of the great Eastern federation. The
Young Turks dreamed of capturing Sukhum and 'defending
Abkhazia from the Georgians' with the help of the Chechens.[32] As
asserted by the pan-Turkist ideologist Ahmed Aga Oglu, that
federation was to be recognized by 'America, Europe and even the
Bolsheviks'.[33]

A fulcrum of the Young Turks was the 'East Caucasian Muslim
Republic' of Azerbaijan, created on 27 May 1918. Independence,
proclaimed on 28 May by the Muslim National Council, in fact
meant that Azerbaijan suddenly found itself completely dependent
on Turkey. Characteristic in this respect was the closing speech by

the leader of the Musavat Party, Mamed-Emin Rasulzade, at the final session of the Muslim National Council: 'The forces that might intervene in our internal affairs are not alien but kindred'.[34] Also characteristic is the speech given in Elizavetpol by Prime Minister Fatali Khan-Khoisky on the occasion of the entry into the city of the troops of the Turkish General Nuri Pasha:

> At long last, the Turks of Azerbaijan are achieving their aim. They are falling into the embrace of their beloved Ottoman Caliphate. The age-old ideal of all Mohammedanism – the rallying of all Muslims under the banner of the sultan – is at last becoming a reality. The Turkish liberation troops are awaited with a quivering heart by the mountain peoples of the Caucasus, the Turks and the Kyrgyz of Turkestan, the Sarts [the name used in the past to denote mainly settled Uzbeks and Tajiks living on the plain], the Khivans [of the Khanate of Khiva, now in Uzbekistan], the Bukharans of the Transcaspian and, finally, Afghanistan and the mighty India'.[35]

The transfer of railways and main roads into the hands of the Turkish command represented 'fraternal aid' to the young Muslim republic. The Austro-Hungarian representatives in the Caucasus had a different assessment of these events. 'The Azerbaijani government is an instrument in the hands of the Turks', the head of the Austro-Hungarian mission in the Caucasus, von Frankenstein, wrote from Tiflis on 4 August 1918 to Foreign Minister Stephan Burián.[36]

Territorial Claims

It was at that time that, contrary to historical justice and the national composition of their population, Karabakh, Zangezur (a southern extremity of present-day Armenia) and Nakhichevan were proclaimed by the Young Turks and the Musavat party (who led the government of Azerbaijan in 1918–20) to be 'Azerbaijani'. 'Musavat, the standard bearer for Azeri nationalism, is putting pressure on the Armenians, taking advantage of their awkward situation, and demanding from them an immediate redrawing of borders as well as the cession of the whole of Karabakh, where the Armenians constitute two-thirds of the population', wrote – on 1 July 1918 – the Tiflis newspaper *Znamya truda*, the organ of the Central Committee of the Socialist Revolutionary Party of

Transcaucasia. Speaking of Karabakh, von Frankenstein stated: 'In Nagorno-Karabakh there live 150,000 Armenians and 20,000 Muslims. Nevertheless, the Turks consider this territory to be Azeri. The Armenians will not give up Karabakh voluntarily'.[37] 'The Turks want to penetrate from Azerbaijan into the purely Armenian province of Karabakh and disarm its population', the head of the German mission in the Caucasus, Friedrich Kress von Kressenstein, reported from Tiflis to Reichskanzler Hermann von Hertling in Berlin.[38]

'To wrench the population of Karabakh forcibly from their ethnic environment, to deprive them of national independence and subordinate them to an authority which is alien in culture and spirit would be the greatest injustice, and one which could only lead to an eternal dispute and enmity between both sections of the population ... ', testified the leaders of the Countrymen's Union of Karabakh and Zangezur to members of the countries of the Quadruple Alliance at the Constantinople conference on 17 July 1918. The Armenian people would never cease to claim their natural property, nor would they reconcile themselves to the infringement of their rights in favour of the Muslim minority, said the memorandum. The authors of the memorandum saw the application of the principle of self-determination of peoples as the only just solution to the question of incorporating Karabakh into one state entity or another.[39]

Meanwhile, as confirmed by reports sent to Berlin and Vienna from the Transcaucasus by the German and Austro-Hungarian diplomatic and military services, 'the Turks explicitly wish for the annexation of the Northern Caucasus, including Dagestan, to the East Caucasian Muslim republic which is here called Azerbaijan' (15 July 1918). As was reported by the newspaper *Kavkazskoe slovo*, the Musavatist government intended – with the help of Turkish soldiers – to disarm the Armenian population of Karabakh and Azerbaijan, to arm the Muslims and destroy the Armenians in their indigenous land, confronting the Constantinople conference with a *fait accompli*.[40]

The Armenians found themselves in a disastrous situation. This was reported to the German government by Johann Heinrich Bernstorff, the German ambassador in Constantinople. On 25 August he informed Berlin as follows: 'The situation deteriorates daily. The responsibility for the death of the ancient Christian Armenian people lies squarely with Germany and Austria-Hungary.

History will not forgive us for the fact that the two great European powers are unable, at least today, to settle the question of the existence of a whole people and are solving that question under pressure from their Asiatic ally'.[41]

The German and Austro-Hungarian politicians were alarmed by the excessive activity of the Young Turks' leaders. 'One can never trust the Turks or believe their words', said General von Lossow to Armenian delegates in Berlin.[42] The German ambassador in Constantinople, Bernstorff, drew the attention of the Armenian delegates to the Pharisaism of Turkish leaders. 'One cannot trust the promises of the Turkish government. Talaat Pasha promised twenty times to amnesty the Turkish Armenians, but did nothing, however. Turkey (especially Talaat and Enver) would not hear of the formation of Armenia and now says it is better the way it is',[43] said Bernstorff. 'Those who have power should spare no effort to keep the Turks in check', said deputy Hugo Haase at a session of the Reichstag on 26 June 1918. 'One should do one's utmost to ensure that the Armenians living in the Caucasus are not subjected to pogroms, that the Turks leave the Caucasus immediately and observe the terms of the Treaty of Brest-Litovsk'.[44] 'The Turks in Turkish Armenia have murdered the men and driven the women and children to the mountains, thereby dooming them to death from hunger. They are acting the same way now with regard to the refugees',[45] von Frankenstein reported to Burián in Vienna on 26 August 1918.

The hypocrisy of Grand Visier Talaat and other leaders of the Young Turks is laid bare in an editorial by the ideologist of pan-Turkism, Ahmed Emin Bey, 'Our Policy in the Caucasus and the Armenians', published in the newspaper *Vakt* on 3 September 1918. 'It will be easier to settle accounts with an independent Armenia than with Armenians enjoying the protection of foreign states'. The pan-Turkists believed Armenia would serve as a buffer state between Turkey and Russia, and that it would be compelled to depend on the territory of Turkey for all lines of communication, both by sea and by land. 'Thus', they thought, 'in a political sense Armenia would find itself under our influence'.[46]

The Young Turks were pushing towards the East, to Baku, which they wanted to take over 'for Azerbaijan, that is, for themselves, for Turkey will in fact dominate in Azerbaijan',[47] Bernstorff stated. 'If Baku passes over to Azerbaijan, that is, to Turkey, then the latter will expand as far as Vladikavkaz',[48] added Austria-Hungary's chief

military representative in Turkey, Pomiankowski. The capture of
Baku was considered a 'duty' by the Turks. 'If Anatolia is today
shedding its blood for the liberation of Azerbaijan, tomorrow
Azerbaijan will save it. In saving Azerbaijan, Anatolia is saving
itself', the Young Turks' leaders kept repeating. They also grounded
a claim that Karabakh belonged to Azerbaijan: 'The local Turks use
pastures there, and it is for this reason alone that it is impossible to
leave that land to Armenia.' Such was the opinion of Grand Visier
Talaat.[49]

From Baku the Turks expected to penetrate Central Asia, their
ultimate objective being the creation of 'the Great Turan' that
would comprise the entire Turkic world lying between the
Mediterranean and China. 'The future Turkic world will be
precisely like that',[50] wrote the pan-Turkist writer Ahmed Emin,
referring to the judgements of representatives of various currents
of the pan-Turkist movement.

Despite the supplementary treaty signed between Germany and
Russia on 27 August 1918 in Berlin, and the Russo-German
warning to Turkey on the need to refrain from taking Baku and to
observe the clauses of the Treaty of Brest-Litovsk, on 15 September
the joint Turko-Tatar forces broke through to Baku. This was
facilitated by the sudden withdrawal of the British military
contingent. Pogroms and acts of violence continued for three days.
The number of Armenians deported and killed reached 50,000.
'Baku has thus been added to the number of places where the
systematic extermination of Armenians is put on the agenda of the
triumphant victor', wrote the newspaper *Kavkazskoe slovo* on 29
September 1918. Recalling the terrible fate of many thousands of
Armenians in various regions contested by Armenia and
Azerbaijan, the expulsion and wholesale killing of the indigenous
inhabitants of these places, the paper demanded an 'explicit answer
from the Azerbaijani government to the question disturbing
everyone: when will there be an end to this?'

The Soviet government, too, was demanding an answer from its
Turkish counterpart. In a note on 20 September 1918 it stressed
that the actions of the Ottoman government virtually annulled the
Treaty of Brest-Litovsk which had established peaceful relations
between the two states, and that such a treaty between Russia and
Turkey no longer existed.[51]

By that time the Entente's victory was becoming more evident,
as were its aims in the Caucasus. On 30 October 1918, an armistice

was signed in Mudros between the allies and Turkey. On 1 November 1918, the Soviet government proclaimed the abrogation of the Treaty of Brest-Litovsk, including its clauses pertaining to the Caucasus.

Turkish Policies after the First World War

Although the Turkish government evacuated its troops from Baku, it expected to keep some of its strongholds in the Caucasus after withdrawal. In addition, after the armistice new territories were seized by the Turks. 'The Turkish command will spare no resources to organize the fraternal Azerbaijani Army, and all the ranks of the Turkish Army stationed in Azerbaijan must be listed in the service of the Azerbaijani state and will remain there as long as they are needed', said Cavad Bey, the chief of the political department of the Muslim Caucasian army. The same point was confirmed by Izzet, Turkey's Minister of War. In a letter to Azerbaijan's Prime Minister, Fatali Khan-Khoisky, he expressed the hope that, after the removal of the Turkish troops from Azerbaijan, the Ottoman government would 'try to create a Muslim state'. This aim would be furthered by a Musavatist army modelled on the Turkish one.

> The fraternal Ottoman Empire which came to the defence of our country, with its renowned army commanded by the best military leaders, set itself the primary task of helping Azerbaijan to form its own military forces. It gives us all we need for a strong army: arms, uniforms, experienced officers and – and this is the main thing – the spirit of national identity which reigns throughout the Turkish army. What is required of us is only the manpower for the defence of our native land. Manpower and the means to keep up our army are what we have in abundance'.[52]

The Turkish armed forces under the command of Nuri Pasha were left in Elizavetpol, those commanded by Halil Pasha in the Northern Caucasus and those led by Sevket Pasha in Kars. 'In the Caucasus we had two divisions. Of late, arms have been distributed to the Muslims of Azerbaijan and the Northern Caucasus. After reinforcing our divisions with Caucasian volunteers, Enver Pasha planned to crush the Armenians and set up a provisional government in Kars, which the states of the Entente cannot reach soon enough'[53] subsequently wrote the future Turkish prime minister and president, then an activist in the Kemalist movement, Celal Bayar.

The so-called 'government of the National Council of Kars' and 'Araxes Turkish government' were set up, to be united in December 1918 into a 'South-Western Caucasian Republic'. The latter comprised the regions of Kars and Batum, the Akhaltsikh and Akhalkalaki districts (now in southern Georgia), Sharur (then in the Erivan province, now in the northern part of Nakhichevan in Azerbaijan (Ilyichevsk district), Nakhichevan, the Surmalu district (in eastern Turkey, main city: Igdir; conquered by Russia in 1828, ceded back to Turkey in 1921) and the south-eastern part of the Erivan district. The republic's government made contact with the 'Society for the Defence of the Rights of Eastern Anatolia 'which had sprung up in Erzerum, in eastern Turkey, with a view to repelling the 'threat of an Armenian takeover'.[54]

The republic lasted until mid-April 1919. The objective of its founders can be seen from the statement by its parliament on 27 March 1919: 'From now on the fate of the South-Western Caucasian Republic will merge with that of kindred Caucasian republics. It is a member of the family of Muslim republics of the Caucasus. In the event of the reconstitution of a unified Russia, its relation to this must be determined by agreement with the other Muslim nationalities of the Caucasus'.[55]

Turkey's aspiration was to annex the whole territory from Erzerum to Daghestan, and also Turkestan (Russian Central Asia). To make this pan-Turkist dream come true, Turkey needed a victory in Armenia, which was the only obstacle in the path of the pan-Turanianist movement. Such were the conclusions of the French diplomats, Colonel Chardigny and Captain Poidebard. They defined the essence of Azerbaijan's policy as achieving independence from Russia and a union with the Mountain Republic of the Northern Caucasus and with Turkey. Turkey, in turn, was striving for unification with the North Caucasian Republic and Azerbaijan.[56] Nor did it renounce the idea of a confederative association, which would mean a separation of the Caucasus from Russia.

Initiatives by the Transcaucasian States

The idea of a confederative association of the Caucasian republics and the mountain peoples of the Northern Caucasus, of creating a

'Caucasian Home', was revived in the period from October 1918 to June 1921. On 27 October 1918, the government of the Georgian Republic came up with a proposal for a conference in Tiflis which would bring together representatives of Georgia, Armenia, Azerbaijan and the Union of Mountain Peoples of the Caucasus. The aim of the conference would be to draw up the principles behind a 'joint' representation of the peoples of Transcaucasia and the Northern Caucasus at a world congress. Conference participants had to agree both on the terms of such joint action and on ensuring mutual accord and aid. This was the general tenor of the note sent to the Armenian government by Georgia's foreign minister. The government of the Georgian Republic proposed to discuss the mutual recognition of the independence of the states and governments invited to the conference, the settlement of all outstanding questions, including those relating to borders, and a common obligation not to enter into agreements, with any state, which would be to the detriment of any nation participating in the conference.

In principle, without denying the need to hold the conference, the Armenian government considered it necessary to increase the number of those taking part in it and to invite – besides those states indicated by the Georgian side – representatives of the governments of Kuban, Terek and other state entities in the south of Russia that were not members of the Union of Mountain Peoples of the Caucasus.[57]

Proposing to hold the conference in Baku, the government of Azerbaijan suggested that the following issues be discussed: mutual recognition of the independence of the Caucasian republics participating in the conference and the promulgation of a corresponding document; joint action at the peace congress, and wherever needed, in defence of the republics' independence; measures to curb possible encroachments on the independence of states participating in the conference, and the peaceful resolution of all border disputes, including by means of arbitration. Along with that, due to the formation in the Transcaucasus, in the areas of the Batum and Kars regions, of the so-called South-Western Caucasian Republic (whose interests were closely linked with those of the other Caucasian republics), the Azeri government deemed it 'desirable and necessary' that this Republic should participate in the work of the conference.[58] This proposal from the Azerbaijani government provoked vigorous objections on the part of the governments of Georgia and Armenia. They viewed the formation of the 'South-Western Republic' as a blow to the independence of the peoples of Transcaucasia and a 'threat from the South'. In a Georgian government note to the Azeri government, dated 9 March 1919, Georgia's foreign ministry let it be known that the presence of the 'South-Western Republic' at the conference would in fact prejudge the issue of its recognition, a circumstance the Georgian government could not possibly agree with.[59]

Deeming the participation of the South-Western Caucasian Republic in the conference to be unacceptable, and suggesting Tiflis as a venue, the government of Armenia put forward its own principles: it held that the promulgation of a solemn declaration recognizing independence before all the powers would be appropriate and possible only after the peaceful resolution, by mutual consent, of the issues relating to the territorial delimitation of the republics which had been formed in the Caucasus. The government of Armenia thought that the same resolution of territorial questions should serve as a prerequisite both for joint actions in defence of the independence of Caucasian republics and for all kinds of agreements on joint steps to guard that independence against possible dangers. It suggested including on the conference agenda the question of defining the terms and procedures for the recognition of citizenship for the nationalities living outside their mother republic.[60]

A new phase of negotiations, conferences and exchanges of notes began. A number of agreements and treaties between Georgia, Armenia and Azerbaijan were concluded, including on free transit and arbitration, and a convention on the railways. The situation was aggravated by the occupation of the Northern Caucasus by the Volunteer Army led by the Russian White General Anton Denikin, who did not recognize the independence of the Caucasian republics. A conference was held in Tiflis to co-ordinate positions and map out joint action. There were no Armenian representatives present. On 16 July 1919, an agreement was concluded between Georgia and Azerbaijan on joint military action against a possible advance by Denikin's Volunteer Army. Armenia did not join that defensive alliance. 'Armenia cannot and should not have a Caucasian orientation. The latter does not proceed from the interests of Armenians',[61] was the official response from the Armenian side. Thus Armenia, according to Henri Poidebard, the French military agent in Erivan, did not wish to foster the ties between Turkey and Azerbaijan.[62] The intervention by the Supreme Council of the Entente, to which the representatives of Georgia and Azerbaijan at the Paris Peace Conference (1919–20) appealed for mediation, and which admonished them to smooth out their differences, did not help. Equally futile were the subsequent efforts by representatives of Georgia, Azerbaijan and the Supreme Council to launch Armenia into the orbit of a Caucasian orientation.

In all discussions, the Azeri delegation continued to insist on its proposal for the creation of a confederation. The Armenian government ruled in December 1919 that talks with Azerbaijan would only be possible on the following conditions: if a road to Sharur and Nakhichevan were opened (both districts were then controlled by Armenia, but an insurgency by the Muslim part of the population, aided by Turkey, was in progress there); if Azerbaijan waived its claims on Zangezur, a disputed region east of Nakhichevan and then controlled by Armenia; if Azerbaijan granted the Armenians on its territory equal rights with the Azeris; and if specific proposals on the confederation were submitted.[63]

At the Armenian-Azerbaijani conference held in Baku from 15 to 22 December 1919, the Azeri side, while reaffirming its position on the need to set up a confederation, evaded discussion of the issues raised by the Armenian delegation, namely those relating to borders and the cessation of hostilities.[64] None the less, the government of Azerbaijan continued to maintain that 'a close and lasting bond between the peoples of Transcaucasia was one of the important factors for their political well-being and economic prosperity'. It insisted on the convening of a conference of representatives of the Transcaucasian republics to discuss and work out constructive forms for the proposed confederation.[65] In a telegram on 4 March 1920, the Azeri prime minister proposed to hold such a conference in Baku on 15 March with a view to 'drawing the Transcaucasian republics closely together in the form of a confederation of independent states'.[66]

Speaking of the general approach taken by Azeri premier Fatali Khan-Khoiski, Armenian prime minister Alexander Khatisian reminded his counterpart in a telegram dated 8 March 1920:

> The government of Armenia still expects a response from your government to a number of concrete proposals sent by me personally to Tiflis and then received by you to be reported to your government. These proposals, which can serve as a basis for continued activity by the Armenian-Azeri conference,

were expressed in the following points: first, a status quo in Karabakh with strict observance by Azerbaijan of the terms of the agreement reached with the Armenian National Council of Karabakh; second, status quo for Zangezur; third, the opening of the Erivan-Julfa railway line [to the Persian border]; fourth, effective recognition of the Sharur-Nakhichevan region as an integral part of the Republic of Armenia.

It was noted that the three-year-long experience of convening the conference had proved beyond a doubt that, without prior acceptance of the above conditions and their strict observance, there was no possibility of a real agreement. Khatisian requested the Azeri government to 'indicate a list of questions to be dealt with at the conference and the concrete form in which the proposed confederation is conceived by the government of Azerbaijan'.[67]

The Armenian delegation likewise defended this viewpoint at the Transcaucasian conference which opened in Tiflis on 9 April 1920. The conference resolved that all the bloody clashes between Armenians and Azeris that had been occurring since 1919 should cease immediately. It appealed urgently to the governments of Armenia and Azerbaijan to take, immediately, stringent measures to rule out any possibility of clashes between the Armenian and Azeri populations within the relevant republics.[68] A sequence of issues to be examined at the conference was also proposed: the immediate cessation of hostilities on all fronts; the setting up of a permanent body for liaison between the three republics of Transcaucasia; the territorial issue; the co-ordinating of action in the field of foreign policy; the confederation of the Transcaucasian republics; economic questions. 'The Azerbaijani delegation proposed to put the question of the confederation in second place. Our delegates and the Georgians were against this',[69] it was reported to Erivan on 12 April. Another letter said that 'the Tatars [Azeris] were calling the establishment of the permanent body the achievement of the new federation'.[70]

The Azeri delegates, enjoying the support of the Georgian delegation, for several days pressed for a discussion of the question of coordinating the foreign policies of the Transcaucasian republics. According to their statement, they were prompted to do so by the news of a certain Bolshevik advance in the direction of the Black Sea port of Sochi and the Caspian Sea port of Baku. The Armenian delegates argued, with reason, that until the territorial question had been resolved and the conflict situations eliminated, there could be no question of taking joint steps in foreign policy matters.[71] The sessions of 19, 20 and 21 April were entirely devoted to issues related to co-ordinating the foreign policies of the Transcaucasian republics while settling internal disputes between them. The head of the Armenian delegation, Amo Oganjanian, reported:

> The Georgian and Azerbaijani delegations, speaking with one voice, insisted that the conference should at once pass a resolution declaring that we will act jointly to defend our republics and their independence from any encroachments, from either north or south. The last addition ('from the south') was made mainly to curry favour with us. Our delegates argued that such actions cannot take place, nor can there be any question of co-ordinated steps between us, until we settle our internal disputes. Therefore our people insisted that we should first of all and simultaneously conclude mutual agreements on these outstanding questions, including economic ones, and then take any joint steps'.[72]

The Armenian delegation's proposed resolution was turned down. The question of co-ordinated action by the Transcaucasian republics was taken off the agenda altogether. In view of the manoeuvring, the profusion of general statements and the evasive approach of the Azeri delegation, the leaders of the Georgian and Armenian delegations put a direct question to Azerbaijan's prime minister, Khan-Khoysky (who had arrived in Tiflis after a long delay), about Azerbaijan's relations with Turkey.

They wanted to find out concretely about a Turkish–Azeri treaty, the text of which had been published in *The Times*. Khan-Khoiski called this report 'a wanton provocation and a lie' which could only have found its way into the newspaper 'through some enemy'.[73] In fact, however, Azerbaijan had indeed concluded a treaty, not only with Turkey, but with the Mohammedans of the Northern Caucasus. 'The Turkish plan was based on religion. The Turks envisaged a unification of the Terek Republic [Mountain Republic] and Azerbaijan. That alliance was concluded in October 1918', reported Colonel Chardigny, drawing attention to the development of the pan-Turkist movement that had transformed itself into a 'nationalist and religious movement of Mohammedan Turks'. Having encompassed nearly the whole of the Northern Caucasus, the Mountain Republic claimed the whole of Kabarda and the territory inhabited by the Cossacks, and laid claim to South Ossetia (which did not wish to recognize the Georgian government), to Abkhazia and the Zakataly region (now in North-Western Azerbaijan). This last region was also claimed by Azerbaijan.[74] Turkish emissaries were strenuously working among the Mohammedans of the Northern Caucasus. 'Direct instigators of pan-Turkist and pan-Islamicist sentiments are active among the mountain peoples. Even after its fall, Turkey will not leave them alone', said a report from Vladikavkaz.

Diplomatic Negotiations

Efforts to unite the Caucasian republics were also made in Europe, notably at conferences in Paris (18 January 1919–21 January 1920), London (February–March 1920) and San Remo (19–26 April 1920), attended by delegations from the Caucasian republics. The Paris Peace Conference was convened by the states of the First World War victors to draft peace treaties with the vanquished Central Powers. Its work led to the signing of the Treaty of Versailles with Germany (28 June 1919) and corresponding treaties with Germany's wartime allies (Austria, Hungary, Bulgaria and Turkey). On 14 May 1919, the Paris Conference stipulated the transfer to the US of a mandate on Armenia (to be rejected by the US Senate on 1 June 1920). The London conference dealt with (and failed to resolve) the question of borders between the still independent Transcaucasian republics, while the one at San Remo was a session of the Supreme Council of the Entente which approved the draft of the peace treaty with Turkey (the future Treaty of Sèvres). At San Remo, it was resolved that Armenia's borders would encompass large tracts of Turkish Armenia with an outlet to the Black Sea. These provisions, enshrined in the Treaty of Sèvres, were bitterly opposed by Turkey, with the support of Bolshevik Russia, and never came into effect.

Robert Vansittart, Private Secretary to Lord Curzon and subsequently Permanent Member of the British Foreign Office, put the British government's political line to members of the delegations of the Caucasian republics in London and San Remo. At the London meetings with the delegations of Georgia, Armenia and Azerbaijan, Vansittart stated bluntly that if the delegations failed to resolve the confederation issue and form a united bloc *vis-à-vis* the allies, the Supreme Council of the Entente would desist from taking any part in the fate of the Transcaucasus. He expressly mentioned that an agreement on a confederation would make a favourable impression on the conference that was due to open in San Remo. Despite this, the questions outstanding between the Transcaucasian republics were not settled in London.[75]

The examination of the issue was resumed in San Remo in the middle of April 1920, where the Georgian and Azeri delegations came to a mutual agreement. The Azeris would recognize Georgia's sovereignty over Batum on condition that Azerbaijan's interests – namely, the right of access to the Black Sea – were guaranteed. The Armenian delegation demanded that a section of the port of Batum and a territorial zone for building a railway line to Armenia be placed at Armenia's disposal. These latter proposals did not meet with understanding on the part of the Georgian or Azerbaijani sides and no agreement was reached on them. Vansittart's statement that, unless an agreement in principle between the republics of Transcaucasia were submitted to Lord Curzon, the allies would not render them material aid, also failed to produce a rapprochement. Vansittart suggested proclaiming Batum a free city under the control of the League of Nations. A meeting of members of the delegations on 21 April 1920 in San Remo ended in failure. A unified economic space was never formed.[76]

The Musavat line aimed at territorial expansion was continued by Azerbaijan, which was sovietized in April 1920. The new government began its foreign policy activity with claims on Armenian lands – Karabakh, Zangezur and Nakhichevan. 'The subjugation and destruction of the Armenian people will be the main task of the Muslim Turks who have put on a Bolshevik mask, for the Armenian people form a wedge in the Turkic-Muslim world and, because of their links with the European Christian world, are a dangerous impediment to the complete domination of pan-Turkism in the East and its extension to the confines of the lands inhabited by the Turkic race', ran the memorandum submitted by the Armenian side to the British military delegation attached to the White Russian General Pyotr Wrangel (whose official title was Commander-in-Chief of the Armed Forces of Southern Russia).[77]

The slogan 'Azerbaijan for the Azeris' was advanced by Enver Pasha on 4 September 1920 at the First Congress of the Peoples of the East, held in Baku. It appeared in a written declaration submitted 'on behalf of' the peoples of Algeria, Morocco, Tripoli and the entire Muslim world, whom Enver claimed to represent as self-styled plenipotentiary.[78] After becoming acquainted with the situation in Azerbaijan and the Muslim East, and after conversations with the leaders of the Communist International and the Azeri authorities, Enver, in a letter to Mustafa Kemal (who shared his opinion on 'the special place of Turkey in the Islamic world'), expressed readiness to send to the Anatolian fronts two divisions made up of Azerbaijani Turks.[79] 'Even if the Red Army does not wish it, we should move onto the offensive and reach the borders of 1877 [that is, before the Russian conquest of Kars, Ardahan and Batum in 1878]',[80] he wrote on 7 September 1920.

In the second half of September 1920, the Turkish armies invaded Armenia, seizing Sarikamis and then Kars and Alexandropol. The Turkish General Karabekir demanded the extension of Turkey's 'rights' to Nakhichevan and the adjoining lands, where an autonomous government was to be set up under a Turkish protectorate.[81]

After the occupation by the Turks of the Kars region and a section of the area around Batum, the question of the unification of the South-Western Caucasian Republic was again raised. This issue was discussed at a session of the Presidium of the Council for Propaganda and Action of the Peoples of the East (this council, set up following a decision of the First Congress of the Peoples of the East in 1920, was composed of both the participants in the Congress and Bolshevik officials and was entrusted with the task of disseminating revolutionary propaganda in the East; it was dissolved in 1922, and its functions transferred to the Comintern). The Presidium declared as follows: 'This apology for a South-Western Republic undoubtedly has pro-Turkish leanings. The greater part of the South-Western Republic is constituted by the Kars region, which is populated by Armenians and forms a component part of Armenia; the issue concerning it should therefore be decided by agreement with Soviet Armenia'.[82]

At the Moscow conference of 16 March 1921 the Turks sought the annexation to Turkey of the Kars region, Ardahan, Kagizman and Surmalu (these regions are now in eastern Turkey, adjacent to the Caucasus), and of Nakhichevan to Azerbaijan. In June 1921 Nagorno-Karabakh was handed over to 'the outpost of Soviet power in the East' – Azerbaijan. The Kemalists and the Azeri leaders were progressing jointly towards a common aim, skilfully using the Bolshevik slogans to their advantage. The question of a confederation was raised anew. Earlier, at the end of November

1920, Mustafa Kemal had written in a telegram to Prime Minister Simon Vratsian of the Republic of Armenia about the 'mutually beneficial relations between Turkey and Armenia', which would provide an opportunity to defend Armenia from 'baleful outside influences.'[83]

At the same time, Cemal Pasha, one of the instigators of the Armenian massacres, posing in the role of 'protector' of the peoples of the Caucasus, drew up a programme for their 'salvation' from Russia. The Young Turks' doctrine on the national question, *A Political Project for the Ottomans, Armenians, Georgians and Azeris*, unveiled by Cemal, rested on the creation of a defensive anti-Russian alliance of Georgia, Armenia, Azerbaijan and the Mohammedans of the Northern Caucasus with Turkey, in order to prevent them from becoming 'victims of Russia' and of a 'possible invasion from Moscow'. Cemal recommended 'exerting all efforts so as not to let the Russian flow overwhelm them by spilling over the Caucasus Range. For this purpose these four states must undoubtedly conclude between them a defensive alliance against a possible invasion by the Muscovites'. And further:

> If the four of us – the Ottoman Empire and the Azerbaijani, Georgian and Armenian republics – do not contract an alliance of peoples of the Middle East to defend ourselves from Russia, if we do not act jointly and do not assist the formation of republics in the Northern Caucasus, we cannot doubt that we shall again become victims of Russia, which has always sought to bring us under its yoke.

Cemal did not conceal the fact that 'for the Turks, who constitute a huge majority in the Ottoman Empire, this project is of immense importance'. It was aimed to bring home to the Armenians the need to 'remain in the Ottoman Empire', to 'be loyal to Ottoman ideals' – this being, in his opinion, 'the only way to forget the bloody past and lay the foundations for a radiant, happy future'.[84]

By that time the representatives of the Caucasian republics that had existed before the installation of the Soviet power – Avetis Agaronian (Armenia), Akaki Chkhenkeli (Georgia), Alimardan Topchibashev (Azerbaijan) and Abdul-Mejid Chermoev (the Northern Caucasus) – imbued with the ideals of independence and mutual alliance, spoke in a memorandum (adopted in Paris on 10 June 1921) of the community of political and economic tasks shared by the four republics, and of the need for establishing a close fraternal union between them.[85] The memorandum recognized the need for union in the military, customs and diplomatic spheres. This document had no legal effect, however: in the republics of Transcaucasia and the Northern Caucasus there existed another power, the Soviet one.

None the less, the search for ways to effect a rapprochement continued abroad. Throughout the 1920s and 1930s, broadly-based activities were launched by the organizations Prometheus and The Caucasus, which were backed by Turkey. The Armenian political parties avoided adopting a pro-Caucasian attitude.

Émigré representatives of the formerly independent republics of the Caucasus – Georgia, Armenia, Azerbaijan and the mountain peoples – gave even stronger recognition to the economic unity of the Caucasus in a second declaration, drawn up in September 1924. As a form of Union of Caucasian Peoples they chose a confederation, vesting it with three main functions – those of common customs frontiers, defence and foreign policy. It was explained that the confederation of states was an International Association of Sovereign States with legal status. In a Draft Pact of Confederation of the Caucasus, drawn up by Caucasian emigrés and published in early 1932 in the émigré press, the Caucasus was viewed as a single political and economic unit. The purpose of the confederation was the defence of that unit from outside danger, particularly from Russia.

Also envisaged were the organs of the common confederative state: a permanent secretariat and a confederative court of law.[86]

In émigré circles, however, there was no unanimity. All the Armenian political parties and public organizations came out against the Pact. The Boston magazine *Airenik* (Motherland) pointed out that it was Turkey that stood behind Prometheus, the organization militating for the national defence of the Caucasian peoples and initiator of the Draft Pact. The Armenian organizations could not co-operate with a group that was merely a tool in the hands of Turkey and in fact sought to replace the sovereignty of the Bolsheviks with that of Turkey over the whole of the Caucasus. That was a change not a single Armenian could countenance. 'We had never been admirers of Soviet power, but if our Caucasian friends wanted to exchange it for a camouflaged Turkish yoke, we would not follow them'.[87] The Pact was never signed.

In the Soviet Union, an experiment with federating the Transcaucasian republics was also short-lived. 1936 became the year of the end of the Transcaucasian Socialist Federative Soviet Republic, set up in 1922. The Armenian, Azerbaijani and Georgian Soviet Socialist Republics each became a constituent part of the Soviet Union. Both the Soviet and emigré attempts at Caucasian federalism have to be regarded as political failures.

'Caucasian Home' and Pan-Caucasian Solidarity

Thus, as shown by historical experience, the form of a confederative association failed to take root in the Caucasus. It again became a subject for discussion, however, after the break-up of the USSR, when General Jokhar Dudaev advanced the idea of a 'Caucasian Home' encompassing all the North Caucasian and Transcaucasian peoples. A special role for Turkey in the Caucasus was again postulated and statements were made about Turkey's readiness to assume 'political responsibility in a region stretching from the Adriatic to the frontiers of China'.[88]

Calls have been and are still being made to the Caucasus to separate itself from Russia, and to Russia to do likewise in relation to the Caucasus. All this is fraught with danger for Caucasian civilization. The noble idea of pan-Caucasian solidarity 'is most often added to their armoury by political speculators of all kinds, who use the pathos of these ideas to turn whole peoples into hostages to their selfish ends, orchestrating moves to foment war in the Caucasus against this background. Moreover, it is the anti-Russian forces that play with the idea of a pan-Caucasian home, which is particularly dangerous for the prospects for preserving the unity of Caucasian civilization.'[89] One cannot but agree with these thoughts by the eminent politician and scholar, the Dagestani Ramazan Abdulatipov. Nor should one overlook pan-Turkism, which is being presented as a promoter of general human values, a champion of true democracy and a banner of freedom, unification, internationalism and the solidarity of all Turkic peoples and those living side by side with them.[90]

In resolving interethnic issues, the will of all the peoples is of paramount importance. Any solution must take into account the community of their political, economic, social and strategic interests and must be based on a civilized and humane realization of the principle of the self-determination of peoples, with a corresponding resolution of territorial disputes in such a way as to eliminate the causes of such interethnic conflicts.

NOTES

1. Magyar orszagos Levéltár. Filmtár – Wien (State Archive of Hungary, Budapest. Films of the State Archive of Austria-Hungary for 1918) – OLFT-W-1110, political archive X Russia, file 156, XI Caucasian countries, 6 July 1918, No.59/P, pp.369–70. OLFT-W is an abbreviation of 'országos Levéltár. Filmtar – Wien'. Before every mention of OLFT below, the words 'State Archive of Hungary' have been added.
2. Ismail Bey Gasprinski, *Russkoe musul'manstvo. Mysli, zametki i nablyudeniya musul'manina* (Simferopol, 1881), p.5. See also S.M. Chervonnaya, 'Ideya natsional'nogo soglasiya v sochineniyakh Ismaila Gasprinskogo', *Otechestvennaya istoriya* (Moscow, 1992), pp.31–4.
3. *Ports* (Experience) (Tiflis, 1897), No.7–8, pp.204–5.
4. See *Golos Moskvy* (16 Jan. 1914); *Kavkazskoe slovo* (15 April 1916); Tsentral'nyi gosudarstvennyi voenno-istoricheskiy arkhiv (Moscow, cited below as TsGVIA), d.2000, op.1, d.973, ll.110–15; Arkhiv vneshney politiki Rossiyskoy Federatsii, f. PA, 1913, d.3470, pp. 40–41.
5. M. Pavlovich (Veltman), *Bor'ba za Aziyu i Afriku* (Leningrad, 1924), p.78.
6. Quoted from the Russian First World War edition: P. Rohrbach, *Voyna i germanskaya politika* (Moscow, 1915), pp.62–4. The main points that later found expression in Rohrbach's book were made on 23 November 1913 at a session of the Deutsch-Asiatische Gesellschaft in Berlin, attended by German politicians, diplomats and military. They were approved by Field Marshal von der Goltz. A Russian military agent in Berlin, Bazarov, was also present among the audience. Bazarov later gave a secret report on the session to the Russian Army General Staff in St. Petersburg (see TsGVIA, d.2000, op.1, d.973, ll.110–15).
7. Yu. Klyuchnikov and A. Sabanin, *Mezhdunarodnaya politika noveishego vremeni v dogovorakh, notakh i deklaratsiyakh* (Moscow, 1926), part II, pp.8–9, 17.
8. E. Ludshuveit, *Turtsiya v gody pervoi mirovoi voiny. 1914–1918. Voenno-istoricheski ocherk* (Moscow, 1966), pp.33–4.
9. W. Gottlieb, *Studies in Secret Diplomacy During the First World War* (London, 1957), p.36.
10. Ibid.
11. A. Emin, *Turkey in the World War* (London, 1930).
12. O. Seyfeddin, *Yarinki Turan Devleti* (Istanbul, 1958), pp. 21–2.
13. K. Karabekir, *Cihan harbine neden girdik, nasil girdik, nasil idare ettik. Ikinci kitap* (Istanbul, 1938), pp.26–30, 487.
14. Karabekir K, op. cit.
15. Z. Sakir, *1914–1918. Cihan harbini nasil idare ettik* (Istanbul, 1944), p.127.
16. S. Aydemir, *Suyu Arayan Adam* (Istanbul, 1967), p.160.
17. See *Genotsid armian v Osmanskoy imperii* (Edited by M. Nersisian) (Yerevan, 1966).
18. State Archive of Hungary, OLFT-W-1110, 156, Caucasian countries, 1918, 84-B/P, supplement to the letter of the Union of Mountain Peoples of the Caucasus dated 5 October 1918, pp.380–81.
19. *Georgia and the War* (Zurich, 1916), pp.33–4.
20. Musavat ('Equality') was the party of Azeri nationalists in power in the Republic of Azerbaijan in 1918–1920. Until the end of 1918 Musavat adopted a pro-Turkish stance, and later a pro-British one.
21. M.D. Guseinov, *Tiurkskaya demokraticheskaya partiya 'Musavat' v proshlom i nastoyaschem. Vyp. 1. Programma i taktika* (Baku, 1927), pp.71–6; S. Sef, *Bor'ba za oktiabr' v Zakavkazye* (Tiflis, 1932), pp.127–31.
22. State Archive of Hungary, OLFT-W-1110, No.84/P, pp.380–81, message dated 5 October 1918 continued (Constantinople).
23. K. Mühlmann, *Das Deutsch-türkische Waffenbündnis im Weltkriege* (Leipzig, 1940), pp.190–91.
24. Central State Historical Archive, Republic of Armenia (here and below: TSGIA RA), f.200, op.1, d.9.
25. *Dokumenty i materialy po vneshnei politike Zakavkazya i Gruzii* (Tiflis, 1919).

26. TSGIA RA, f.200, op.1, d.9.
27. State Archive of Hungary, OLFT-W-1110, No.60/P, do, 7369, n.702.
28. Ibid., N 84-B/P, pp.405–7.
29. Ibid., p.368.
30. Ibid., N 83/P, p.108; pp.159–64.
31. TSGIA RA, f.200, op.1, d.180, ll.51–5, 60–61.
32. State Archive of Hungary, OLFT-W-1110.
33. TSGIA RA, f.200, op.1, d.664; *Kavkazskoe slovo* (2 Nov. 1918). Translated from the Turkish newspaper *Vakt* .
34. A. Steklov. *Armiya musavatistskogo Azerbaidzhana* (Baku, 1928), p.7.
35. *Airenik* (Boston, MA, 1925), No.9, p.68.
36. State Archive of Hungary, OLFT-W-1110, 98/2, p.30.
37. Ibid., No.12, 921, pp.14–15; OLFT-W-1112, PA/P, A/C, 8987.
38. *Deutschland und Armenien, 1914–1918, Sammlung diplomatischen Aktenstücke. Herausgegeben und eingeleitet von Dr. Johannes Lepsius* (Potsdam, 1919), pp.420–21.
39. State Archive of Hungary, OLFT-W-1110, pp.31–4; TSGIA RA, f.457, op.7, d.3, p.1; d.8, pp.1–6.
40. *Kavkazskoe slovo* (17 June 1918).
41. *Deutschland und Armenien*, op. cit., p.431.
42. TSGIA RA, f.200, op.1, d.658, ll.49–50.
43. Ibid., d.11, ll.39–42, 86–91.
44. State Archive of Hungary, OLFT-W-1112, XI-157, pp.542–6.
45. Ibid., No. PA/P A-C, 8967.
46. *Kavkazskoe slovo* (23 Oct. 1918). Article reproduced from the Constantinople newspaper *Vakt*.
47. TSGIA RA, f.200, op.1, d.13, ll.10, 14, 19.
48. Ibid., f.222, op.1, d.12, ll.102–3.
49. Ibid. Archive of the Institute of History, National Academy of Sciences, Republic of Armenia, F.M. Tumanian, l.14.
50. A. Emin, *Turkey in the World War* (London, 1930), pp.187–204.
51. *Dokumenty vneshnei politiki SSSR* (Moscow, 1957), pp.490–91.
52. *Azerbaijan* (16 Oct.; 1 Nov. 1918).
53. C. Bayar, *Ben de yazdim. Milly müladeleye giris* (Istanbul, 1967).
54. Rossiyski tsentr izucheniya arkhivov novoy istorii, f.5, op.1, d.158, ll.9–10.
55. Ibid., f.544, op.3, d.20, ll.2–3.
56. 'Zakavkazye. 1918–1920,' *Svobodnaya mysl'* (1991), pp.40–49. Survey of the situation in the Caucasus. Documents of the Deuxième Bureau of France's General Staff: report of the military mission in the Caucasus headed by Colonel Chardigny, 22 Jan. 1920 (pp.40–46). General Staff. Bureau A., 20 Jan. 1920. Analysis of Captain Poidebard's report on pan-Turkist movement (pp.47–9).
57. TSGIA RA, f.200, op.1, d.154, ll.1–2, 25–6, 39–41.
58. Ibid., f.149, l.15-16, Nos.1076, 1078.
59. Ibid., l.34, No.1704.
60. Ibid., l. 21, Nos.1075, 1080, 1081, 1082.
61. Ibid., d.252, l.46.
62. 'Zakavkazye. 1918–1920', *Svobodnaya mysl'* (1991), No.16, p.49.
63. TSGIA RA, f.200, op.1, d.411, l.6–7.
64. Ibid., d.365, ll.1–49.
65. Ibid., d.411, l.7, Nos.76/20, 1/364, 1974.
66. Ibid., l.23, Nos.74101, 1642.
67. Ibid., l.26, No.76, 1382; l.60.
68. Ibid., l.34, Nos.76/20, No.1713; ll.60-61.
69. Ibid., l.81.
70. Ibid., l.78.
71. Ibid., l.89a.
72. Ibid., l.91.
73. Ibid., l.90.

74. 'Zakavkazye. 1918–1920', *Svobodnaya mysl'*, No.16 (1991), pp.40, 44.
75. *Prometei. Organ natsional'noi zaschity kavkazskikh narodov* (Paris, 1932), No.72. On the London Conference, see *Documents on British Foreign Policy 1919–1939*. Vol.VII.
76. *Prometei* (1932), No.72. On the San Remo Conference see *The Armenian Review*, Vol.30, Nos.4–120, pp.398–413, and 3–119, pp.229–53.
77. TSGIA RA, f.200, op.1, d.385, ll.62–5.
78. *Pervyi s'ezd narodov Vostoka 1–7 sentyabrya 1920 g.* (Baku, 1920), pp.108–12.
79. C. Kutay, *Atatürk – Enver Pasha Heldişeleri* (Istanbul, 1956), p.36.
80. Kazim Karabekir, *Istiklal Harbimizde Enver Pasha ve Ittihat Terakki erkani* (Istanbul, 1967), pp.40–47.
81. TSGIA RA, f.200, op.2, d.79, ll.19–20.
82. Rossiiski tsentr izucheniya arkhivov novoi istorii, f.544, op.3, d.26, ll.13–14.
83. TSGIA RA, f.200, op.2, d.79, l.21.
84. *Zapiski Dzhemal-pashi. 1913–1919* (Tiflis, 1923).
85. *Revue des études arméniennes*, IV (Paris, 1923).
86. *Prometei* (1932), No.70.
87. *Airenik* (Boston, 18 Sept. 1932), No.6196.
88. *Izvestia* (27 July 1992).
89. *Nauchnaya mysl' Kavkaza*, No.1 (Rostov-on-Don, 1995), pp.55–7.
90. *Kavkazski dom* (Grozny, 2 April 1992).

4

'Caucasian Home': A View from Azerbaijan

RAFIG ALIEV

After the break-up of the Soviet Union, the Caucasian region (Transcaucasia and the Northern Caucasus) turned into a hotbed of extremely grave tensions, with a conflict potential surpassing that of the other 'hot spots' of the former USSR. This situation requires conceptualization on both the analytical and prognostic levels. Of special interest is the repeatedly advanced idea of a 'Caucasian Home'. The question is to what extent this idea may contribute to the achievement of peace in the region at the present crucial period in its history. The starting point for further debate is a thesis that there is a certain analogy between the 1917 revolution and the perestroika which began 70 years later. The October Revolution was primarily a Russian revolution. It had taken by surprise the oppressed peoples of the Russian Empire, for whom its aspirations had been alien and who quite by accident found themselves following in its wake.[1] As a result, 'in Transcaucasia generally and in Baku particularly the revolution had turned from a struggle between classes into a war between hostile nationalities'.[2] The perestroika of the 1980s was also aimed at resolving Russian problems above all.

As for the non-Russian peoples, with the exception of those of the Baltics, who met with full understanding and support in the West, these were caught unawares by events. They became entangled in a sharp internecine struggle to survive and to gain possibly greater advantages amid the confusion of *perestroika*. And just like the Bolsheviks – who had undertaken to extend their power to all the borderlands of the former Russian Empire, against which they had waged such bitter struggle in the past – the Moscow authorities of today are likewise not prepared to relinquish the legacy of the USSR.[3] So although it is the deeply rooted internal factors of a primarily socio-economic and ethnocultural nature that underlie the conflicts and bloody clashes in the Caucasus, it would be a mistake to overlook completely the role of the neighbouring powers, including the major ones. In this situation, how is it possible to contribute to the resolution of interethnic conflicts in the Caucasus? It appears that the realization of the idea of a 'Caucasian Home' may play a positive role in this.

The notion of a 'Caucasian Home' calls for the unification of all the peoples and states of the region into a single family, with all of them enjoying equal rights. This idea is nothing new. As far back as April 1918, the Transcaucasian Diet proclaimed the Transcaucasus a federal republic, independent of Russia.[4] One may also refer to the example of the Transcaucasian Federation (ZSFSR) that existed from 1922 to 1936, and which comprised Azerbaijan, Armenia and Georgia.[5] There were also other associations of a federal nature in the region, for example, the Mountain Republic in the Northern Caucasus which existed from 1920 to 1924 and comprised Chechnya, Ingushetia, North Ossetia, Kabarda, Balkaria and Karachai.

An interest in this idea comes quite naturally at present, in the conditions of instability engendered by the break-up of the USSR – an instability no newly independent state (including Russia) can cope with. Different ideas on how to build the 'Caucasian Home' are being proposed. Some people associate the 'Caucasian Home' with the religious unity of the peoples of the region. True, religion has played and today continues to play a major role in the cultural and political life of the Caucasian communities. This role is especially appreciable in the Northern Caucasus. It was in religion that the Moslems of this area have always found a rallying point for their struggle against the imperialist policy of Tsarist Russia. A sense of religious unity compensated for the lack of cohesion and organization in their worldly life, consolidating their forces. Under the leadership of Naqshbandiya preceptors,[6] even the individualistic tendencies of the mountain tribes were overcome. In the philosophy of Islam there is no opposition between religion and political liberty. But along with this, in the Caucasus, the concept of *tariqat*,[7] perceived in all other Moslem regions as an order of hermits and pious ascetics, acquires a lay meaning pertaining to this world. Whereas in other Islamic regions the leaders of the tariqats are called *sheikhs*, here they are designated as imams like the first Moslem caliphs. This was how Imam Shamil, who led the 25 years' war (1834–59) by the North Caucasian tribes against Russian Tsarism, was perceived. Mansur (Ushurma), leader of the mountain peoples' liberation movement (1784–91), had also been called an imam.

The experience of peaceful and, moreover, fraternal relations between all religions in the Caucasus, the activities of the leaders of all faiths stemming from peace-making aims, from a noble desire to work out mutually acceptable solutions along with a solicitous retention of their faith, allow one to hope that religion may play a major role in bringing together the peoples of the Caucasus. However, account must be taken of the fact that religious differences become an essential factor of internal policy when they interact with class and ethnic, linguistic and regional forms of social differentiation.[8] This means that religious institutions per se may both impede and assist the forces pressing for change. In the process, they in turn are themselves subjected to transformation. Therefore – and also because in the period of socialist cultural construction the peoples of the Caucasus, just like the other peoples of the Soviet Union, moved away from religion and had time to forget many of the spiritual and moral values of religion – it cannot be viewed as a firm basis for unity.

Some researchers advance economic unity as a basis for a 'Caucasian Home'. Thus a well-known Azerbaijani cultural figure, Ibrahim Bairamly, refers to the unified Caucasian Home programme worked out by the Institute for State Construction and International Relations in Baku. The policy of encouraging narrow specialization in the region, pursued during the Soviet period, is seen as one of the factors allowing the construction of the 'Caucasian Home' on an economic foundation. That policy has resulted in a situation where the newly independent states of the region simply cannot survive in isolation from each other.[9] According to another view, the road to large scale integration begins with intensive regional economic co-operation, while the similarity of the socio-economic problems of the peoples of the Caucasus calls for an integration of the national markets of these peoples into a single 'Caucasian Common Market'.[10] Thus there is no lack of concepts of the 'common home'.

The importance of religious and economic factors in achieving the unity of the peoples of the Caucasus should not be neglected.

Still, it would be wrong to single out any one specific factor at this stage. A concept of interethnic reconciliation must be considered a central component of the 'Caucasian Home' philosophy at present, for the idea of a 'Caucasian Home' proceeds first and foremost from a recognition of the earnest wish of all the peoples of the Caucasus to be free and independent. This does not, however, relieve these peoples of an equal responsibility for peace in the region. This is also attested to by the concrete experience of the organization bearing the name of Caucasian Home. The study and analysis of this experience enables us to make certain corrections to the concepts of a 'Caucasian Home' currently being developed.

On 4–5 September 1992, a round table was held in Grozny, the capital of Chechnya. The participants adopted a statement addressed to 'peoples, states, public and religious organizations and associations, political parties and movements of the Caucasus'. This document contained a call to render every kind of assistance in the creation of a 'Caucasian Home', in which each people will be assured of its security and of the possibility of free development. Under the influence of the deposed president of Georgia, Zviad Gamsakhurdia, who was staying in the Chechen Republic at the time, the round table, however, adopted an appeal that subsequently had a very negative effect on the activity of the Caucasian Home organization itself. At issue was the 'denunciation of the military coup and criminal actions of the so-called State Council of Georgia headed by Shevardnadze and the leadership of the Russian Federation *vis-à-vis* the Georgian and Abkhazian peoples' as well as the 'demand for the prompt restoration of the constitutional power in Georgia and the withdrawal of punitive forces from the territory of Abkhazia'. Despite the fact that there were no official representatives of states of the region among the round table participants who signed the statement, some persons holding official positions in a number of Caucasian states took part in it. The participation of the then state councillor of the Azerbaijan Republic, Arif Gajiev, for instance, was quite problematic from the perspective of Georgian–Azeri relations. Such a statement by an organization which had just been founded contributed in large measure to the fact that, on an official level, all the Transcaucasian republics distanced themselves somewhat from the Caucasian Home.

Needless to say, of no small importance here was the role played by other factors: preoccupied above all by their own socio-economic, political and military problems, and not wishing to damage their already tense relations with Russia, they were interested in the idea of the 'Caucasian Home' only to the extent that it could serve their own political and economic interests. The round table also adopted a Declaration providing for the setting up of a working group to examine and prepare documents for the Caucasian Home round table with the mandatory participation of all the parties concerned.

Within the framework of Caucasian Home, the establishment of the Supreme Religious Council of the Peoples of the Caucasus and a United Information Centre of the Caucasus was announced. The leader of Azerbaijan's Moslems, Sheikh-ul-Islam Allahshukur Pashazade, a Doctor of Historical Sciences, was then elected Chairman of the Supreme Religious Council. Worthy of special note is the item contained in the Declaration on 'the need to create a Confederation of Caucasian States'. This proposition was premature and insufficiently thought out, as thus far even the discussion of such an idea would create sharp discord and have an extremely negative influence on the work of the Caucasian Home.

The International Caucasian Home Forum

The International 'Caucasian Home' Forum was registered as a public association in the Chechen Republic on 27 September 1992. The president of Chechnya, Jokhar Dudaev, was confirmed as leader of the Forum. Subsequently, a Programme for the unification of the peoples of the Caucasus was worked out along with the mechanisms for putting it into practice (the permanently operating Caucasian Home Forum, the Supreme Religious Council within its framework, socio-political and cultural associations, state and government bodies). The legislative and legal basis underpinning the Programme was determined (besides documents of international law, the constitutions of sovereign states of the Caucasus and proceedings of the International Caucasian Home Forum (ICHF), this also included the statutes of various socio-political organizations in the region), and ways of achieving a unified policy in the Caucasus were indicated. The Declaration adopted by the participants of the ICHF, its Statute and Programme were proclaimed as a single strategic basis for its policies. It was noted that the Consultative Council, the Supreme Religious Council, the Security Council and the Union of Socio-Political Forces of the

Caucasus were to work out the legislative (legal) basis of state (national) relations and monitor the execution of Caucasian policy. Decisions were to be carried out by the executive bureau of Caucasian Home and by the leadership of the socio-political bodies.

Also deserving of attention is the resolution of 8 April 1993 by the Bureau of the ICHF Consultative Council, which states that the purpose of creating the ICHF Security Council was to contribute to the cessation of military, interstate and interethnic conflicts and wars raging in the Caucasian region as well as to prevent the appearance of new ones. In accordance with its Statute, the chairman of the ICHF, Jokhar Dudaev, was entrusted with the leadership of the Security Council.

A great deal of work was done by the Supreme Religious Council, which held a number of international Caucasian conferences of religious figures, including those held in Grozny on 17 October 1992 and in Baku on 23–24 November 1992. In their appeals and statements, both conferences called on the peoples of the Caucasus, the leaders of the countries of the region, the international community and 'all those not indifferent to the preservation of the sacred gift of life on Earth', to join in their efforts 'to resolve interstate and interethnic conflicts and outstanding issues exclusively by peaceful means; to use the power of religious teaching to bring peoples together on the basis of the principles of tolerance and the equality of human beings before the Most High; to favour the peaceful and least painful transition of peoples and states of the Caucasus on to the path of religious and cultural rebirth'. The Council managed to settle some religious-based conflicts that had broken out in Ingushetia and other regions of the Northern Caucasus.

The second conference of the ICHF was scheduled to be held in Baku in the autumn of 1993. But it never materialized, although in March 1993 and February 1994 two more sessions of the Consultative Council and the Supreme Religious Council were held, the last of which was timed to coincide with Chechnya's Independence Day and the reburial of the remains of Zviad Gamsakhurdia in Chechnya. After that, no further undertakings of any importance within the framework of 'Caucasian Home' were observable.

The Assembly of Mountain Peoples of the Caucasus and the Confederation of Mountain Peoples of the Caucasus

Of interest is the comparison between the activities of the ICHF and a kindred body, the Assembly of Mountain Peoples of the Caucasus (AGNK). The AGNK was set up at the end of the 1980s in the Northern Caucasus. Of all the North Caucasian peoples, it was the Chechens – who had suffered the most from Stalinist repression – who, thanks to their historical traditions and geographical position, were bound to play the greatest role in the process. Perestroika seemed to promise Chechnya full national independence, and it assumed the leadership of the region. Russia's sharply negative reaction *vis-à-vis* Chechnya's attempts to achieve independence enhanced the status of the latter among the other territories of the region. The personal authority wielded by the Chechen leader, Jokhar Dudaev, also had a role to play in this.

The formation of the AGNK was proclaimed on 26 August 1989 at the congress of the mountain peoples of the Caucasus, which was held in Sukhumi. It was set up on the initiative of the Abkhazian People's Forum. The Assembly was chaired by a Kabard, Yuri Shanibov, a lecturer in Marxist-Leninist theory at Nalchik University, who was then still unknown to anyone. In spite of Shanibov's efforts, the AGNK failed to consolidate its positions in the Northern Caucasus at once. In autumn 1991 General Dudaev took the Assembly under his patronage. After that, changes were introduced in the structure of the AGNK: already in early November 1991 in Sukhumi the AGNK was transformed into the Confederation of Mountain Peoples of the Caucasus (KGNK).

The new organization had a markedly anti-Russian attitude. For that reason, the Ingush did not join it, while the Turkic-speaking mountain peoples (Kumyks, Balkars, Karachais) – with the exception of the Meskhetian Turks, and also the Nogais and the Azeris of Daghestan – also refused to become members, preferring to join the Association of Turkic Peoples. As a result, the core of the KGNK was formed by the Chechens and the representatives of Adyghe peoples (Kabards, Circassians, Adyghes, Abazins) as well as the Abkhaz and certain ethnic groups from Ossetia and Daghestan. AGNK chairman Yuri Shanibov became chairman of the KGNK and assumed a Muslim name, Musa, on this occasion. 16 vice presidents were elected, one from each of the peoples represented in the KGNK.

It should be noted that the KGNK leadership took great exception to the refusal of certain groups to participate in the Assembly's activities. The resolutions of the extraordinary congress of member peoples of the KGNK (October 1992) included a call to declare the authorities of the North Caucasian republics to be anti-popular if they refused to co-operate in building the Caucasian confederation and repudiated the Declaration of the extraordinary congress. In such an eventuality, it was proposed to launch a campaign to organize a referendum in the region, as well as mass peaceful actions of protest and civil disobedience. Only a few months later, it became evident that it was not Musa Shanibov who was the real leader of the KGNK, but a Chechen, Yusup Soslambekov, the chairman of the Confederation's parliament.[11] It should be emphasized that the armed detachments of the KGNK consisted mainly of Chechen army fighters.

In summer 1992, serious disagreements arose between Dzhokhar Dudaev and the KGNK leadership on account of the Chechen leader's friendly attitude towards Zviad Gamsakhurdia, the former president of Georgia, whom many in the KGNK viewed as a common enemy of all mountain peoples and all Moslems in the Caucasus. The Confederation leaders believed that, under the influence of the ex-president of Georgia, who had emigrated to Chechnya, Dudaev was slowly but surely abandoning the idea of a North Caucasian confederation in favour of Caucasian unity, in which – if Zviad Gamsakhurdia returned to power in Tbilisi – the leading role would naturally be played by Georgian–Chechen unity.[12]

These disagreements vanished at once, however, after the Georgian–Abkhazian conflict broke out in September 1992. This conflict gave new impetus to the activity of the KGNK, which had by then gained widespread popularity and support among the North Caucasian peoples. That organization, in which the Chechen Republic played a leading role, has turned into the most authoritative political force and has begun to exert a considerable influence on the situation in the Northern Caucasus as a whole.

As was noted earlier, the KGNK acted in parallel to the ICFH and, simultaneously, formed part of the latter's structure. It was the Confederation, however, that represented the real force. When the situation in the region became sharply aggravated due to events in Abkhazia and Kabardino-Balkaria, the KGNK declared that if the State Council of Georgia sent 40,000 fresh soldiers into Abkhazia, the same number of experienced fighters from the republics of the

Northern Caucasus would come to the aid of the Abkhaz freedom fighters.

The KGNK aimed at the unity of mainly the North Caucasian peoples. At the extraordinary congress of the KGNK in October 1992, Musa Shanibov said: 'Only by joining a union of mountaineers can we make our land a prospering Caucasian Switzerland!' The KGNK held the Federal Treaty, signed by the Russian centre with the subjects of the federation, to be null and void, and proposed a new treaty. The Confederation also demanded the recognition of the independence of Chechnya and the creation of forces for regional security and defence. This focusing on the mountaineers of the Northern Caucasus frequently furthered efforts to use the KGNK against Azerbaijan as well. As noted by a perceptive observer (Radik Batyrshin of the Moscow-based *Nezavisimaya Gazeta*):

> The confederates will doubtless stand up with greater zeal for a fraternal people if blood is spilt in the Lezghin regions of Azerbaijan. But a second 'great game' of the KGNK [after the Abkhaz events – R.A.] in the context of Daghestan, which is populated by 36 nationalities, is fully capable of severing not only this republic, but the whole Northern Caucasus, from Russia, making the world overjoyed at the appearance of another state – the Caucasian Confederation.[13]

Jokhar Dudaev, too, was openly using the 'Lezgin' card. In one of his interviews he stated that, if Azerbaijan agreed to sign a treaty on military co-operation with Chechnya, the Lezgin issue would not be included on the 'agenda', as in that case he would persuade the Lezgins to co-operate with both Chechnya and Azerbaijan.[14] Thus he let it be understood that if Azerbaijan did not sign such a treaty or if it spoiled its relations with Chechnya, it would be faced with the inevitable challenge of the Lezgin problem.

At the above-mentioned extraordinary congress of the KGNK of October 1992, Jokhar Dudaev made a move that bears witness to his indisputable talent as a pragmatic politician. To extend his influence on other peoples of the Caucasus besides those from the mountains, the congress, on his initiative, passed a motion to transform the KGNK into the Confederation of Peoples of the Caucasus (KNK). The congress paid special attention to the Cossacks. It noted, in particular, that the Cossacks had the right to a discussion of the issue of their autonomy in the places where they represented a large percentage of the population.

Other 'Caucasian Home' Projects

Still another structure should be mentioned. In spring 1992, again on Dudaev's initiative, and in parallel to the official ecclesiastical authority, another religious body was set up: the Islamic Centre of the Northern Caucasus. This came to be headed by Gaji Mukhammad Alsabekov, a young but authoritative religious figure and politician from Chechnya.

For a true understanding of the trend of integrationist efforts and the relationship between the centrifugal and centripetal forces in the Caucasus, one should also mention the activity of the so-called Co-ordination Council of the Northern Caucasus (KSSK), set up by the leaders of North Caucasian republican administrations as an alternative to both the Caucasian Home and the Confederation of Peoples of the Caucasus. The KSSK met every three months in its headquarters in Pyatigorsk to examine, discuss and make decisions on the most topical issues in the socio-political and economic life of the republics of the Northern Caucasus. The proceedings of the KSSK conferences on the Georgian–Abkhazian and Ossetian–Ingush conflicts attest that this organization shapes its activity by taking note of the positions of Moscow on the issues under discussion.

Conclusions

The material examined in the present chapter thus allows one to reach the following main conclusions:

(1) In the present critical period, interethnic and interstate relations in the Caucasus develop by and large under the influence of two main trends: one towards rapprochement, co-operation and greater solidarity between individual Caucasian republics, the other towards an aggravation of the conflicts between the countries of the region. The differentiation of political and economic interests, differing official approaches to the formation of ideological doctrines, the absence of a single integrationist ideology, satisfying all the parties: all these complicate the already difficult process of overcoming the potential for conflict (which has been accumulating for years) between the countries of the region.

(2) Objectively, the concepts of a 'Caucasian Home' cannot be free

from contradictions, as they try to reconcile two opposing principles: that of the self-determination of nations and that of the inviolability of state borders. Naturally, in this case what is involved is not the establishment of a confederation or some other type of multinational state, but the creation, on more reasonable and democratic foundations, of an international forum that would combine the efforts of all its subjects to achieve peace, interethnic accord and progress in the region. Under present conditions in the Caucasus, such a variant of political compromise – which would envisage a combination of the principles of the self-determination of nations and the inviolability of borders – is possible.

(3) One reason for the lack of appeal of the idea of a 'Caucasian Home' lies in the contradiction between its content (pan-Caucasian in its aims and aspirations) and its ethnic form (Chechen, Georgian, Azerbaijani, and so forth). Having originated almost simultaneously in different places in the Caucasus and having met with the approval and support of independent states in the region, the 'Caucasian Home' idea failed to rise to a pan-Caucasian level, to shape itself into a regional, unifying idea. Despite the subjective strivings of the leaders of the region's mass popular movements and heads of state, and despite the objective need for it to become a pan Caucasian unifying idea, 'Caucasian Home' began to be interpreted in the interests of individual political groupings.

(4) The very prevalence and remarkable tenacity of the idea of the unity of Caucasian peoples, and the existence of historic examples of its translation into reality, confirm the need for a continued search for reasonable and democratic ways of implementing this idea in modern conditions. Despite substantial differences in the forms of self-awareness of the peoples of the Caucasus – ranging from a religious and cultural self-image to a tribal or national identity – a single Caucasian orientation is also clearly discernible. The very notion 'Caucasian' implies a native of the Caucasus – a common home for all who belong to one of the indigenous peoples of the region, regardless of any other aspects of their self-awareness – be they Georgian, Azeri, Armenian, Chechen, Abkhaz, Muslim, Christian, Sunni or Gregorian.

(5) Efforts to assess the prospects of a particular 'Caucasian

Home' concept without regard for the position of the three Transcaucasian states are futile. Since the achievement of independence, the political life of the Transcaucasian countries has been crisis-ridden. The nationalist-minded forces that came to power in each of these states found themselves programmatically unprepared and politically inexperienced, and soon they had to give way to representatives of old Soviet elites. This led to the weakening of extreme nationalist motives, improved the prospects for interethnic dialogue and strengthened democratic tendencies. Thus quite a reasonable basis has been laid for a more constructive dialogue between all patriotic forces in the Caucasus interested in overcoming ethnic conflicts and in seeking a new – perhaps more moderate and well thought-out – idea of Caucasian unity.

(6) One may thus conclude in a general way that the idea of a 'Caucasian Home' is capable of making a contribution to the achievement of political stability in the Caucasus. In the process, the democratic character of a Caucasian Home would ensure equal rights for all the autonomous structures of which it is formed.

NOTES

1. G. Imart, 'Un Intellectuel azerbaijanais face à la revolution de 1917. Samad Aga Agamaly oglu,' *Cahiers du monde russe et soviétique*, Vol.8, 4 (1967), p.528.
2. R. Suny, *The Baku Commune. 1917–1918. Class and Nationality in the Russian Revolution* (Princeton, NJ: Princeton University Press, 1972), p.171.
3. A. Saydam, 'Kuzey Kafkas. Yoldaki Bagimsizlik Hareketleri', *Avrasya etüdleri*, No. 1, Ankara, 1995, p. 89.
4. True, the Diet was disbanded on 26 May 1918, the eve of the proclamation of the independent Azerbaijan Democratic Republic.
5. See S. Kharmandarian, *Lenin i stanovlenie Zakavkazskoi Federatsii* (Yerevan, 1969); G. Galoyan, Oktiabr'skaya revoliutsiya i vozrozhdenie narodov Zakavkazya (Moscow, 1977). Together with Russia, Ukraine and Byelorussia, the Transcaucasian Federation joined the USSR which was formed on 30 December 1922.
6. Naqshbandiya is a Sufi brotherhood founded in the 14th century in Central Asia. It was called after Baha-ad-din Naqshband (1318–89), a preacher from Bukhara. In the first quarter of the 19th century, Naqshbandiya teaching reached the Northern Caucasus.
7. Tariqat (from the Arabic for 'way, road'): (1) mystical path of a Sufi towards knowledge of God; 2) synonym of a Sufi brotherhood, a term denoting particular Sufi monastic orders.
8. B. Toprak, *Islam and Political Development in Turkey* (Leiden: E.J. Brill, 1981), p.18.
9. I. Bairamly, 'Kavkazskiy dom' – real'nost', *Azerbaijan*, 25 June 1993.
10. D. Aliev, 'Chto takoe Kavkazskiy Obshchiy Rynok?' *Azerbaijan*, 5 Jan. 1993.
11. *Kuranty*, No. 116 (2 Sept. 1992).
12. *Azerbaijan*, 16 Jan. 1993.
13. *Nezavisimaya gazeta*, 15 Sept. 1992.
14. *Azerbaijan*, No.10, 1992.

5

The Armenian and Azeri Communities in Georgia: On Georgia's Nationalities and Foreign Policies

ALEXANDER KUKHIANIDZE

This chapter analyses the situation of the Armenian and Azeri communities in Georgia, taking as its point of departure the role of Georgia in the conflict between Armenia and Azerbaijan. Both Georgia's foreign policy and its policy on nationalities will be examined. First, the geopolitical situation in the Caucasus, Georgia's interests in the global competition between Russia, Iran, Turkey and Western powers, and Georgia's policies in the conflict between Armenia and Azerbaijan will be analysed. Secondly, relations between the Azeri and Armenian minorities and the Georgian authorities will be investigated, and the possibility of granting those minorities some form of political autonomy critically assessed.

Conflicts in the Caucasus

In the 1990s, the Georgian media were describing Georgia as the main strategic link in the Caucasus. 'Georgia must act as an overland bridge between East and West', wrote the Georgian newspaper *Rezonansi* in January 1996, citing the words of the President of Chevron and the President of Georgia.[1] At the beginning of the 1990s, the Georgian political leadership spoke about a Transcaucasian Europe–Asia transport corridor, which in their view would radically increase Georgia's independence *vis-à-vis*

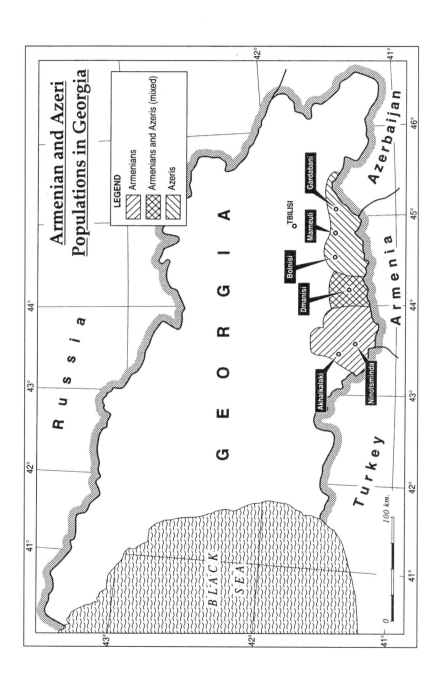

Armenian and Azeri
Populations in Georgia

LEGEND

Armenians

Armenians and Azeris (mixed)

Azeris

R u s s i a

G E O R G I A

BLACK SEA

Turkey

A r m e n i a

Azerbaijan

TBILISI

Gardabani

Marneuli

Bolnisi

Dmanisi

Akhalkalaki

Ninotsminda

100 km.

0

43°

42°

41°

42°

43°

44°

45°

46°

41°

Russia. Independent strategy plus Western orientation – these were the expectations of Georgian society after the overthrow of the regime of the former President, Zviad Gamsakhurdia, in January 1992. Yet these expectations of a rapid stabilization and democratization of the country, turning it into a leading regional power, were not fulfilled. In the beginning of 1993 the Georgian opposition newspaper, *Iberia-Spektr*, wrote that 'Georgia did not become a 'shop-window of democracy' or an 'island of stability'. Internal conflicts prevent it from playing the role which the West was ready to acknowledge – that of builder of regional security and mediator in disputes between the Caucasian peoples, and first and foremost between Armenians and Azeris'.[2]

Georgia was able to increase its political stature in the region thanks to the Armenian–Azeri conflict. Had this conflict not taken place, Georgia would not have been a key player in Transcaucasia, because Azerbaijan would have developed its communication links with Turkey through the territory of Armenia, and Armenia would have had access to the Black Sea and Russia through Turkey and Azerbaijan. The blocade of Armenia organized by Azerbaijan increased the significance for Armenia of the transport routes through Georgia to Russia and the Black Sea. The conflict in Nagorno-Karabakh favoured the formation of alliances between Russia and Armenia and between Turkey and Azerbaijan, whose paths all cross on the territory of Georgia. Moreover, it is only through Georgia that Turkey can establish communication links with the peoples of the Northern Caucasus and Central Asia. Due to its own internal strife, however, Georgia has failed to perform the role of independent player on the international scene outside the Russian sphere of influence.

In themselves, nationalism or the lack of democratic traditions are not enough to explain why ethnopolitical armed conflicts took place in Georgia. In order to force Georgia to accept Russian military bases on its territory and to join the Russian-led Commonwealth of Independent States (CIS), Russia supported separatist movements in South Ossetia and Abkhazia, and might have done the same in the eastern and southern regions of the country (where large Azeri and Armenian communities are living) if Georgia had not accepted Russian dominance in the region after its defeat in Abkhazia in September 1993. At that point, in the words of Eduard Shevardnadze, Georgia had been 'brought to its knees'.[3] The Armenian newspaper *Vremya* described the logic of

Russian policies in the Georgian–Abkhaz conflict as follows:

> At first, Russia supported Abkhazia in this war, and then when Georgia was defeated and refused to continue the war, Russia played the role of mediator and guarantor of an armistice. It is evident from several speeches by the Georgian leader [Eduard Shevardnadze] that Georgian approval for the stationing of Russian military bases had been conditional on Russia's promise to make it possible for Georgian refugees to return [to Abkhazia] and to facilitate a solution to the conflict which would respect the territorial integrity of Georgia.[4]

The Armenian newspaper expressed its fear that Russian policies in Abkhazia could serve as a precedent for its policies in Nagorno-Karabakh, and pointed out that Azerbaijan was refusing to join the CIS, just as Georgia had done since its independence. It also presented Russia's possible gains in the Nagorno-Karabakh conflict as being important from a geopolitical point of view:

> It is quite a tempting perspective: to drive a wedge between Azerbaijan and Turkey, to frustrate the political plans of Pan-Turkism and to re-establish control over Baku and Caspian oil. An agreement on the joint guarding of Azerbaijan's borders with Turkey and Iran and the stationing of Russian military bases along them would be an essential step in that direction. Under certain conditions … the Russian scenario for Abkhazia could very well be repeated.[5]

Russia's strong military presence cannot hide its economic weakness. The country's economic crisis, the breakdown of transport communications between Russia and the Transcaucasus as a result of the war in Abkhazia, the economic blocade officially declared by the Supreme Soviet of Russia against Georgia in 1993, and the new blocade due to the war in Chechnya in 1994/95, have all led to a decrease in the importance of Russia's market share in Georgia in the period 1993–mid-1995, to the advantage of Turkey.[6] Russia's share in Georgia's foreign trade turnover rose again however in 1996, mainly due to natural gas imports.

The Georgian public compares the costs and benefits of its relations with Russia with those with Turkey – the Russian military fist and the Turkish economic honey-cake. The officially-supported Russian policy of repression towards 'persons of Caucasian nationality' – especially Azeris and especially in Moscow, on the pretext of the struggle against crime – adds to Russia's negative image in Georgia. Parallels are drawn between Russia's part in the Georgian–Abkhaz and the Georgian–Ossetian conflicts and its role in the Nagorno-Karabakh conflict. Russia's support for Armenian separatism against Azerbaijan, and the occupation by Armenian troops of the territory of Azerbaijan outside Nagorno-Karabakh, favour a rapprochement between the Georgian and the Azeri positions regarding the preservation of the territorial integrity of their countries and the refusal to allow their national minorities the right to self-determination. The Armenian population of Nagorno-Karabakh demands the complete separation of its region from Azerbaijan, ignoring the right of Azeri refugees to return to their homes. The newspaper *Golos Armenii* (The Voice of Armenia) regrets that the primacy of the principle of territorial integrity over the principle of the nation's right to self-determination is receiving support from major Western states, such as the US. The return of Azeri refugees to Karabakh is condemned as an attempt to 'restore the ethnic picture of 1988'.[7]

The majority of the Armenian population in Abkhazia has supported Abkhaz separatism, thereby reviving anti-Armenian sentiments and mistrust on the part of the Georgian population, and especially among Georgian refugees from Abkhazia. According to the account of the war in Abkhazia given by Helen Krag and Lars Funch, 'the Abkhaz were supported not only by the North Caucasian minorities but by local Armenians and Russians'.[8] Information about the activities of the Armenian organization 'Krunk' in Abkhazia, together with rumours of the brutality of the 'Marshal Bagramian' Armenian battalion against the civilian Georgian population (even though this brutality was partly in response to acts by Georgian marauders[9]), also poisoned Georgian–Armenian relations. MPs from Armenia who arrived in Sukhumi at the beginning of the conflict stated, however, that 'the actions of some Armenian politicians cannot be identified with the opinion of the whole Armenian population of the autonomous republic'.[10]

Armenia has roundly condemned the repeated acts of sabotage and the bombing of the railway and gas pipeline which run to Armenia via the eastern part of the territory of Georgia (Marneuli district), where a large Azeri population lives, and criticized the inability of the Georgian authorities to prevent such crimes. The explosion in the hall of Tbilisi's Armenian Petros Adamian Theatre in May 1994 was qualified by the President of Armenia as 'a terrorist act, which is undoubtedly a provocation, directed against traditional Armenian–Georgian friendship'. A link between this terrorist act and the Armenian–Azeri conflict has never been established.[11] In the declaration by the Armenian Charitable Society of Georgia, this diversion was described as a terrorist act calculated 'to provoke the next ethnic conflict'.[12]

In 1992–94, Armenia sent repeated messages of protest to the Georgian government concerning the numerous robberies of humanitarian and commercial goods transported through Georgian territory and the extortion of money from Armenian businessmen and drivers on the roads of Georgia. During a meeting of the leaders of Armenia, Georgia and Turkmenistan at the beginning of December 1994 in Ashgabat (Ashkhabad), the Georgian Head of State, Eduard Shevardnadze, promised the unhindered delivery of Turkmen gas through Georgia to Armenia, adding, however, that the Georgian authorities were not capable of controlling the entire length of the pipeline which transited their territory.[13] The Georgian government, like many others, is indeed confronted by enormous difficulties in its struggle against terrorism. It is doubtful whether Georgia has the means to prevent all acts of diversion until the Armenian–Azeri conflict has been fully regulated. During another meeting, the Azeri President, Geidar Aliev, and the Armenian President, Levon Ter-Petrosian, argued over the sabotage of a rail bridge linking Armenia to Georgia. Ter-Petrosian claimed that Azerbaijani special agents had been behind the attack. Aliev, in a statement, accused the Armenian leader of making a 'far-fetched assessment' deliberately intended to raise the level of tension in their relations.[14]

With the breakdown of Georgian–Russian economic relations in recent years, Georgia has become highly dependent on Azerbaijan for its energy imports, particularly supplies of electric power and fuel. As Azerbaijan was itself organizing an economic blocade of Armenia, it was anxious lest energy exports to Georgia be diverted to Armenia. The Georgian government, however, which was confronted with mafia groups controlling the petrol business, was not able to keep the transportation of energy resources under its control. According to a report in May 1994 in the newspaper *Svobodnaia Gruzia*, the Georgian customs could not halt the smuggling of copper, leather or petrol across the Georgian–Armenian border. The 'Javakh' organization, from the Armenian-populated district of Akhalkalaki, was said to play the main role in this smuggling.[15] The situation changed only after the crackdown on the mafia by the Georgian authorities, which was enforced after a failed attempt on Shevardnadze's life on 29 August 1995.

Competition for access to Azeri oil resources, and for a distribution of spheres of influence among the big powers in the Transcaucasus, play a role in both the Armenian–Azeri and the Georgian–Abkhaz conflicts. The Turkish attempt to expand its influence towards Central Asia, the Northern Caucasus and the Volga region is perceived in Russia as a threat. In Transcaucasia, the interests of Ukraine and Russia collide. Ukraine, trying to affirm its independence, is under enormous economic and political pressure from Russia, particularly where oil and gas supplies are concerned. It is thus seeking alternative ways of getting energy, from Azerbaijan via Georgia, and from Iran via Armenia and Georgia. Ukraine has similar interests to Turkey to defend in the Transcaucasus: 'Not only the limitation of Russia's sphere of influence is in the interest of Ukraine: Kyiv supports the territorial integrity of post-Soviet states, and sees parallels between separatism in Transcaucasian republics and the secessionist movements in the Crimea and Moldova'.[16] Although relations between Russia and Ukraine are improving, the latter's dependence on Russia for energy and its fear that Russia may use this as a weapon against Ukraine remain. Concerning Ukraine's decision to increase tariffs for the 715-km Lvov 'export' section of the 'Druzhba' (Friendship) oil pipeline, the newspaper *Izvestia* wrote that 'the Russian side could blackmail Ukraine by turning off the pumping through the northern pipeline. Today Ukraine is almost completely dependent on the export of Russian oil (about 20 million tons annually), and plans for the construction of the oil terminal in Odesa (4 million tons with proposed expansion to 40 million tons) are unlikely to be implemented in the near future'.[17]

For obvious geopolitical reasons, Armenia has voluntarily opted for a pro-Russian position. Georgia, on the other hand, was forced into this role of strategic ally of Russia – or, as the 'Zviadists' (the supporters of the former Georgian president Zviad Gamsakhudia) say, that of a Russian 'gendarme' in the Caucasus. The Georgian government gave its full support to Russia's intervention in Chechnya, despite the condemnation of Russia's methods of waging the war by public opinion worldwide.[18] Azerbaijan managed to follow another policy and keep the Russian military out of its territory. It signed 'the oil deal of the century' with Western companies in autumn 1994. The Turkish magazine *Turkish Probe* wrote in this regard: 'The strategic significance of this agreement ... is clear. It puts Azerbaijan – the only country in the Caucasus which Russia has been unable to penetrate fully with political and military influence – in a different league ... . Azerbaijan knows this agreement gives it more leverage in settling its undeclared war with Armenia. It also knows it will be instrumental in consolidating its independence and keeping Moscow at arm's length'.[19] Such a turn of events greatly worried Armenia, but it did not lead to a breakdown of the cease-fire on Nagorno-Karabakh, for several reasons. First, Armenia has already acquired Nagorno-Karabakh, and does not seek new territorial gains in Azerbaijan. Second, Azerbaijan needs peace in order to carry out its oil plans and attract Western capital. Third, Russia's 'derzhavniks' (those who support the restoration of the USSR or the Russian empire) are not in as strong a position as they have been in the past. Especially after its intervention in Chechnya, Russia has decreased its support to separatist forces (which have won everywhere in the Caucasus, including Chechnya). It is trying to carry out mediating and peacekeeping functions and is seeking international recognition of these efforts from the UN and the OSCE.

Investments for oil and gas transportation on Georgia's territory necessitate internal political stabilization, the regulation of all potential and already existing conflicts, and the prevention of acts of diversion on its territory in the transit of oil and gas to Armenia. But Russia, seeing Georgian co-operation with both Azerbaijan and Western companies as a threat to its own interests, could play a destabilizing role.

Georgia is not under any circumstances going to send peacekeeping forces to regulate the Armenian – Azeri conflict. First, according to UN norms, its position as a neighbouring country would not allow it to do so. Secondly, its eastern and southern regions are mainly populated by Azeri and Armenian minorities, and Georgia has reason to fear that it would not be perceived as neutral when performing peacekeeping duties. Georgia has a delicate balance to keep in the Armenian–Azeri conflict. Thirdly, Georgia is a small country in disastrous economic shape, unable to regulate its own conflicts. But it could be a mediator at meetings between the two parties. This has not happened at an official level, but Georgian political parties and NGOs have already initiated some meetings. Joint Transcaucasian cultural and academic initiatives have been organized on the territory of Georgia, with the active participation of representatives from Armenia and Azerbaijan. Cross-border trade takes place in Sadakhlo in the Marneuli district – at the meeting-point of the borders of Georgia, Armenia and Azerbaijan, where traders from the three republics trade in a free and friendly manner.[20]

In order to substantiate its claim to be a 'bridge between East and West' as well as a 'strategic ally of Russia', Georgia will have to find an equilibrium between Iran, Russia and the West. It is just as interested in participating in the co-operation projects between the Central Asian republics, Azerbaijan, Turkey and the West as it is in those between Iran, Armenia and Russia. It does not want to side with one particular group of countries against the other. And such a position is impossible to maintain without complete neutrality in the Armenian-Azeri conflict.

Azeri and Armenian Minorities in Georgia

There are several regions in Georgia with compact Azeri and Armenian communities. According to the 1989 census, Azeris numbered 307,556 (5.7 per cent of the total Georgian population). They live mainly in the eastern districts of the country – Marneuli, Gardabani, Bolnisi, Dmanisi – in the region of Kvemo Kartli, which shares a border with Azerbaijan. According to the same census, there are 437,211 Armenians (8.1 per cent), who live mainly in the southern districts, in the region of Meskhet-Javakheti, for the most part at the Javakheti side, with the most populated centres in Akhalkalaki (the capital of Javakheti) and Ninotsminda (formerly Bogdanovka), which has a common border with Armenia. The same census showed that Armenians also made up a significant proportion of the population of Abkhazia (14.6 per cent). In Tbilisi, which has a population of 1,246,936, there were 824,412 Georgians (66.1 per ent), 150,138 Armenians (12 per cent), and 17,986 Azeris (1.4 per cent).[21] The Azeris from Kvemo Kartli and the Armenians from Javakheti do not speak Georgian. But Azeris and Armenians from Tbilisi, who have their own schools and theatres, speak and write Georgian well.

Despite Georgia's cautious policies towards its Armenian and Azeri minorities, there were serious Georgian-Azeri collisions in 1989 when Azeris from the Marneuli, Bolnisi and Dmanisi districts wanted to set up a so-called 'Borchalo Autonomous Republic', which met with the resistance of the majority of ethnic Georgians. At that time, Georgian public opinion considered that the primary aim of autonomies of the Soviet type was not to express the interests or to protect the rights of national minorities – these federal divisions were seen as time bombs set by the Kremlin and ready to be blown up at will. The Georgian public suspected that the Kremlin was using the national minorities in the autonomous regions or republics as a 'fifth column', and that the creation of new autonomous units would lead to new secessionist movements. At the end of the 1980s, in conditions of rapidly-growing nationalism and mistrust among all ethnic groups, national minorities demanded autonomy not only in order to guarantee their national rights in the newly-independent states, but also to secure a degree of independence from central government and to mobilize further political support in Russia or among their ethnic kindred in a neighbouring state. Under these conditions, it was difficult to distinguish between demands for autonomy and separatist claims.

The 'autonomist' ambitions of the Azeri community in Georgia never received any support from Baku as, since 1988, Azerbaijan was involved in a war in the autonomous region of Nagorno-Karabakh and, in addition, it opposed the creation of federal institutions on its territory. There is also a second reason for the weakness of the Azeri secessionist movement in Georgia: the secession of the Azeri districts would have far-reaching consequences for the population involved. The dissolution of the Soviet Union and the drawing of new international borders between Georgia and Azerbaijan has demonstrated that the Azeri communities in Georgia would face serious practical (and especially economic) difficulties if they seceded. Marneuli and other Azeri districts produce mainly agricultural goods for sale in the nearby capital, Tbilisi. A new border between this district and the Georgian capital would make their trade extremely difficult. This fact may help to explain why demands for secession are so much weaker in this region than in other parts of Georgia.

A compact Georgian population lives on a part of the territory of Azerbaijan (Zakataly) which belonged to Georgia before the Bolshevik invasion in 1921. Azerbaijan and Georgia have a mutual interest in protecting the rights of their respective national minorities. After 1993, the two republics agreed to develop mutual supervision of the rights of their minorities on each other's territory. An Azeri delegation went to Georgia in December 1994[22] and a Georgian one to Azerbaijan in July 1993 and again in July 1995.[23]

Relations between Georgia and Armenia are tenser and more complicated than those between Georgia and Azerbaijan, but they have never escalated into an open conflict. Georgia is closer to Azerbaijan than to Armenia, due to their respective geopolitical positions and views on the right to self-determination. Georgia, confronted with the separatism of the Abkhaz and Ossetians, who have received Russian support, looks warily and carefully at its southern Armenian-populated districts with their Russian military bases and common border with Armenia. In the period 1991–93, the complete breakdown of law and order in Georgia led to a strengthening of centrifugal tendencies in the districts with a mainly Armenian population. Unlike the Marneuli district – where more than three-quarters of the population is Azeri, and where the jurisdiction of the central authorities has always been maintained – the Akhalkalaki district, where Armenians constitute 91.3 per cent of the population,[24] resisted the authority of Tbilisi. Historians from Georgia and Armenia had already been arguing about the historical identity of Javakheti (or, in Armenian, 'Javakhk') and such scientific polemics could (as had previously been the case with historic debates concerning the historic borders and origins of Karabakh, Abkhazia or South Ossetia) lead to an open political – and even military – conflict.[25] It was difficult to predict if 'potential claims' would, in the case of the Alkhalkalaki district, evolve into 'latent claims' and thence to 'open public demands'.[26]

Since independence, the Armenian-populated district had in practice been outside the jurisdiction of the central power of Georgia. Under the government of Zviad Gamsakhurdia, it refused to accept the prefect appointed by the central authorities, and under Eduard Shevardnadze local leaders expressed their complete mistrust of his representative in the Meskhet-Javakheti region. The Armenian inhabitants of Javakheti refused to serve in the Georgian army in 1992–95, but seem to have been enrolled in the local 'Fidain' paramilitary detachment, and even to have taken part in battles for Nagorno-Karabakh.[27] Arms belonging to the Russian army stationed in Akhalkalaki were used in Nagorno-Karabakh, as well as fuel and lubricants for heavy weapons. In 1996, several thousand men serve in the Russian army located in this district. Police reports in 1992–95 referred to the huge quantity of weapons

collected here. In 1992–94, the Javakheti district was considered to
be infested with criminals. Roads were unsafe and it remained
largely isolated from the rest of the country. The Georgian
authorities feared being faced in this region with one more
secesssionist movement and, at first, did not dare take any decisive
action to disarm the criminal and paramilitary groupings.

At the beginning of 1995, with the consolidation of central
power in the whole of Georgia, it proved possible to stabilize the
situation in Javakheti. As S. Alexanian, who at that time represented
the Akhalkalaki District in the Georgian parliament, declared on 14
July 1995 to the Armenian newspaper *Respublika Armenia*, 'Unlike
the situation several years ago, when the tension caused by the
general situation in the republic caused fears that the fire of
conflicts could spread to here too, today everything is quiet. We do
not differentiate between Armenians and Georgians, Javakhetians
and Tbilisians. Everybody is a citizen of Georgia and that is the
main point.'[28] This opinion, however, did not accord with that of
the region's more radical forces, who intervened in the debate on a
new Constitution – which took place in Georgia in 1995 – in order
to enhance the status of their region. A federal state structure was
discussed at the time, as a possible way of settling the conflict with
Abkhazia and South Ossetia. It was finally decided that this
discussion on a federal constitution should be postponed until the
territorial integrity of the Georgian state had been re-established.
The Co-ordinating Council of Socio-Political Organizations and
Movements of Javakheti, however, wanted to take advantage of this
discussion. In summer 1995, it sent a request to the Head of State
and the Parliament of the Republic of Georgia asking them to grant
their district 'the constitutional right of political self-government
within the framework of a united Federal Republic of Georgia'. The
Council claimed that this request had the support of the entire
Armenian population of the district.[29]

The request did not have any practical consequences. The central
authorities ignored it, and the local administration even questioned
the Council's claim that it was based on a general consensus within
the population. For the Georgian people, the idea of creating a new
autonomous region or republic on the territory of Georgia, with
the risk that that region or republic (following the example of
Nagorno-Karabakh and Abkhazia) might subsequently claim the
realization of its 'right to self-determination', was simply
unacceptable. But although the central Georgian authorities refused

to discuss a federal status for the region, they perfectly understood that they could not take rough action against national minorities if they wanted to avoid accusations of oppression and prevent ethnic conflicts from escalating into open war.

The central authorities of Armenia are not interested in openly supporting separatism in Javakheti, as this could lead to a new conflict with neighbouring Georgia and a full blocade of its land communications with Russia – its main patron. It would also put the hundreds of thousands of Armenians living in Georgia in a very difficult position. In spring 1996, a Yerevan Court banned the daily Armenian newspaper *Lragir* for three months for having published an article advocating the annexation by Armenia of the predominantly Armenian-populated regions of southern Georgia.[30]

Conclusions

Despite the open war between Armenia and Azerbaijan and tense Russian–Turkish and Iranian–Western relations, Georgia has succeeded in staying on good terms with all its neighbours and with the other countries involved in the region. The wars in South Ossetia and Abkhazia have led to Georgia's forced entry into the CIS and its acceptance of Russia's military dominance in the region, but they have not had far-reaching consequences for Georgia's capacity to keep a careful geopolitical balance between all regional powers. Throughout the period of the war in Nagorno-Karabakh, Georgia succeeded in maintaining full neutrality and to prevent collisions between the Armenian and Azeri populations on its territory. Due to the country's difficult geopolitical position, the government of Shevardnadze has not been able to act as mediator in the regulation of the Armenian–Azeri conflict, but at an unofficial level several meetings of representatives from the three Transcaucasian republics have taken place on Georgian territory. This may be seen as a good omen for Georgia's future role as a stabilizing power in Transcaucasia.

NOTES

1. *Rezonansi*, 11–12 Jan. 1996.
2. *Iberia-Spektr*, 17 Jan. 1993.
3. *Sakartvelos Respublica*, 29 Sept. 1993.
4. *Vremya*, 12 July 1995.
5. Ibid.

6. *Svobodnaya Gruziya*, 19 Aug. 1995.
7. *Golos Armenii*, 13 July 1995.
8. Helen Krag and Lars Funch, *The North Caucasus: Minorities at a Crossroads*, (Manchester: Manchester Free Press, 1994), p.36.
9. *Belaya kniga Abkhazii. Documenty, materialy, svidetel'stva, 1992–1993* (Moscow, 1993), p.218.
10. *Svobodnaya Gruziya*, 1 Sept. 1992.
11. *Svobodnaya Gruziya*, 17 May 1994 .
12. *Svobodnaya Gruziya*, 18 May 1994.
13. *Covcas Bulletin*, Vol.IV, No.24, 21 Dec. 1994.
14. Ibid.
15. *Svobodnaya Gruziya*, 17 May 1994.
16. Yuri Pavlenko, 'Ukraine and Modern Civilisations', *Political Thought* (Kyiv, 1994, No.3), pp.199–200.
17. *Izvestia*, 6 Jan. 1996.
18. *Covcas Bulletin*, Vol.IV, No.24, 21 Dec. 1994.
19. Semih D. Idiz, 'Sale of the Century. Deal Signed in Baku', *Turkish Probe*, 23 Sept. 1994.
20. *Svobodnaya Gruziya*, 27 July 1995.
21. *Zaria Vostoka*, 10 March, 1990.
22. *The Georgian Chronicle*, Dec. 1994. Vol.3, No.12.
23. *Svobodnaya Gruziya*, 1 Aug. 1995.
24. *Eri*, 10 April 1991.
25. Ibid.
26. N. Petrov, 'Chto takoe polietnizm? Territorialno-etnicheskie pritiazanya i konflikty na territorii byvshego SSSR', *Polis*, No.6, 1993, pp.9–10.
27. Information about the Javakheti region was mainly collected by the author through interviews with the representatives of central and local administrations, security and police officers.
28. *Respublika Armeniya*, 14 July 1995.
29. *Svobodnaya Gruziya*, 1 Aug. 1995.
30. *Omri Daily Digest*, No.63, Part I, 28 March 1996.

6

Conflict and Co-operation in Russo-Ukrainian Relations

ARKADI MOSHES

The new political forces which came to power in Ukraine in July 1994 as a result of President Leonid Kuchma's election victory had made it absolutely clear during the pre-election campaign that their top priority would be to improve relations with Russia. Addressing the parliament on 11 October 1994 on the concept of market reforms, President Kuchma stressed that developing 'strategic partnership' relations with Russia and other CIS nations would be his policy of principle – although, unfortunately, Ukraine's president did not explain what he meant by partnership. The political will of Kuchma himself to reach a compromise with Russia has not been in great doubt. Despite this, however, one can state with certainty that this has not been fully translated into practice. There were too many complex questions to be resolved in the sphere of Russian–Ukrainian relations. Put in general terms, the most challenging of these runs: 'Is it at all possible to raise the level of the bilateral relationship so that it could become to that of a partnership?'

Even if the answer is affirmative – and this cannot be taken for granted, despite the very powerful role played in the post-Soviet political world by the subjective factor in general and personalities in power in particular – it is essential to take into account the legacy of the past which, in the context of relations between Russia and Ukraine, means mutual dissatisfaction, apprehensions and complaints, leading to mutual frustration. This legacy cannot be eliminated and forgotten overnight.

In fact, a great deal has been done in the period 1995–97 to overcome the legacy left by the political course steered by President

Leonid Kravchuk, whose image in Russia was reflected in the formula 'promise and never fulfil'. Russo-Ukrainian relations attained with the first visit of President Boris Yeltsin to Kyiv and the signature of a treaty in May 1997 a certain degree of stability – a guarantee against a speedy transition into a phase of crisis in the majority of predictable situations. Nevertheless, statesmen in both countries need to realize, first of all, that for many years to come the conflict potential accumulated earlier will remain on the political agenda of bilateral relations and may overburden them, making the whole construction barely manageable, and, secondly, they need to understand the nature of every single problem in every area. Otherwise, all the good intentions will result in mere hand-shaking, with no practical results. This is the reason for focusing the present research on the potential for conflict rather than the potential for co-operation. A full-scale confrontation between Russia and Ukraine would be a catastrophe for both countries, and the truth of this conclusion seems to be fully understood in both Moscow and Kyiv. The author of this chapter, however, shares the view of some Ukrainian experts who concluded that 'an open confrontation between the countries before the year 2000 is very unlikely ... , but from time to time hidden controversies will re-emerge'.[1] If this is the case, then a thorough analysis of all the existing problems between Russia and Ukraine, as well as of all the spheres from which conflicts of various kinds may arise – be they economic or diplomatic – is even more necessary.

The sum of contradictions forms a potential for conflict. The task of politicians and experts on both sides is to prevent situations in which this potential could escalate into a conflict detrimental to bilateral relations and dangerous for European security. Understanding the problem in this context means taking the first step towards a solution. The purpose of this work is to describe and analyse key problems that have accumulated in bilateral relations – an elucidation of the problems seeming, to a certain extent, an even more important task than their detailed study, which perhaps makes for a somewhat cursory treatment of the matter. The author deems it necessary, without claiming completeness, to outline the problems as seen from Moscow, without aspiring to establish who is right or wrong in the process. It must also be stated from the outset that the present chapter is not a study of the foreign policies of Russia or Ukraine; an analysis of questions that, while important, are extraneous to the chosen topic (the Ukrainian policy of Western countries, specific political steps taken by Russia and Ukraine in the CIS, etc.) will therefore remain outside the scope of this chapter.

Seeking Common Security

Russia and Ukraine, the biggest and most powerful of the Soviet Union's successor states, could theoretically form an alliance to promote stability in the post-Soviet space. But conceptual differences in the two countries' approaches to national security preclude the hope of achieving that aim in the foreseeable future. Among the ruling Ukrainian elites – and not only these – there is a widespread belief that the main threat to Ukraine's independence comes from Russia,[2] which is easy to explain when one takes into account that the concept of Ukrainian independence is construed precisely as independence from Russia. Interpretations of this point may vary. When Ukraine's Deputy Foreign Minister Tarasyuk says in diplomatic language that 'imperial ambitions manifested in different ways are a major threat to the region',[3] this means the following: 'Ukrainians undoubtedly have every reason to consider their statehood in danger from the outside – from the former 'parent' state, which ruthlessly thwarted all Ukrainian attempts at emancipation over the centuries, and even now does not show any particular respect for Ukrainian independence'.[4]

The pattern of thinking characterized by the sentences quoted above is so deeply rooted in the mentality of many Ukrainian politicians and academics that it probably represents the major obstacle to an improvement in bilateral relations.[5] Once it had appeared, the notion of 'imperialist revanchist Russia' – an extremely useful one, easily perceived by the population, distracting it from analysing the whole picture and, consequently, advertised daily by the coalition of Ukrainian nationalists and former communists which was in power until mid-1994 and whose management of the country's economy brought it to a wretched condition – is a notion which arouses fear and mistrust of Russia's actions, whatever Russia's intentions might be. Such an approach, in turn, cannot but evoke a feeling of irritation and frustration on the other side,[6] including in people with a genuine wish for an improvement in bilateral relations, thereby leading to increased mutual incomprehension. One may, moreover, observe a mirror effect, as it were: sharply-worded statements by Ukrainian politicians are taken up by those in Russia who have no interest in normalizing relations between the two countries, while their reaction, in turn, is given wide coverage in Ukraine, and so on, *ad infinitum.*

The basic assumption that Russia's aim is to weaken Ukraine's sovereignty is manifested in the following fears:

– that on a bilateral level Russia will try to use the ethnic Russian (12 million) and Russian-speaking population – concentrated in the eastern and southern regions of Ukraine and, politically, mainly Russia-oriented – to destabilize the situation and bring about the secession of some parts of the country, starting with the Crimea; and that to this end Russia will use economic pressure;

– that Russia will use CIS mechanisms and integration processes within the CIS to create a Russian-dominated confederation in which other states will play the role of satellites;

– that, at an international level, Russia will try to isolate Ukraine, not allowing it to receive financial assistance from the West.

Correspondingly, Ukraine needs to find ways of its own to neutralize or at least resist these challenges. It should be noted that Ukraine's apprehensions, especially on the first point, are not completely groundless. Certain potential for secession does exist, above all in the Crimea, where two-thirds of the population are composed of ethnic Russians, most of whom have resettled there after the Second World War and who identify to a negligible degree with Ukrainian statehood. Living standards in Ukraine (and attempts made before 1994 to introduce Ukrainian as the only official language) caused social dissatisfaction. The economic situation in Russia is far better, and this made the idea of joining Russia attractive to people living in border regions. One cannot rule out the possibility that, if Russia tries to exploit existing attitudes to subvert Ukrainian statehood, a destabilization of Ukraine could ensue.

The separatist potential of Eastern Ukraine and, consequently, the likelihood of a break-up of the state was, however, clearly exaggerated. It should not be forgotten that during the referendum on independence in December 1991, 83.9 per cent of the residents of the Donets'k and Lugans'k regions voted in favour.[7] Numerous opinion polls conducted in 1993 virtually throughout the country showed that, if a fresh referendum were held, the only region where the number voting against Ukrainian independence would exceed the number for was the Crimea.[8] The political demands of the population of Eastern Ukraine, even during the mass strikes in summer 1993, did not seem to go beyond changes in the internal policies of the Ukrainian leadership, a fact which underscored the loyalty of these regions to Ukrainian statehood. Kuchma's administration has succeeded in weakening even further the desire of the Eastern Ukrainian regions for autonomy.

It cannot be denied that some statements by Russian politicians on the need to defend the Russian-speaking population in other countries, such as those made by Russia's Foreign Minister, Andrei Kozyrev, greatly increased the fears on the Ukrainian side. In this context, a special role was played by the resolution adopted by Russia's Supreme Soviet on 9 July 1993, which declared that the city of Sevastopol belonged to Russia. This resolution, provided the Ukrainian side with proof of Russia's 'aggressive plans' and substantially increased Kyiv's suspicions regarding Moscow's intentions.

In addition, however, one cannot fail to see that, in its practical policy, Moscow proceeded from an understanding of the inadmissibility of destabilizing the situation in Ukraine, whether by political or economic means. In the political sphere, there was a virtual renunciation of the demand for dual citizenship. Moscow has refrained from interfering in Crimean events. Both in May 1994, when Ukraine was on the verge of an outbreak of armed conflict between the Crimean and Ukrainian authorities, and in September 1994, when an acute political crisis erupted between the Crimean President Yuri Meshkov and the parliament of the Crimea – a time when many politicians in the peninsula would have welcomed the engagement of Russia – the latter managed to stay neutral. In March 1995 – and despite appeals by the Speaker of the Crimean Parliament, Sergei Tsekov, which were viewed with approval by a section of the State Duma – the careful position adopted by the Russian executive became, in effect, one of the major factors contributing to the return of the Crimea into Ukraine's legal fold.

In the sphere of economic relations, the only indication that pressure was being put on Ukraine was an attempt made during the Massandra summit (September 1993) to use Ukraine's indebtedness as a trump card to obtain concessions from Kyiv on dividing up the Black Sea Fleet and nuclear weapons. The failure of that attempt proved the utter futility of such a policy. Throughout 1994, Russia, which was aware of Ukraine's complete insolvency, continued to supply it with energy without receiving any payment. In October 1994, at an international conference on Ukraine held in Winnipeg, Russia declared its willingness to defer payment by the Ukraine of its debt and accrued interest for the period from October 1994 to February 1995 ($635 million).[9] After that it was entirely logical for Russia to accede to the IMF's demand to sign an agreement on rescheduling Ukraine's debts, the essence of which is that the debts for 1992–93 (approximately $22.5 billion) will be paid off between 1998 and 2008 (a separate agreement was also signed with the Russian joint-stock company, Gazprom, on the principle of settling the issue of indebtedness for gas supplies).[10]

Ukrainian policy, on the whole, was aimed at neutralizing possible Russian action in those areas where it thought such action could have most destructive effect. At the bilateral level, Ukraine was concerned with the question of how to avoid making any concessions to Russia, or to political movements which supported close co-operation with Russia, on issues which were perceived as potentially threatening Ukraine's territorial integrity (dual citizenship, the introduction or recognition of Russian as the second official language and the federalization of Ukraine).

In the CIS, Ukraine was the first country which started to set up independent armed forces, since an army of its own was recognized as an indispensable attribute of statehood. It refused to take part in the Commonwealth's collective security system (a fact related to its declared principle of not joining any blocs), did not sign the CIS Charter and refused to become a full member of the CIS Economic Union. Despite President Kuchma's declared intention to become an active participant in the CIS, Ukraine kept the status of associate member of the CIS Economic Union and did not sign the document establishing the Interstate Economic Committee, the first executive body to have supranational powers. Ukraine preferred to build up its bilateral relations with the CIS countries, especially with those (and on those matters) which opposed Moscow, if only on an *ad hoc* basis. In this respect it is worth mentioning a military agreement with Moldova and a bilateral treaty with Georgia, both signed at the beginning of 1993 (that is, before Georgia joined the CIS) and designed to counterbalance the influence of Moscow in Transdniestria and Transcaucasia. Later on, Ukraine formed a *de facto* alliance with Kazakstan and Uzbekistan to combat Russian policy on dual citizenship.

Russia's attempts to have its peacekeeping efforts inter-nationally recognized are an area of specific Ukrainian concern in the CIS. Ukraine's Deputy Foreign Minister Tarasyuk has qualified the desire 'to assume the role of the only country responsible for maintaining peace and stability in the region' as a manifestation of 'imperial ambitions.'[11] Quite understandably, Ukraine feared that in the event of an open conflict in the Crimea Russia might claim involvement in the settlement process, whereas Ukraine would consider this to be a violation of its state sovereignty. By and large, however, such an approach, which denies the positive side of Russia's peacekeeping commitment – that is, the fact that in many cases Russia has been able to settle or de-escalate crises, thus promoting general stabilization, in particular in the Black Sea region – is also a factor which negatively influences the state of bilateral relations.

In the international arena, Ukraine has tried to seek security guarantees from the West. Its attitude towards the enlargement of NATO in 1993, unlike Russia's, was positive. Ukraine welcomed the NATO 'Partnership for Peace' programme, was the first CIS country to join it (on 8 February, 1994) and became an enthusiastic participant. It agreed with an Individual Partnership Programme with NATO in September 1995 and spoke of its interest not only in maintaining regular political and military ties with the bloc and creating a consultation mechanism, but also in direct participation in certain NATO bodies.[12] Such a position, which at the time was completely at variance with Russia's approach, had a negative effect on the development of bilateral relations.

Realizing the impossibility of rapid integration into Western security structures, Ukraine tried to find a substitute in Central Europe. Kyiv was very active in promoting the idea of Baltic/Black Sea co-operation and in putting forward the initiative to create a Central European security zone (announced on 28 April 1993). Both concepts, especially the latter one, appeared to be aimed at isolating Russia.[13]

In one respect, the policies of Western countries, and in particular the USA, seem to have played a negative role regarding the problem of ensuring Ukraine's security *vis-à-vis* Russia. From May 1992 to November 1993, the absence of a firm stance on Ukrainian nuclear policy in the policies of Western countries – which have, beyond any doubt, a priority interest in the nuclear disarmament of Ukraine – not only encouraged those with pro-nuclear tendencies but also spread the illusion among the Ukrainian political elites that, in the post-Soviet political space, the West was interested in transforming Ukraine into a security counterbalance to Russia. These forces did not realize that such an outcome would be possible only if Russia really chose the path of forcible neo-imperialist expansion. The West's willingness and ability to come to the rescue of the ineffective Ukrainian economy and military machine, thereby running the risk of antagonizing Russia, were obviously misjudged by Ukrainian politicians – nevertheless, this had serious political repercussions in Russia, adding another cause for concern to bilateral relations.

After Kuchma's electoral victory, there was no radical change in Ukraine's general approach to security. Apprehensions regarding Russia's role in the post-Soviet world are still present, if not dominant, in geostrategic planning by Ukrainian analysts, and this cannot but have implications for practical policy. Thus the background for preserving the conflict potential remains in many ways untouched.[14]

Military Relations

The military-political field of bilateral relationships was for a long time the one where a materialization of the conflict potential was easy to see. Ukraine was the first CIS country which openly refused to stay within CIS security structures and be subordinated to the Joint Command, a fact which was unexpected for Moscow and, due to the latter's unpreparedness for such a turn of events, drew a sharp reaction.

As early as 3 January 1992, implementing resolutions of the Verkhovna Rada of 24 August and 22 October 1991, on bringing the armed forces deployed on Ukrainian territory under its jurisdiction, the Ukrainian government started taking an oath of allegiance from servicemen. Such a step, re-subordinating to Kyiv about 700,000 servicemen from the Kyiv, Odesa and Carpathian military districts – which, along with the Belarussian military district, were the best equipped and manned in the Soviet Union – caused shock waves in Moscow. Russian political leaders at that time (that is, before 7 May 1992, when Russia announced the creation of its own armed forces) intended to preserve the united armed forces of the CIS. Ukrainian policy not only made this impossible but left unprotected the European part of Russia with its weak military districts in the rear area. In addition, Russia had to cope with shortages or a complete lack of some specific types of equipment, especially in strategic aviation, which at that juncture could not be withdrawn from Ukraine.[15]

Moscow's inability to counteract what Ukraine regarded as the natural policy of an independent state lasted until 6 April 1992, when President Kravchuk issued a decree declaring the Black Sea Fleet the property of Ukraine, while the next day President Yeltsin declared it the property of Russia. Both decrees put the two countries in a position of open confrontation, prone to violent actions by radicals on both sides, and they were withrawn by the respective presidents on 9 April. Since then, Russia and Ukraine have had an eventful history of controversy over the fate of the Black Sea Fleet.

In the history of this process, the main landmarks are as follows: On 23 June and 3 August 1992, in Dagomys and Yalta, Boris Yeltsin and Leonid Kravchuk agreed to withdraw the Black Sea Fleet from the Strategic Forces of the CIS and to regard it as being subordinate to the two presidents, who were Commanders-in-Chief in their countries. After a transitional period (of three years), the Fleet was to be divided. The Ukrainian approach was to divide it in half, the Russians apparently wanted to postpone the very procedure of division. Later, Ukraine added one more issue to the agenda, pointing out the impossibility of dividing coastal facilities, which belong to Ukraine, and for which Russia was supposed to pay rent. The way out appeared to have been found at the Yeltsin-Kravchuk summits in Zavidovo near Moscow and Massandra in the Crimea, in June and September 1993. At the first summit, Russia gave its consent to the principle of equal division, the joint use of the coastal facilities and parity financing. At the second one, the two presidents agreed that the whole Fleet, together with its infrastructure, would belong to Russia, but that the Ukrainian part (half of the fleet) would be counted as payment of debt. Illusions about the possibility of implementing this agreement lasted only a few days. Back in Kyiv, President Kravchuk, accused by influential nationalist forces of high treason, realized that ratification in the parliament was highly improbable and *de facto* disavowed his signing of the document.[16]

There was a new crisis in April 1994, when Ukrainian air-borne units took by storm the Black Sea Fleet facilities at the Odesa military base. Negotiations at the level of prime ministers and ministers of defence brought no results beyond a confirmation of willingness to divide up the ships. After the Odesa incident, the Russian approach stiffened. Russia continued to declare its readiness to divide the ships, recognizing Ukrainian ownership of the infrastructure, but insisted that the Ukrainian and Russian navies be based separately, with the Russian ships to be stationed in Sevastopol and the Ukrainian ones at other naval bases on the Ukrainian Black Sea coast.

The willingness of the new President Kuchma to improve relations with Russia did not help in finding a lasting solution to the naval dispute. Although some progress was undoubtedly made in the negotiating process, the lists of ships to be split up were agreed upon, as were the main principles of mutual settlements. The Black Sea Fleet handed over the bases in Izmail, Ochakiv, Donuzlav and Balaklava to the Ukrainian Navy, together with a number of other items. During the Sochi summit in June 1995, Russia agreed to the formulation 'the Russian fleet will be based in Sevastopol', having agreed to withdraw the expression used earlier: 'Sevastopol is the main base of the Russian fleet' – this wording could have been construed as expressing Russia's claim to attain exterritorial status for the city, and had aroused apprehension on the Ukrainian side. The use of the expression 'Sevastopol' could mean that only the Russian Fleet would be based in all four harbours of the Sevastopol naval base, whereas the formulation 'in Sevastopol' not only does not call into question Ukrainian sovereignty over the city, but in principle leaves open the possibility that the two navies could be jointly based there. In November 1995, 26 agreements – all relating in one way or another to the issue of the division of the fleet – were signed by the defence ministers of the two sides. None the less, the list of problems remaining was long enough. The main one was the question of separate basing, which was rejected by Ukraine as a matter of principle.[17]

Besides the question of basing the Black Sea Fleet and the Ukrainian Navy, there was an acute financial problem, which was not confined to defining the amount of rent Russia should pay for utilizing bases in the Crimea in the future. There were two sides to the problem. The first concerned the financing of the Black Sea Fleet, which was still under the joint control of the two countries. As mentioned above, in accordance with the agreement reached in Zavidovo (June 1993), the Black Sea Fleet was to be financed on a parity basis. In fact, however, Ukraine's share in the allocation of funds for the fleet accounted for just 6.7 per cent, while on 6 December 1993 payments stopped altogether.[18] Ukraine's backlog of payments for the fleet, arising from unpaid expenses for the maintenance and training of conscripts from Ukraine, the maintenance of ships that were to go to Ukraine after the division of the fleet and maintenance of the coastal infrastructure claimed by Ukraine, was estimated to have reached the sum of $81 million between 1 January 1994 and 30 May 1995.[19]

The second aspect was linked to the heavy taxation Ukraine imposed on the Black Sea Fleet. The fleet was being forced to pay Ukraine 42 different kinds of taxes which, in 1994 alone, amounted to about one trillion karbovantsy (comparable to half the budget of the Crimea). The Crimean and Sevastopol local authorities imposed additional taxes on the fleet. In December 1994, the Crimean government introduced a land tax, which for the Black Sea Fleet came to roughly ten times the amount of similar land taxes for Ukrainian land users, including military units. The fleet had to pay in 1995 an estimated $133 million for the use of land.[20] The fleet's lack of funds led to the emergence of a number of other (less serious) conflicts, when the fleet found itself unable to pay Ukrainian enterprises for ship repairs or to appropriate funds for the upkeep of the social infrastructure of the city, or when the Sevastopol authorities switched off the fleet's power supply.

The attempt to divide the military legacy of the Soviet Union in general, and the Black Sea Fleet problem in particular, illustrate how difficult it is for Russia and Ukraine to find common language in the areas most closely connected with security concerns. Even the virtual loss of combat readiness and modern character by the Black Sea Fleet has not induced the parties to be more active in seeking a compromise. Yeltsin's first official visit to Kyiv, which settled the row over the fleet and Sevastopol, took place in May 1997. It had previously been postponed at least six times owing mainly to disagreements over this issue.[21]

The Economic Sphere: On the Eve of a Final Farewell

By the end of 1994, the order of priority in the list of problems in bilateral Russian–Ukrainian relations had changed considerably. The attention of the majority of politicians and experts switched from the military-political to the economic field. The problem of

Ukraine's debt to Russia seemed to take on a new significance at the interstate level, and it is in this field that a lessening of the conflict potential has been registered. As is well known, in the course of 1994 the Ukrainian debt to Russia increased rapidly, approaching $5 billion.[22] Ukraine had to pay more than one billion dollars for gas and oil alone.

Such a situation was the logical outcome of Russia's decision to stop subsidizing the post-Soviet states by providing them with sources of energy at prices equal to those of the internal market.[23] In the Ukrainian case, this immediately had catastrophic consequences, making its economy – and its very statehood – vulnerable to Russian pressure. Evidence of this 'soft' pressure may be found in the Massandra agreements already mentioned, according to which Ukraine had to give up its half of the Black Sea Fleet (a major symbol of its sovereignty) to repay its debt. These agreements were, notoriously, never implemented. None the less, despite non-payments Russia has continued supplying energy to Ukraine. In the first place, as mentioned earlier, it would be risky to destabilize the situation in Ukraine, as social unrest could spill over into Russia; and secondly, Russian exports to Europe are dependent on Ukraine (pipelines cross Ukrainian territory), so Ukraine could simply pump the fuel out of the pipelines.

The Kyiv administration seems to have been well aware of the motives driving the Russian side and, in turn, sought to find mutually acceptable solutions. Since the signing, in March 1995, of an agreement on rescheduling the Ukrainian debt for 1992–93, the country's debt situation has been greatly improved through bilateral efforts. Despite Russia's general satisfaction with the payment for current deliveries in 1995, Ukraine's debt has still continued to grow.[24] In trying to pay for current deliveries at least (which it does at the expense of Western credits, too), Ukraine was proving its desire to avoid a return to the confrontational model in this sphere. Russia, in its turn, has sensed the futility of using the 'debt' trump card in an effort to gain political dividends. Since the package principle fell apart, non-governmental agents (the Gazprom shareholding company on the Russian side and its Ukrainian partners) have been playing a major role in settling the issue. Naturally, the general scope of market reform in Ukraine is the main factor which, among other things, would lead to the promotion of resource-saving technology and to decreased volumes of consumption of Russian energy in Ukraine.

Reduction in Incentives to Co-operation

By 1995, there were already not very many areas left where Russia might have been interested in co-operation. Once powerful, the military-industrial complex of Ukraine, which had been integrated into the Soviet system, was now not much use to Russia. In the first place, Russia had reoriented the broken economic ties and needed to restore them only a little and, in the second place, it did not have enough money to finance its own military production and its conversion to peaceful uses. Russia and Ukraine are competitors for the sale of certain types of arms (tank production), so it would be reasonable for each to prevent the other from having access to new technology.[25] A separate item is competition in the trade in arms inherited from the Soviet Union and, accordingly, in servicing those arms in the importing countries. In addition, taking into account the differing approaches to security, Russia cannot rely on Ukraine for military production, which would give Ukraine an extra card in the game.

Russia no longer depends on Ukraine for food deliveries. It has the possibility of purchasing food on the world market, where it is of better quality and sometimes cheaper than Ukrainian produce. Furthermore, Ukrainian agriculture, being highly dependent on Russian fuel, is declining along with the whole economy, making Ukraine an unreliable supplier. The only sphere where there is still considerable potential for co-operation is communications. Russia needs Ukrainian ports as well as pipelines. This dependence, however, is not absolute and will be lessening as Russia constructs two gas pipelines through Belarus and Poland and a sea port in the Leningrad region.

Conclusion: Can the Conflict Potential be Eliminated?

In the period 1995–97, the overall crisis in Russian-Ukrainian relations – which in 1992–93 had been acute, with mutual criticisms, accusations and appeals to the world community – had transformed itself into a chronic malaise, where on the surface everything seemed quiet enough, but deep down there simmered the same problems that used to divide the two countries in the past. The situation with bilateral relations is not hopeless, however. The general answer to the question whether the conflict potential can be overcome (and this is not at variance with the conclusions which have been or may be drawn from this chapter) may be positive. It may be positive, because Russia and Ukraine share one overwhelming common interest – keeping Ukraine stable. Their reasons for this are different, and rather egoistic on the Russian side. For Russia, preventing the destabilization of Ukraine means protecting itself from an influx of refugees spilling over on to its territory, bringing with them social upheavals that could wipe out the results of Russian economic reforms, strengthen nationalist forces within Russia and send new recruits into criminal networks. It means preventing ecological disasters at nuclear and hydro-electrical power-stations and at chemical plants, obviating the need to undertake the economically unaffordable burden of responsibility (including in the military sphere) for crisis management in the neighbouring country.

The answer, however, may be positive only if some requirements are met. The main one is that the mentality of the political and intellectual elites in both countries must change. Realizing that both sides need each other, however limited this need might seem, the Ukrainian elites should give up looking for hidden, anti-Ukrainian intentions in Russian policy, shake off their suspicions and stop looking at Russia through a prism of fears; while the Russian elites should accept at bottom that independent Ukraine has legitimate interests in various fields, and that these cannot be the same as Russia's. If these are their starting points, the two countries will find the way which leads to co-operation. Even in the medium-term, there is no point in speaking of some abstract strategic partnership lacking in substance – the interests involved are too different at present – but such an outcome should not be completely ruled out for the more distant future. In order to move in that direction, Russia and Ukraine should start the process of co-operation on a case-by-case basis, striving to achieve a good-neighbour relations model.

NOTES

1. See *Strategii rozvitku Ukrainy: vyklyki chasu ta vybir* (Kyiv: National Institute of Strategic Studies, 1994), p.34.
2. From about the middle of 1994 an increasing number of analysts in Ukraine has begun to understand that the main danger to the existence of a sovereign Ukraine comes from inside the country, from socio-economic conditions in the state. Russia, however, is still cast in the role of main external challenger to Ukraine's security.
3. B. Tarasyuk, 'Nebezpeky ta destabylizuyuchi chinnyky v Tsentralnii ta Skhidnii Evropi', *Polytychna Dumka*, No.2 (Kyiv, 1994), p.94. Interestingly enough, this official does not

speak about the ambitions of Russia's imperialist forces, but levels his criticisms directly at the present government.

4. M. Ryabchuk, 'Demokratiya i tak nazyvaemaya 'partiya vlasti' na Ukraine', *Polytychna Dumka*, No.3 (Kyiv, 1994), p.41.

5. It is, for example, manifested in the attempts to concentrate analysis on a possible Russian policy aimed at undermining Ukraine's stability, instead of studying the course which Russia – or its executive bodies, at least – is really pursuing in relation to Ukraine. See *Strategii* ... , op. cit., pp.32–4.

6. It would be wrong to deny the presence of forces on the Russian political scene that demand the forcible reintegration of Ukraine with Russia or the restoration of the Soviet Union, thereby abolishing Ukrainian independence. But the dominant way of thinking within Russian elites is completely different. As a telling example, one may quote a passage from a document prepared by the influential non-governmental Council on Foreign and Defence Policy, which says that it is the situation in Ukraine – but not Ukraine itself – that represents the most serious challenge to Russia's security and internal stability. *Nezavisimaya gazeta* (27 May 1994). Such an approach points out the problem to be solved, not the country to be blamed.

7. 'The Birth and Death of a Country', *The Economist* (7 May 1994) – Survey, p.16.

8. For a more detailed treatment see *Strategii* ... , op. cit., p.21.

9. *Segodnia* (28 Oct. 1994).

10. For more on this, see *Segodnia* (21 March 1995 and 24 March 1995); *Nezavisimaya Gazeta* (23 March 1995).

11. B. Tarasyuk, op. cit., p.202.

12. For more on this, see H. Udovenko, 'European Stability and NATO Enlargement: Ukraine's Perspective', *NATO Review*, No.6 (1995), pp.15–18.

13. An American researcher, St. Larrabee, believes that the concept of a Central European security zone looked like an anti-Russian alliance. See St. Larrabee, *East European Security after the Cold War* (RAND, CA, 1993), p.108.

14. In analysing the basic differences on the issue of ensuring security, one cannot pass over in silence the legacy of Ukraine's nuclear policy in 1992–94, which was one of the main factors contributing to the conflict potential. Ukraine's unwillingness to honour its commitments on nuclear disarmament promptly was causing resentment in Russia. However, after the signing on 14 January 1994 by Ukraine, Russia and the US of a tripartite agreement that suited Ukraine (and eventually led to its accession to the Nuclear Non-Proliferation Treaty as a non- nuclear power in December 1994), Russia's position gradually began to soften. By the end of 1995, as a result of the strict observance of their commitments by all parties, the legacy of the 'nuclear dispute' virtually disappeared from bilateral relations. This issue is a positive example of how the most serious conflict-forming challenges can be neutralized by common international effort.

15. Ukraine received 19 TU-160 bombers and 23 TU-95 strategic bombers (none of the machines of the first type had been stationed in Russia). Bilateral negotiations on the purchase of the aircraft by Russia failed, because the Ukrainian side demanded payment of 700 billion roubles at 1994 prices, while Russia was ready to pay only 200 billion. Russia had to build a new squadron of TU-160 aircraft. Only four planes of each type were operational in Ukraine in spring 1995. The fate of the planes has not been fully clarified to this day. There have been reports that they were to be transferred to Russia in exchange for spare parts for tactical aviation or in payment of the Ukrainian debt; however, there has also been contradictory information. See details in: *Segodnia* (1 June and 12 July 1994, 25 Feb. 14 March, 6 April and 8 June 1995).

16. On the Ukrainian opposition to the Massandra agreements, see *Izvestia* (7 Sept. 1993, 8 Sept. 1993) and *Krasnaya Zvezda* (9 Sept. 1993). Speaking in Kyiv, President Kravchuk said he had never signed such an agreement. See the account of the press conference in *Nezavisimaya Gazeta* (7 Sept. 1993).

17. At a meeting with the the Ukrainian Naval Command on 22 Aug. 1995, Leonid Kuchma said that 'moving the Ukrainian Naval Headquarters out of Sevastopol [was] impossible from any standpoint', *Segodnia* (23 Aug. 1995). The need to resettle a substantial number of officers from Sevastopol in Donuzlav, a move which is financially burdensome and

fraught with social consequences, plays a key role in shaping the Ukrainian position on this question.

18. See more detailed treatment in *Segodnia* (7 Dec. 1994); see also interview with the chief of the financial department of the fleet, Colonel A. Zhukov, in *Krasnaya Zvezda* (18 May 1995). Ukrainian experts explained the suspension of the allocation of funds to finance the fleet by saying that the fleet de facto came under Russian control. However, Ukraine did not officially denounce the corresponding agreements, did not abandon its claims to part of the fleet and continues to send its conscripts for service in the Black Sea Fleet.

19. As the Deputy Commander of the Black Sea Fleet, Rear-Admiral A. Aladkin, informed the newspaper *Krasnaya Zvezda* (25 July 1995).

20. As told by A. Senchenko, Vice-Premier of the Crimea, to the newspaper *Segodnia* (26 July 1995).

21. *The Economist*, 24 May 1997.

22. *Segodnia TV broadcast*, 15 Nov. 1994.

23. In 1993 alone, according to the estimates of the head of the Russian delegation at negotiations with Ukraine, Ambassador Yuri Dubinin, Russia granted Ukraine $7 billion by supplying Ukraine with oil and gas for significantly less than world prices. *The Economist* (7 May 1994), p.14.

24. *Segodnia* (2 Nov. 1995).

25. Naturally, there are fields where co-operation is still mutually beneficial (aircraft construction, missile construction). In most cases, however, the party which should be most interested in military-industrial co-operation is precisely Ukraine, which has no closed cycle of arms production; for Russia, co-operation between the two military industrial complexes is not imperative, so in itself this factor will not contribute to a *rapprochement* between the two countries.

7

Ukrainian Foreign Policy:
Between Russia and the West

SERGEI VLASOV

For Ukraine, withdrawing from the USSR involved, from the very beginning, the need to distance itself from Russia. One would have thought that Russia, which had initiated the Belovezha Agreement, would have to have an interest in an independent Ukraine. In fact, however, Kyiv was soon feeling pressure from Moscow – a pressure which it perceived as a blatant encroachment on its independent status. Nevertheless, as the years went by it became apparent that there was no question of formally depriving Ukraine of independence. Russia's aim was more probably to retain it as a weak state within its own sphere of influence.

At the time of its formation, while Russia already had the formal attributes and adjusted infrastructure of a central power, Ukraine was only starting to create its own power structure and was unable to compete in this area with Russia. All its institutions of power, including the infrastructure for foreign policy, had previously occupied only a subordinate position in the Soviet state hierarchy. The process of identifying its own interests was difficult and long drawn out. Its basic problem in international multilateral institutions was to overcome its foreign policy partners' traditional perception of Ukraine as a former dependency, and this also applied to bilateral relations with Russia. The need to move away from Russia, which was using all existing infrastructure links to exert pressure on its foreign and security policies, was forcing Ukraine to break not just the threads of dependence that really handicapped it, but often useful links too. Ukraine perceived Russia's activity as a threat to its sovereignty and security. As a result, it was faced, in its foreign policy priorities, with the problem of choosing between

Russia (CIS) and the West (NATO, EU and WEU).

Moving away from Russia and towards the West

Ukraine received large-scale economic assistance, especially from the United States and Canada, on the eve and after its declaration of independence in August 1991. This engendered a host of illusions regarding the West. At the time it was felt to be perfectly possible (using support organized by the Ukrainian diaspora) to build an entire foreign policy network. The diaspora's aid was instrumental in supporting the Rukh (Ukrainian People's Movement), whose creation as the first large-scale political force marked the end of the single-party system in Ukraine. From its resources diplomatic representations of Ukraine were first created and maintained in the USA, Canada and several other countries. Still, the influence and the resources of the diaspora were insufficient to adjust Ukraine's entire system of international links.

After looking to the diaspora, it was Germany's turn. Ukraine intended to lean on Germany in moving away from Russia and towards the West. This tallied with the fact that a tacit agreement had emerged among the countries of the West that Germany was 'responsible' for Ukraine. Germany played a significant role in establishing the latter's independence. It is sufficient to recall that, even while the USSR still existed and after the adoption of Ukraine's Declaration of Independence in August 1991, Leonid Kravchuk's trip to Bavaria as Chairman of the Verkhovna Rada (Ukrainian parliament) had made a breach which opened up the process of *de facto* recognizing Ukrainian independence. This was Ukraine's idea – to obtain meetings with Germany's political leadership by formally making trips not to Germany but to Bavaria.

Because of its dual concern to move away from Russia and please the West, immediately after independence Ukraine, of its own accord, linked itself to the commitment to a non-nuclear stance and neutrality. Ukrainian politicians feared, however, that, as a result of the non-nuclear policy, the West's interest in Ukraine might wane and Ukraine might become all the more vulnerable in the face of Russia. Moreover, the loss of significant industrial resources, largely due to neglect, and of tens of thousands of experts proved to be irreparable for the country. The commitment to nuclear non-proliferation, which in itself appeared advisable from the point of view of international stability, especially in the region of Eastern

Central Europe, has led to a severe loss of power. Ukraine managed to evade utter defeat in this matter only through receiving, after immense efforts, 'guarantees of nuclear security' from the USA and Great Britain in 1995 – the value of which, however, many in the West do not consider to be very high.

This policy increased regional and European nuclear stability, in so far as it removed the problems linked to the presence of nuclear weapons in Eastern Central Europe. This was particularly to the advantage of NATO, Russia and Ukraine's other neighbours, above all Poland. Not a single country in the world had hitherto taken this step. The nuclear disarmament decision has considerably increased Ukraine's international stature, but up to now the West, Russia and its other neighbours have failed to value this decision at its true worth.

The Idea of a Black Sea–Baltic Union

The Ukrainian Republican Party was the first to put forward the idea of a Black Sea–Baltic Union. This was that the states of Eastern Central Europe, and subsequently the whole of Europe, should unite around Ukraine to resist both Russia and the USA. In fact this was an emotional reaction to the Russian–American *rapprochement* after the end of the cold war against the background of the USA's failure to take Ukraine's interests into consideration. With Kravchuk, who reformulated this idea in 1992, the project of a Black Sea–Baltic Union looked rather more well-thought-out, as it was now territorially limited to a regional, vertical European Black Sea-Baltic belt, and not presented as an alternative to the USA and Russia. The basic overriding idea of this union was to counterbalance Russian influence. Just after being proclaimed by the Ukrainian president, however, and thus before it had time to take proper political shape, it was laid to rest by a series of factors:

(1) Having been conceived as an alternative to Russia in the Eastern Central Europe region, it did not meet with support either in the East or the West. Having agreed to delimit the spheres of influence of NATO and Russia along the Western borders of Moldova, Ukraine and Belarus, the West itself, without Russia's participation, brought in a verdict on the idea of the Black Sea–Baltic Union. A broad political process of movement by Eastern European states, especially Poland, into NATO and the European Union, and the

unfolding of NATO's 'Partnership for Peace' programme, absorbed all the previously existing variants of regional alliances in the sphere of security policies.

The CIS countries rejected the BSBU idea as being a new confrontational model, with a tripolar structure, of the European international order. The existing Russia–NATO model, while retaining a certain potential for confrontation, was predictable. From the Western perspective, the bipolar model was more attractive than the idea of a BSBU. The existence of a Black Sea–Baltic Union counterbalancing Russia would give rise to a Black Sea–Baltic arc of instability.

(2) The second major factor which made the BSBU impossible was constituted by the differences between Ukraine and its neighbours regarding national minorities and the territorial problems associated with them. The idea of a union was accepted with reservations by Ukraine's neighbours, who feared the strengthening of Ukraine and the removal of the opportunity to lay claim to disputed territories which had been settled by national minorities: Romanian, Hungarian, Ruthene and Polish. In reality, this factor made any regional security model in Eastern Central Europe impossible. This was a basic reason for all Eastern European states to strive for a definitive settlement of all territorial issues.

(3) There remained some uncertainty regarding the question of regional leadership in the context of the BSBU idea. Poland and Ukraine both laid claim to this role. It is no mere coincidence that, after Kravchuk's initiative in 1992, Lech Wałęsa's initiative on NATO Mark II soon followed, with the same idea of a regional security structure, but this time one in which Poland would dominate.

Recent events have shown that the BSBU idea still partly exists as an element in the diplomatic game, in fact if not in name. On the very day of the signing of the Russia–NATO Founding Act in May 1997, the presidents of Poland, Ukraine and the three Baltic states met in Tallinn to work out what many observers characterized as a common strategy enabling the Baltic states and Ukraine to join NATO as part of the 'second wave' of applicants, with Poland, an undoubted 'first wave' member, acting as a promoter of these states' plans to the Western Alliance.

The 'Strategic Partnership' with Poland

The beginning of an independent foreign policy in Ukraine relied closely on collaboration with Poland and the formation of a 'strategic partnership' with that country. The crucial factor, from Ukraine's point of view, was that such a partnership was advantageous to both sides in their *rapprochement* with Western institutions. Ukraine also considered that Poland would need its support in its relations with Russia. Initially this was so. Poland played up to Ukraine. An inter-presidential committee was even created, charged with co-ordinating a 'strategic partnership' policy.

Nevertheless, everything seemed easier for Poland but more complicated for Ukraine. Unexpectedly, Russia 'released' Poland, and the Baltic states, so that they had more freedom in their own foreign policy choices. Having tasted freedom, after 1994 Poland made a considerable leap forward in its own strategic movement towards NATO and lost interest in the partnership with Ukraine, and any other partnership in the Eastern European area. As a result, Ukraine remained without any prospect of a strategic partnership in a Western direction. A Polish–Ukrainian tandem was out of the question, and furthermore, Poland, in moving away and towards the West, gave a considerable stimulus to Ukraine to reconsider its own opportunities *vis-à-vis* the West, provoking opposing tendencies in its thinking and its policies.

Ukraine has finally abandoned the idea of being part of a Polish tandem. Furthermore, it sees significantly negative potential in the actions of Warsaw:

(1) Poland views as one of the key elements of its entry into the common European structure the opportunity to create 'a Weimar triangle' of Poland, France and Germany. From the Polish perspective, the present *rapprochement* with Germany is needed to compensate for 'barriers which have remained between Poland and Germany since the time of the Second World War'.

(2) It is quite possible that Poland needs the rapprochement with the West in order to create opportunities for future claims on the East, including on Ukraine.

(3) Poland does not single out Ukraine in its overall approach to the countries in the CIS, where it sees Russia alone as its major partner.

A joint Kuchma–Kwaśniewski declaration in May 1997 allayed some of Ukraine's fears regarding Poland. Both sides undertook to bury the historical enmity between the two nations and promote co-operation. Other successes of Ukrainian diplomacy in 1997 were Ukraine's co-sponsorship of the agreement between Moldova and the Trans-Dniester region, the agreement between Ukraine and Belarus on border issues, and a treaty with Romania eliminating the latter's territorial claims on Ukraine.

The Black Sea Economic Co-operation Zone

For the time being, the practical and most effective regional structure, in which Ukraine has its very own part to play and chances for influence, is the Association of Black Sea Co-operation with its Parliamentary Assembly and Black Sea Economic Co-operation Zone (BSECZ). A declaration on this organization was signed in 1992 by 11 states from the region, including Ukraine and Russia. It was the first international regional organization which Ukraine entered as an independent state with the same rights as Russia, that is, where it was not burdened with the complex of being an inferior member, as it was for example in the UN and its agencies.

Ukraine supports the idea of long-term reorganization of the BSECZ in an EU-type union and sees in it a chance to participate in economic programmes of co-operation without Russian domination. In appraising BSECZ opportunities, mention must, however, be made of the significant differences between the foreign policies of the participants, of the considerable potential for crisis in the area, and of a series of economic problems. All of this reduces the BSECZ's attractiveness for Kyiv. First, foreign trade policies in Greece, as an EU member, operate on the supranational level and a regulatory infrastructure between CIS members has not yet been developed. Secondly, not only do the regulating mechanism and instruments differ substantially, but also strategies and tactics: from liberalizing policies in this sphere on the basis of advanced tariff policies (Turkey, Greece) to the practical lack of any effective policies in given fields (CIS region, partially – Bulgaria, Romania, Albania).

Co-operation with Turkey

Co-operation with Turkey was promising to start with. Ukraine was counting on Turkey in order to create a counterbalance to Russia in the BSECZ. This hope was based on the combined dissatisfaction of both countries with NATO expansion to the East. Ukraine is dissatisfied that it has not been included among the prospective members, while Turkey fears that this expansion could destroy its monopoly position in defending NATO interests in the Black Sea area. But Ukraine also perceives a huge threat from Turkey in the context of the Crimean Tatar problem. The Crimean Tatars aim to create their own autonomous republic within Ukraine, gradually dislodging the peninsula's Russian population from its dominating economic, political and cultural positions in the Crimea. Their population has been growing through immigration from places to which Stalin deported Crimean Tatars in 1944. Turkey, which remembers vividly that the Crimean Khanate was its vassal before the Russian conquest of the Crimea, seems to welcome this prospect. Everything points to an increasing economic presence of Turkey in the Crimea through the Crimean Tatars, and even to an affirmation of its political presence there in the future. Ukraine thus fears an international conflict if, in response to possible Crimean Tatar (Islamic) terrorism, Russia decides to defend the Russian population in the Crimea.

Ukraine in the NATO Partnership for Peace Programme

The Partnership for Peace Framework Document was signed by Ukraine on 8 February 1994. This programme for military co-operation with NATO shifted Ukrainian security policy closer to the West. In future, Ukraine could receive institutional backing from NATO if it came forward with an initiative on the demilitarization of the Black Sea basin. This would be a logical extension of declarations already made on the transformation of the Baltic–Black Sea region into a zone of peace. This way of implementing the BSBU idea would both save that idea and, in the sphere of security policies, promote Ukraine to the level of a regional leader. But up to now the road to demilitarizing the region has been littered with a series of Ukrainian–Russian problems surrounding the division of the Black Sea Fleet.

After the 1994 elections and changes in the ruling coalition, there was, however, a radical reassessment of Western priorities in Ukraine's foreign policies, in particular concerning NATO. The Chairman of the Verkhovna Rada, Alexander Moroz, once declared: 'It is time to cease frequenting the corridors of NATO, as it is doing nothing for Ukraine'. President Kuchma kept his distance from the Verkhovna Rada on economic and political reforms and, above all, on that of the political system, but, nevertheless, conceptually agreed with Moroz regarding Ukraine's strategic orientation. He advised 'not deceiving ourselves on the issue of where Ukraine is going'. The 'East or West' alternative was not to be regarded as a real alternative for Ukraine as, in his words, there was no necessity for Ukraine to go anywhere, since its place was determined historically and geographically.

The NATO military co-operation programme is also encountering other difficulties. NATO calls for the observance of a series of conditions, including transparency in national defence planning and in military budgets, and also the maintenance of civilian control of the military. Such obligations seem very difficult to fulfil, due to the criminalization of the military-industrial complex. Civilian control over the military would require a thorough reform of the country's politics and economy, including the legalizing of the black economy. Resistance from the black market sphere of the military-industrial complex may thus be one of the biggest obstacles to co-operation with the West.

In spring 1996, on the eve of elections in Russia, Kuchma declared that moving closer to NATO constituted a foreign policy priority for Ukraine. But it is noteworthy that he did this after a series of consultations with Boris Yeltsin. Consequently, experts assessed the Ukrainian president's statement as demonstrating how closely Ukraine's security policy matches that of Russia's. But the co-operation between Ukraine and NATO is also designed to counterbalance Russia's position. Ukraine's drift towards NATO became more pronounced in the first half of 1997 in response to repeated statements by Russian politicians (and a Federation Council resolution) that Sevastopol remained a Russian city. The requirement that prospective NATO members must have no territorial disputes with their neighbours may have played a part in the signing of a full-scale Russo-Ukrainian Treaty on 31 May 1997, in which Russia pledged to respect Ukraine's territorial integrity. The Treaty formally put an end to the two countries' dispute over the Black Sea Fleet, providing for a 20-year lease of Sevastopol's main harbours to Russia, and for the two countries' fleets to be based in Sevastopol. Critics of the Treaty on the Ukrainian side pointed out that NATO would never accept a country that had foreign soldiers on its soil.

The Future Role of the OSCE in the Eyes of Ukrainian Politicians

The strengthening of European security remains one of the priority trends in Ukrainian politics. The OSCE is viewed now, and will be viewed in the future, as a key element in the security policy system. In Ukraine it is considered that it was precisely the position of the OSCE countries that prevented Russia from playing a rerun of Chechnya in the Crimea. In the Crimean dispute with Russia, Ukraine feels real support from the OSCE. A more effective framework for the problems of disarmament, human rights and environmental safety is so far lacking, and the OSCE is consequently considered by Ukraine as the only effective institution in which to discuss and solve these issues in Europe, allowing it to make good use of this organization's mechanism for raising questions on security policies.

Ukraine gives preference to preventive diplomacy. In this respect, the OSCE has a major advantage over NATO's Partnership for Peace programme, which does not offer such an opportunity. The fact that the priorities of all NATO structures are determined by Western interests has made the OSCE much more acceptable to Ukraine. Ukraine supports a reform of OSCE structures. According to one scenario, which has been a subject for discussion in the Verkhovna Rada's Committee for International Affairs, the OSCE should be attributed supranational functions in Europe, with the creation of a single European army made up of national divisions, but under a single command and stationed on national territories at the expense of national resources. NATO does not, however, fit into this system, and its relationship with a reformed OSCE remains unclear.

Ukraine's Relations with the European Union

The EU–Ukraine Partnership and Co-operation Agreement (PCA), signed in March 1994, opened a new chapter in their relationship. It paved the way for an institutionalization of their political dialogue. Ukraine was expecting more support in the political sphere and would have liked to be recognized as a constituent member in the process of European integration, and would have liked to be recognized as a future member of the European economic area. In particular, it was expecting support on the issue of territorial integrity. In 1991–97, the border issue was a problem in Ukraine's relations with Russia, Romania and also, to some extent, Hungary and Slovakia. Ukraine was then also anticipating more active assistance with its institutional integration into European structures, for example, in obtaining a formal status at the Western European Union (WEU).

The EU has adopted a cautious pace in relation to Ukraine: it has taken anti-dumping measures against goods of Ukrainian origin that are competitive; it has expressed criticism concerning Ukrainian economic reform and nuclear security policies. The closure of the Chernobyl nuclear power station has been a major issue in their negotiations.

Ukraine does not conceal its expectations of wide-ranging EU financial support, concerning, for instance, mutual credit arrangements between financial organizations and non-member states; the diversification of its foreign trade; the extension of privileges to Ukrainian goods exported to the EU. It hopes to obtain assistance in solving problems related to the balance of payments deficit, in receiving a stabilization fund (US$1.5 billion) and in financing the closure of the Chernobyl nuclear power station (US$4 billion).

Ukraine and the Council of Europe

Ukraine was accepted into the Council of Europe on 9 November 1995. It was accepted before Russia, at a time when not all the Council of Europe's requests to Ukraine had been granted: the death sentence had not been abolished, although a moratorium had been imposed on its enforcement; the conditions for privatization had not all been completely satisfied. Ukraine, after having gained international recognition as a member of the European community of democratic states, may also expect some material advantages from joining this organization. It may benefit from the economic and humanitarian programmes of the Council of Europe. Meanwhile, Ukraine has to pay out $2 million annually in membership fees. True, it is said that the financial benefits exceed the amounts of the fees, but the whole issue comes up against the fact that payment of Ukraine's fees falls to the population, that is, it comes out of the budget, while the investments and income from these fees go into the black economy. Membership of the Council of Europe will also have other consequences: national minorities will be stirred up and thousands of complaints will emerge in the International Court of Justice and the Commission for the Defence of Human Rights.

The CIS Problem in Domestic Policy Discussions in Ukraine

There are three foreign policy approaches in Ukraine: pro-Western, pro-Eastern, leaning towards Russia and the CIS and a third way, peculiar to Ukraine. Among the advocates of the last variant it is possible to distinguish a small group favouring the regional Central-East European alliance with some kind of leading role for Ukraine, and a larger group supporting the formula 'with Russia and the West'.

Supporters of integration into Western structures defend a simultaneous movement away from Russia. This group is primarily represented by the Rukh (Ukrainian People's Movement) and a number of small National Democratic parties. The CIS is seen exclusively as an instrument for Russia's influence and thus a threat to Ukrainian independence. Their basic attitude towards Russia is very well expressed in a quotation from the American politician and scholar Zbigniew Brzezinski: 'Without Ukraine, Russia does have a chance of becoming a democratic state, with Ukraine it does not'. Some Ukrainian researchers combine a pro-Western stand with the consideration that Ukraine should not dramatically alienate Russia in its movement towards the West. Moreover, the CIS, for the time being, should be supported and used as a form of 'divorce suit'.[1] It is indeed not sufficient for Ukraine to distance itself from Russia in order to be integrated into Western structures. This integration presupposes several conditions, namely:

(1) To announce clearly its intention of joining, with equal rights, the Western political and economic system on the basis of a corresponding reform of its society;

(2) To support unequivocal membership of NATO and the EU by the Visegrad Group, which would be regarded as Ukraine's first steps towards entry into these institutions;

(3) To consider NATO and the EU as the institutional bases of a
    pan-European commonwealth and actively secure full
    membership of these organizations.[2]

Supporters of closer relations with Russia and the other countries
of the CIS are mainly to be found among the members of the
Ukrainian Communist Party (UCP) which is the biggest party in
the country and a conglomerate of small political forces affiliated to
it. The programme for the reconstruction of the USSR was adopted
at the UCP congress which took place in March 1995. This
defended the position that the CIS should be significantly
transformed and given Union-wide functions. The programme
took into account two possible scenarios:

– initial unification with the subsequent reform of the economic
  sector geared towards dismantling market reforms which already
  existed in some states;

– the cancellation of market reforms in some states and, only after
  this, unification into the 'neo-USSR'.

It can be said with certainty that 97 communist deputies out of the
403 in the Rada, with 140 sympathizing socialists and agrarians, give
strong political backing to this project.

The centrist 'third way' orientation consists of two wings with
considerable differences of principle. The less numerous wing
promotes an independent direction for Ukraine – leaning neither
towards the West nor the East, but taking the role of regional leader
capable of gathering around itself the many states of Central and
Eastern Europe in a 'buffer' function. Politically, this wing
comprises parties and forces of the 'national patriotic' tendency,
above all, the Ukrainian National Assembly – Ukrainian National
Self-Defence and the Ukrainian Republican Party. They do not see
any positive function in the CIS and consider Ukraine's
participation in it to be a mistake, with no political prospects in the
context of genuine Ukrainian independence.

A politically more influential tendency in this centrist 'third
way' approach strives to combine the positive aspects of co-
operation with Russia and integration with Western institutions.[3]
Advocates of this position realize the impossibility of severing the
mental and historical – not to speak of economic – links with Russia
and the region of the former USSR. They also stress the difficulties
attached to the process of integrating with the West, in particular

when current economic conditions in Ukraine are taken into account. The queue of Eastern European countries waiting to join Western European structures is also depressing. Ukrainian President Kuchma and the Chairman of the Ukrainian Parliament, Moroz, may be regarded as supporters of this course. They view friendly relations and integration with Russia as a strategic priority. Developing co-operation with the West should not go ahead at the expense of Ukrainian–Russian links. Such a policy is tailored according to the tasks of internal integration and achieving stability of Ukrainian society. It rejects any display of confrontation, attempts to use the anti-Russian mood, and attempts to set the West against Russia. In this instance, Ukraine can play a decisive role in preventing the restoration of a geopolitical bipolarity on the continent. Rejecting a plain, 'either/or' choice should not be regarded as isolationism or amorphousness. From among the supporters of this trend can be heard a warning against enthusiasm for messianism and appeals not to deceive oneself with images of 'a Eurasian bridge', 'buffer' or 'mediator' or with the utopian task of politically unifying East and West. This centrist position, which favours maintaining the CIS and Ukraine's participation in it, stipulates as a condition that its current structure will be significantly reformed.

The Outlook for a CIS Economic Union

Ukraine is not officially advancing proposals for reforming the CIS economic union, but will give preference to bilateral relations, should the functioning of the CIS bodies prove to be ineffective. The positions of Ukraine, in its economic co-operation in the CIS region, are as follows: first, not to consider the restoration of economic links as an end in itself but as a condition of economic development; second, to accompany the restoration of economic links with their diversification, along with the task of overcoming dependence on this region – and of a balanced assignment of this dependence to other regions, in particular the West.

The economic structures which were created within the CIS framework – the IECC (Interstate Economic Committee), Payments Union, etc. – cannot be effective unless they are given supranational functions. But Ukraine, for the time being, is categorically against any supranational structure, so the problem of CIS economic efficiency is, in its view, stuck in the political sphere.

The only matter on which it agreed concerned the arbitration bodies. In Ukraine's opinion, the priority of international negotiations over national legislation cannot be applied to a constitutional document. This means that, in the event of a dispute over the documents signed in the CIS, it will be guided by its own constitution and statutes on economic independence. Ukraine does not support the speeding up of the integration process on the part of Russia and Kazakstan. For Ukraine, the principles of participation are, on the one hand, 'a multi-speed CIS' by analogy with 'a multi-speed Europe', and on the other, selective participation in specific programmes or simply in a certain part of a programme. In other words, the speed of integration will depend on its direct effects on the Ukrainian economy.

Ukraine's support for CIS integrationist and economic formulas will depend to a large extent on how it manages to solve, with their aid, the economic problems it has with Russia and Turkmenistan. In 1997, these were few in number:

– the difference in the approaches of Russia and Ukraine to the problem of cargo transit and the utilization of infrastructure (gas and oil pipelines, electricity transmission lines);

– its debts to Russia and Turkmenistan for energy supplies. A solution may be found in the shape of one of the following compromises:

(1) Russia and Turkmenistan could have an appropriate quota of the resources which Ukraine receives from international financial institutions;

(2) debt rescheduling;

(3) converting debts into other assets (for example, Russia/Turkmenistan's ownership share of gas pipelines, enterprises, etc. in Ukraine);

(4) writing off debts in exchange for Ukraine's full membership of the CIS;

(5) assistance in obtaining for Ukraine fresh credits from international financial organizations (a form of deferred debt).

A positive solution to the debt problem for Ukraine could be crucial in changing its attitude to the CIS and to the process of integration into the CIS.

Military Collaboration with Russia

The military integration of Ukraine and Russia is developing at a fairly fast tempo. In 1995 alone, the Russian and Ukrainian governments signed about 30 co-operation agreements in the military sphere. Experts consider that the unification of anti-aircraft defence, anti-missile defence and defence against attacks from space necessarily entails considerable integration and standardization of military technology. Russia gained significant advantages in all pacts signed, such as, for example, the one on joint anti-aircraft defence, the weightiest of all the agreements. Ukraine does not have any nuclear anti-aircraft defence weapon components at its disposal, nor any means to destroy enemy ballistic missiles: everything is in Russia. In essence, the pact comes down to Russia's using Ukrainian territory for early warning purposes and for the permanent allocation of anti-aircraft defence components. At the same time, Ukraine is still fulfilling its present function as a 'security buffer zone'. Ukraine is bound by Russia's military doctrine, which is not defensive. As a result of this integration, Russia already has a significant hold over Ukraine. A military union exists de facto, despite the statements from the Ukrainian authorities asserting their country's unwillingness to enter into a CIS military union.

Conclusion

The five-year experience of Ukrainian foreign policy shows that Ukraine has become a factor in its own right in international life, appearing as an autonomous player in relations with Russia, Turkey, Poland and the West. By giving up nuclear weapons, Ukraine has increased nuclear stability in the region of Eastern Central Europe, thereby creating for itself a significantly positive image in international affairs. This may be helpful in securing support for its policies towards the Crimea, an area which remains a potential source of conflict between Russia and Ukraine and even – due to the presence there of the Muslim Tatars – between the Christian and Islamic worlds.

NOTES

1. V. Bilynski, 'Vneshnepoliticheskaya integratsiya Ukrainy na poroge XX veka', *Politicheskaya mysl'*, No.3 (Kyiv, 1994), p.81–2.
2. Ibid.
3. See A. Dergatchev, 'I Rossiya i Zapad', *Politicheskaya mysl'*, No.3 (1994), p.72.

8

Turning Away from Russia: New Directions for Central Asia

ALEXEI MALASHENKO

History does not consist simply of a change in social systems and political doctrines, and a succession of scientific and technological revolutions. It also involves the coexistence of centuries-old regional civilizations, of religious communities which have, despite the evolutionary process, preserved the material aspects of everyday life, the genetic features and value systems which determine people's standards of behaviour and their perception of the world. Among the various contradictions between these civilizations, a particular role has been played by religious differences.

As religion is less dynamic than 'the economic formation of society' (*ökonomische Gesellschaftsformation*), to use a Marxist idiom, it imparts a degree of stability and, one could say, conservatism to society. Without this, what we are accustomed to calling progress can easily become extreme, destroying the existing norms for human relations by means of revolution, and leading to cataclysm at a national and social level, amongst others.

The majority of researchers, and above all political scientists, deliberately relegate the mutual opposition between civilizations to second place, with an indirect and weak link to the immediate peripeteia of socio-political development. Experts serving the political establishment in the USA, Europe and Russia tend to reject publications such as Huntington's 'Clash of Civilizations'. The sociological approach, with its emphasis on socio-economic factors, dominates the social sciences. Civilizational aspects remain, as usual, on the periphery of academic research. The fact that the revolution in Iran was, in name, an Islamic one is either directly or indirectly ignored, as is the fact that the Soviet Union contained within it segments of two civilizations, Christian and Muslim. The fact that both of these coexisted within the boundaries of one state always concealed an inner potential for conflict.

Of course, the problems caused by the interaction of these different civilizations were not a direct cause of the collapse of the Soviet Union. But it would be wrong not to take into account the fact that the Muslim territories within the Union were forcibly annexed by Russia, and that relationships between people in Central Asia, on a personal and societal level, were informed to a great extent by Islamic tradition, and that these lands could therefore be considered to be Muslim[1] and Soviet in equal measure. Thus we must not ignore the civilizational factor when evaluating the prospects for the integration of the states of the former USSR, or, in the case of Central Asia, for a more pronounced reorientation towards the Muslim world.

The opinion of the Russian orientalist G.V. Miloslavski is an interesting one. He considers that an 'integral civilizational system was formed' within the Soviet Union.[2] This statement, which presupposes the formation of a new civilizational system in the former Soviet Union, may raise some doubts, if only because Estonia and Turkmenistan can on no account be included in a common civilization (that is, of course, if we use the classical definition of the term). Here, the thesis of the cultural historian, Boris Yerasov, seems more accurate. He argues that the Soviet system was a substitute for the universal order formed by a civilization, by its spiritual and social structures.[3]

Experience has shown that it is not within the power of socio-economic relations or of a political system to destroy a civilizational constant which has formed over time, and which is based on a religious tradition. This civilizational constant has the capacity to regenerate in the face of any impingement by external or internal forces. The civilizational factor, alas, 'cannot be counted' with the aid of statistics and cannot be accurately or thoroughly described using sociological categories. On the one hand, it is the backdrop against which economic development and political peripeteia take place. On the other, it is a composition of the resiliant stereotypes and norms of behaviour which determine interpersonal relations. To put it simply, Islam will not disappear as a result of any economic reforms or developments in science and technology, in the same way that Muslims will always be Muslims, which is to say they will – with minor adjustments, of course –

preserve their socio-cultural stereotype. In Islam this stereotype is more stable and, if I may use the expression, 'more penetrating' than in other civilizations, for the following reasons: first, this has to do with Islam itself, in which, unlike in Christianity, there is no strict division between the secular and spiritual. Secondly, the Muslim world is not as developed as the Euro-Christian world in the spheres of economy and science and technology, and has thus not experienced such cruel pressure from permanent modernisation.

The region of Central Asia is part of this Islamic world. Let us make a preliminary note that the very concept of 'Central Asia' as a region appears to some extent to be artificial. Geographically, the territories included in this region fall into three massive enclaves; the northern, north-eastern and southern, this last of which is also very heterogenous. Only with some reservations can we call Aral (and the area adjacent to it) a geographical segment which is common to the entire region. The interaction between the Pamir mountains and the river system and deserts of Uzbekistan and Turkmenistan is more organic, but then these are not connected with the northern lands. It seems that there was no common economic system for the peoples who settled these lands: firm ties were not established to link the systems of the nomads of Kazakstan and Turkmenistan with the settled dwellers of the other territories. Their external economic links were also different, and were directed more outside the region than inside it. There are no fixed regional borders between the ethnic groups living in Central Asia. There is no watershed between 'Soviet' Uzbeks, Tajiks, Turkmens and those who share the same faith in countries to the south and east, such as Afghanistan, Iran and China. The religious persuasion of the region cannot be seen as a sign of its unity, as all the countries to the south of Central Asia are also part of the Muslim world.

Of course, one should not stress intra-regional differences by maintaining that there is nothing at all in common between the countries and peoples of Central Asia. Yet the majority of specialists continue, as before, to regard and analyse Central Asia as one economic and socio-cultural community. We talk of the affiliation of the majority of the population to the Turkic peoples, or of a certain similarity in historical development. In evaluating Central Asia's prospects, researchers place the main emphasis on the fact that it is a post-Soviet region, or, more broadly, a region which has been part of the Russian empire, a factor which is essentially seen as a sign of its unity.

Recently, attempts have been made to change such perceptions of Central Asia. In Russia, the political scientist Vyacheslav Belokrinitsky has replaced the definition 'Central Asia' with the term 'Central Asian region', which includes the former Soviet republics and also Afghanistan, Iran and Pakistan.[4] His idea has not yet been widely adopted by Russian experts. It does, however, allow us to go beyond the confines of the customary approach and seek the key to resolving many of the problems of former Soviet Central Asia, not only within the region, but also in neighbouring countries. Such an approach requires more intensive study of bilateral (or wider) relations within the borders of Central Asia and also beyond, and of the activities of old and newly-emerging groups and organizations such as, for example, the Economic Co-operation Organisation (ECO). It would also require an analysis of all the processes of integration and disintegration taking place between the Southern Urals and the Indian Ocean.

Nevertheless, as was mentioned earlier, all this does not mean that the approach to Central Asia as a common region in some respects – albeit an artificial one – has been exhausted. While there are increasingly diverse internal problems, and particularities in the relationships between the individual states, the question of Central Asia's relations with Russia is a uniting factor. In other words, Central Asian countries face the prospect of either integrating into a common space with its own pattern of development at the same pace as Russia, or the opposite – distancing itself from the former mother country.

Sometimes, the 'problem of choosing a path of development' is added to all this as another element in common. All of Central Asia is confronted with the costs of the social system out of which, strictly speaking, the new states emerged. This question, however, is being decided independently by each country, and in some cases it is already apparent that the chosen 'path' is connected not so much with regional co-operation as with co-operation abroad. Each state is deciding these issues firstly according to its own needs as a nation-state, and then in terms of its sense of belonging to the region. Furthermore, all the countries of Central Asia are oriented towards foreign models of development.

Taking into account all that has thus far been said, and remembering the social, economic and political diversity of Central

Asia, we shall now concentrate our attention on the prospects for these countries' relations with Russia, in particular with regard to the influence of the civilizational factor on these relations. In this instance we are not going to equate this factor with religion. In principle this would be possible, but it would understandably limit the analysis. We are talking rather of a combination of traditions which were preserved in spite of the three driving forces of the Soviet system: industrialization, collectivization and the cultural revolution.

The civilizational factor is, in its own way, apparent in economics. In the first half of the 1990s, the opinion prevailed among specialists and political scientists that the rebuilding of relations between Russia and Central Asia would begin in the sphere of economics. This theme was evident in the speeches of the Russian premier Viktor Chernomyrdin, and presidents Akaev, Nazarbaev, Karimov and Niyazov, who, to begin with, genuinely saw a panacea for all economic and financial ills in the restoration of economic links between their countries and the Russian Federation. Russian technocrats took a more reserved position from the start, not forgetting that, in 1995, 37.7 per cent of Russia's entire foreign debt went to the states of Central Asia. These former Soviet republics are in no hurry to clear this debt, nor are they in a position to do so.

At the same time, intensive co-operation between Russia and Central Asia may involve the risk of preserving the low standard of technology, labour productivity and product quality which existed in Soviet times. It may also lead to a reproduction of the centre-periphery relations characteristic of the Soviet period. The Soviet economic system was created without taking into account the specific nature of Central Asian society. Olga Dmitrieva writes that 'the same methods were applied to Central Asia as to the European parts of Russia in the USSR', and that 'contrary to any criteria for economic effectiveness or consideration of the social order' the most profit-making options were chosen.[5] The lack of qualified personnel for the creation of a modern industrial sector in Central Asia is also well known. The overwhelming majority of the population of Central Asia worked in agriculture, and the urban population was involved mainly in cottage industry and trade. 'Industrial work is not only psychologically difficult for the Uzbeks', writes the Uzbek academic Talib Saidbaev, 'but it also requires lengthy training.'[6] The majority of the indigenous population have not had this lengthy training, a fact borne out by numerous statistical data. Even in the relatively urbanized Uzbekistan, members of the indigenous nationality involved in industrial production number no more than 35 per cent. In the other Central Asian republics, this percentage is lower still. We can agree with Yuri Aleksandrov when he writes that, in Central Asia, society is divided along 'a line which runs between industrial work and those forms of economic activity which do not contradict the value system'.[7] As a result, a large proportion of the population of the Central Asian republics remained outside the modern industrial sector. In theory, traditional economic methods could have been included in an interregional division of labour. In practice, however, the distribution within Russia of agricultural produce from Central Asia was limited, and sometimes led to the destruction of traditional farming methods.

The traditional sector, in which a large part of the indigenous population worked, served the domestic needs of society, and did not have many links with the modern sectors of the USSR. High technology equipment is not necessary for agricultural work in Central Asia, nor is the widespread use of fertilizers (the incorrect use of herbicides has had serious ecological consequences). Moreover, the modernization of the traditional sector inevitably led, and continues to lead, to a massive rise in unemployment (kept hidden under Soviet rule), with subsequent social instability.

The traditional sector, which remained separate from the Soviet economic system, provided the material basis for the preservation of traditional behavioural norms in Central Asia. This sector of the economy, which remains practically self-sufficient, has no need to develop relations with Russia. Even if we consider the development of economic links between Russia and Central Asia to be inevitable, it will hardly incorporate traditional pre-industrial production methods. We might suppose that with the gradual establishment of trading in agricultural produce in exchange for Russian goods, the traditional sector could to a certain extent become a factor in economic integration with Russia. There would, however, be considerable difficulties in this, due to problems of transport, taxation, the high cost of Russian industrial production and its poor quality in comparison with goods from countries such as China, Turkey, or the states of South-East Asia. The wide availability of cheap consumer goods from Asia is demonstrating the superiority of foreign countries, including Muslim ones, over Russia.

According to Aleksander Akimov, it is quite difficult to determine the prospects for the economic integration of Russia and the Central Asian region. There are few objective reasons for economic co-operation: they do not deal in similar specialized areas of export, their economies are not mutually complementary, and there is no need for their markets to be merged.[8] Also, Russia cannot set a good example for the countries of Central Asia on how to create a market economy. In this respect, China's experience is far more interesting for them.

Nevertheless, the economy – which plays an ambivalent role in the sphere of Russian–Central Asian integration – is not a decisive factor in their mutual estrangement. The fact that Russia and Central Asia belong to different civilizations is more important. This thesis will certainly be disputed by the majority of political scientists and academics who insist that communication between different civilizations leads to the mutual enrichment of peoples and promotes the perfection of their cultures. In saying this, however, they overlook the fact that a potential for conflict has built up specifically on the frontier between Christianity and Islam. The events which have followed the collapse of the bipolar world confirm this. According to Samuel Huntington, conflict will break out in the north of the 'Muslim region' between the Russian Orthodox and Muslim populations.[9]

Boris Erasov notes that during the Soviet period, Russia was already unable to conduct a civilized dialogue with orthodox Islam.[10] In the Muslim Volga Basin, there could be no talk even of dialogue, since Islam was as harshly suppressed in this region as Orthodox Christianity. In Central Asia, though, where Muslims were in the majority and religious tradition showed a strong capacity for resistance, there was something resembling dialogue between the Soviet authorities and Islam. As a result of this very specific dialogue, the local religious elite was suppressed, Muslims were cut off from other centres of Islamic culture, the process of Islamic reform (jadidism) was halted and the system of religious education was destroyed. This led to the indisputable predominance of so-called people's syncretic Islam, in which true Islamic norms and traditions were interwoven with pre-Islamic customs. Even the communists could not get rid of this 'people's Islam', which was part of the way of life of the local population of Central Asia. In this way, Islam was preserved on an everyday level and remained one of the basic factors affecting relationships between the individual and the community. Since the majority of local populations live in the countryside, the force of religious culture is beginning to make itself felt in the large towns and especially in teaching institutes that draw their students from the countryside, as Eden Naby writes.[11]

It is appropriate to mention here that in the first years following the collapse of the Soviet Union, Islam and the feeling of ethnic identity were practically one and the same. 'The beginning of the Islamic renaissance is connected with the growth of nationalism and a slowly growing awareness among the intelligentsia that was reflected in the rebirth of Islamic traditions.'[12] It was precisely at this time that the peoples of Central Asia developed a strong desire to be a 'fully-fledged' nation, a religious-cultural community, and not a part of the Soviet people. 'Homo tajicus' and 'homo uzbecus' were summoned to replace the 'homo sovieticus' who had left them such a difficult legacy.[13] According to a short survey carried out by the Giler Independent Institute in Kazakstan in 1994, 80 per cent of the respondents declared that they considered the USSR to be a 'great evil'.[14] It is appropriate also to mention the negative reaction in Central Asia to the decision to annul the Belovezha agreement taken by the State Duma of Russia in February 1995. Local politicians and the media unanimously detected pretensions to reviving the USSR. The president of Uzbekistan, Islam Karimov, had a poor opinion of the 1996 agreement between Belarus and Russia on setting up the Community of Sovereign Republics. This reaction was due in part to the fact that its abbreviation – SSR in Russian – reminded him of 'the sonorous name of the USSR which is dear to the hearts of several of its authors.'[15] The proposal by the President of Kazakstan, Nursultan Nazarbaev, to create a Eurasian Union (EAU) has also not found favour with the majority and was, in Karimov's opinion, 'dead from the start.'[16] The President of Turkmenistan, Saparmurad Niyazov, also had an unfavourable opinion of the EAU.

At the root of Karimov and Niyazov's scepticism were their confidence in their own strength and their hopes of aid from foreign countries. The President of Turkmenistan places paramount importance on his seemingly inexhaustible hydro-carbon resources, dreaming of turning his country into a 'second Kuwait'. The case of Uzbekistan is less straightforward, based on the intensive development of complex links with many different Western and Eastern states, and also on the intention of playing a role similar to that played by Tunisia in the 1960s or even that of Turkey in Central Asia today. Practical considerations are to the forefront here. Yet we must not forget to mention that this scepticism is also backed up by ideological motives. It must be remembered that the Eurasianist idea first arose in Russian public thinking, that it came from Russia, and reflected first and foremost Russia's state interests, in particular its striving to maintain control over the territory it had conquered and assimilated. Muslims, Soviet and Russian alike, could never understand this idea – it was alien, or at least unfamiliar to them. While advocates of Eurasianism saw in the creation of the EAU an opportunity to 'prevent a conflict of civilizations' and 'an attempt to avert a new estrangement of Russia and Asia',[17] for many Central Asian politicians this appeared essentially to be a way for Russia to 'gather in' the former republics of the USSR. In a sense, the Eurasianist idea is the antithesis of both the Central Asian states' aspirations to be independent of Russia, and of their firm orientation towards the Muslim world, a fact which strikes fear into the hearts of both Moscow rulers and their opposition.

In September 1996 the militarized Islamic 'Taliban' movement seized Kabul, the capital of Afghanistan, and imposed its control over the major part of the country. The Kremlin took vigorous measures to present itself as the main guarantor of stability in the face of potential fundamentalist expansion northwards. Over the course of a few autumn weeks in September and early October, in the first wave of fear of the Taliban, the Central Asian states did see Russia as the force which could contain them. By winter, however, fear had given way to attempts to find a compromise with the Taliban and the forces that were supporting them. Following the initial shock of the Taliban offensive, the governments of countries bordering on Afghanistan tended to see the events more as 'intra-Muslim affairs', in which both Pakistan and Turkmenistan were playing a prominent role. Pakistan had been involved in the creation of the Taliban movement, of which the US was also informed. The Taliban was, moreover, acting with the agreement of the President of Turkmenistan, Saparmurat Niyazov (although this has yet to be proven with documented evidence): the construction of a gas pipe-line from Turkmenistan to Pakistan is being planned through Afghan territory under Taliban control, with the participation of the US company UNOCAL and the Saudi Delta Oil Company.

As Martha Brill Olcott notes, Islam proved to have been much more pervasive in the Soviet era than had been imagined before the independence of the Central Asian states.[18] Religious differences have distanced Central Asia from Russia, but Islam is only one factor – albeit a very important one – in the widening cultural and psychological gap between the two largest civilizational enclaves of the former Soviet Union. The reorientation of the historical memory of the indigenous peoples is among the other factors: they feel more and more acutely that they have been conquered by Russia, while in Russia itself the Russians believe themselves to be conquerors. The notion of a common victory in the Great Patriotic War is being erased from recent historical memory. Nor should we ignore what may be defined as 'psychological fatigue' resulting from the cohabitation of different ethnic groups and religious denominations in one state; a state which gave to some the right to seniority and assigned to others the role of 'younger brothers'.

The increase in cultural distance is felt particularly keenly by the indigenous 'Russian-educated' intelligentsia, by writers and artists, who are beginning to realize that their art is becoming an archaism, the property of the past. Echoes of this bitterness can be heard in the latest works, and particularly in the journalistic articles, of Olzhas Suleimenov, Chingiz Aitmatov and other prose writers and poets whose talent came to light in the Soviet period. A growing ethnic consciousness which was at least ignored, if not repressed, under Soviet rule, is also helping to discourage closer links with Russia. This is now becoming one of the leading factors not only in public opinion, but also in the official ideology of the Central Asian countries. 'National sensibilities are felt more keenly by those creating the new, independent states than they were by their historical predecessors within the Russian empire and the USSR.'[19] This process of turning away from Russia is being indirectly confirmed by the growing wave of emigration from Central Asia by the Russian-speaking population who, judging from their own experience, sense a 'sudden increase in ethno-cultural distance, particularly between the Slavic and indigenous populations.'[20] They can also see Russia's dwindling authority, her lack of interest and inability to preserve the influential position she once held here.

We must recognize that in future, as long as nothing out of the ordinary happens (and this cannot be ruled out in the post-Soviet space), the distance between Russia and Central Asia will continue to grow and, for the generation born in the 1980s, the period when their country was part of the USSR, and the 'special relationship' with Russia, will seem like a dream of the past. It is possible, however, that at some stage Russia and some of the states of Central Asia will be pushed together more strongly than at present by their long-term economic interests. Nationalist tension may decrease, and the inferiority complex before the once 'older brother' may gradually fade away. Religious difference, although it has tended lately to remain somewhat overshadowed by social and ethno-political clashes, is, however, more fundamental, and the gap between different religions cannot be bridged. The dialogue between religions, which has been pursued in the 1990s with due persistence by religious and secular leaders alike, does not signify that the borders between them are being dissolved; it would appear that, on the contrary, not only are they not disappearing, but they are becoming more pronounced. This stubborn opposition can be seen as a reaction to a globalizing world culture.

Thanks to the 'renaissance' of Islam, the future Russian leadership will have to deal with a new generation of Central Asian leaders whom it will not be possible to characterize simply as 'post-Soviet'. For the coming ruling elite – and equally for the opposition, who will have a different attitude from that of the Soviet period – Islam will be not just an instrument of political intrigue, but also one of the pillars of their personal convictions. Working in a Muslim society they will, to varying degrees, prove to be the bearers of Muslim political tradition. This tradition entails the recognition that secular and religious principles are indivisible, a predisposition to 'Islamic theocracy', and authoritarianism. They will appeal to notions of 'Islamic solidarity', 'Islamic economy', 'jihad' and so on, which are dear to Muslims and are unlikely to be taken lightly by their Russian neighbours.

Finally, political Islam, or 'Islamism',[21] occupies a certain, and possibly influential, niche in Central Asia. The Islamists are already an appreciable force in Uzbekistan in the 1990s, and their influence is growing slowly but steadily in Kazakstan and particularly Kyrgyzstan. Here, in the spring of 1995, several Islamist groups were active in the south, in the towns of Batken, Jalal-Abad and Osh, demanding official recognition by the authorities.[22] This is to say nothing of Tajikistan, where they were once in government, have since formed the basis of the United Opposition, and are now securing seats in the coming ruling coalition. In Turkmenistan, which lacks any legal opposition, Islamism could turn out to be the only way of expressing social protest.

The experience of post-war historical development has shown

that mass discontent with unsuccessful social and economic development in Muslim countries has been expressed by Islamism. This was the case in Iran at the end of the 1970s and early 1980s, in Sudan at the end of the 1980s, and Algeria at the start of the 1990s. Turkey can be included in this list, after the electoral victory of the Islamic Welfare Party in the parliamentary elections of 1995. Politicians and experts in Central Asia would do well to follow closely the situation in Turkey, where secular authorities are enlisting the participation of Islamists in a coalition government. Russia, which already has to negotiate with the Party of Islamic Revival in Tajikistan, should also bear such an option in mind. Islamist individuals or political parties could in the future join the administrative organs of Uzbekistan and other Central Asian states.

Some members of the Russian political establishment are beginning to acknowledge the fact that Islamism is the natural political force for the Muslim world. They consider it necessary from a pragmatic point of view to conduct dialogue with this force in the interests of Russia. Political Islam is seen by Moscow both as an adversary and as a partner in a geopolitical system in which the Islamic world and Russia are in danger of being left behind due to Western domination and the growing influence of the Far East, including China. A certain continuity can be seen here with the foreign policies of the USSR, which used the Palestinian Islamists and the Libyan leader Muammar Kaddafi to further its interests, and even tried to play the card of Islamic revolution in Iran. In the mid-1990s, Islamic radicals, in turn, have apparently stopped regarding Russia exclusively as 'Satan' and are also ready for dialogue.

The revival of Islam in Central Asia, and the appeal on an official level to Islamic tradition, does not preclude integration with the wider international community.[23] It is however apparent that the 'Islamic factor' – a combination of religious and cultural revival, an appeal to Islam by local politicians and the activization of political Islam – is widening the cultural gap between Central Asia and other countries that belong to other civilizations, primarily Russia. It is by no means an obstacle, however, to the expansion of Central Asia's contacts with the rest of the world, including Western Europe and the USA. The reasons for this are easy to find: the first has to do with the economic advantages of co-operation with developed countries. In sociological research in Kazakstan and

Uzbekistan, the majority of those questioned felt that in the first instance they should approach the West and Japan for economic aid, and not Muslim countries.[24] Second, the narrowness and ideological xenophobia of Soviet society is no longer accepted in Central Asia, particularly by the youth. Third, the ruling classes of the former Soviet republics are attempting to take their proper place among the world's political elite. The states of Central Asia have been accepted into all of the major international Muslim organizations, and are increasingly influential in intra-Muslim affairs. The new Central Asian elite's striving for recognition by the international community is also a factor in the development of Central Asia's relations with the non-Muslim states of the East, with Japan, China and South Korea (in this last case, the Korean diaspora living in the region plays an important role).

Co-operation between Central Asian countries and Turkey has not brought the expected results for either side. The idea of collaboration between Turkic peoples under the aegis of Turkey has proved untenable. But co-operation with Iran is even more problematic. Iran is making concerted efforts to initiate collaboration on an intra-regional level, in the broad sense of the term. One of the more obvious successes of this policy is the construction of the Tedjen-Serakhs-Mashkad railway line, and Iran's participation in developing Transasiatic-European fibre-optic communications. But Iran is itself suffering ongoing economic hardship and is seen by Central Asian politicians as a revolutionary threat. Several Iranian religious figures of a radical persuasion were expelled from Turkmenistan and Uzbekistan in 1995. Central Asian leaders such as Karimov, Nazarbaev and Akaev declared that their states were acting as barriers to the spread of Islamic fundamentalism. Islam may therefore be regarded as one of the factors preventing closer relations between Iran and the Central Asian states, although in the public appearances by leading politicians, and particularly religious leaders, the religious unity of the region is stressed.

The waning significance of Central Asia's main unifying feature – the fact that it was part of the Soviet Union – will lead to a greater differentiation between the countries of the region. Each state is concerned first and foremost with its own concrete national interests, which, increasingly, involve going beyond the boundaries of the region, in various directions. The common regional issue for all the states of Central Asia is their attitude to Russia. In spite of the efforts of Kazakstan and Kyrgyzstan, a tendency has emerged of moving away from Russia, whose interests conflict more and more often with the internal and foreign policies of the Central Asian elite. The boundary between the civilizations of Islam and Christianity is turning into a political one. But this tendency may also have undesirable consequences for the Central Asian states themselves. Some parts of Central Asia may become subordinate to China, and others to their more powerful Muslim neighbours.

NOTES

1. This question has been convincingly covered by the ethnologist S.P. Polyakov in his works, *Traditsionalizm v sovremennom sredneaziatskom obshchestve* (Moscow, 1989) and *Istoricheskaya etnografiya Srednei Azii i problemy areal'noi tipologizatsii i periodizatsii,* academic paper (Moscow, 1993).
2. G. V. Miloslavski, 'Integratsionnyi potentsial regiona', *Vostok,* No.5 (1996), p.8.
3. Boris Yerasov, 'Rossiya v tsentral'noaziatskom geokul'turnom komplekse', *Rossiya i musul'manskii mir,* No.1 (1994), p.6.
4. See V. Ya. Belokrinitski, 'Genezis i osnovnye kharakteristiki regiona', in *Tsentral'naya Aziya. Puti integratsii v mirovoe soobshchestvo,* Moscow, 1995, pp.9-38.
5. O.G. Dmitrieva, 'Regional'naia ekonomicheskaia diagnostika', SPb (1992), pp.203–6.
6. T. S. Saidbaev, 'Mezhdu vchera i zavtra', *Zvezda vostoka,* Tashkent, No.8 (1991), p.11.
7. Yu. G. Aleksandrov, 'Srednyaya Aziya: problemy strategii razvitiya', in *Rossiya i Vostok: problemy vzaimodeistviya,* Part 1, Moscow (1993), p.175.
8. A. Akimov, 'Rossiya – Tsentral'naya Aziya: perspektivy ekonomicheskoi integratsii', *Aziya i Afrika segodnia* No.6 (1994).
9. Quoted from: *Biznes i politika,* Moscow, No.5 (1995), p.62.
10. Boris Yerasov, op. cit., p.11.
11. Eden Naby, 'The Emerging Central Asia. Ethnic and Religious Factions', in Mohiaddin Mesbahi (ed.), *Central Asia and the Caucasus after the Soviet Union. Domestic and International Dynamics* (Gainesville, FL: University Press of Florida, 1994), p.51.
12. Alexei V. Malashenko, 'Islam versus Communism. The Experience of Coexistence', in Dale F. Eickelman (ed.), *Russia's Muslim Frontiers. New Directions in Cross-Cultural Analysis* (Bloomington, IN: Indiana University Press, 1993), p.67.
14. *Karavan,* Almaty, 11 Nov. 1994.
13. Stephane A. Dudoignon, 'Changements politiques et historiographie en Asie Centrale (Tadjikistan et Uzbekistan, 1987-1993)', *Cahiers d'études sur la Méditerranée orientale et le monde turco-iranien CEMOTI,* Paris, No.16 (1993), p.67.
15. *Narodnoe slovo,* Tashkent, 13 April 1996.
16. *Nezavisimaya gazeta,* Moscow, 21 June 1994.
17. Vladimir Myasnikov, 'Yevraziiskaya ideya i yeyo perspektivy', *Biznes i politika,* (Moscow, 1995), No.5 p.63.
18. Martha Brill Olcott, 'Islam and Fundamentalism in Independent Central Asia', in: Yaacov Ro'i (ed.), *Muslim Eurasia: Conflicting Legacies* (London: Frank Cass, 1995), p.21.
19. Alexei Arapov, Yakov Umanski, 'Tsentral'naya Aziya i Rossiya: vyzovy i otvety', *Svobodnaya mysl'* (Moscow, 1994), p.78.
20. *Migratsiya russkoyazychnogo naseleniya iz Tsentral'noi Azii: prichiny, sledstviya, perspektivy,* ed. Galina Vitkovskaya, Carnegie Endowment for International Peace, Moscow Carnegie Centre, academic papers, edition 11, (Moscow, 1996), p.6.
21. I shall deliberately avoid the question of different definitions of 'Islamism', 'Islamic fundamentalism' and so on. In this context, I am talking about the activity of Islamic political organizations which, in their search for alternatives to the Euro-Christian

model of social development, advance as their aim the reconstruction of the state and society along Islamic lines. In their work they use Islam as much as possible to influence public opinion, and as a weapon in the struggle for power.

22. *Slovo Kyrgyzstana*, Bishkek, 15 July 1995.
23. Nancy Lubin, 'Islam and Ethnic Identity in Central Asia: A View from Below', in Ro'i, op. cit., p.70.
24. Of the 1,000 questioned, those in favour of the West and Japan numbered 519 in Uzbekistan and 423 in Kazakstan; 66 were in favour of the Muslim countries, ibid., p.70.

9

Russian and Western Interests in Preventing, Managing and Settling Conflicts in the Former Soviet Union

DMITRI TRENIN

Russia's politico-military involvement in the conflicts along its periphery and, even more importantly, the methods of such involvement, have become one of the sticking points in the country's relations with the West. Even before the start of the war in Chechnya in December 1994, Russian activities were said to differ fundamentally from the traditional United Nations peacekeeping practices, especially as regards impartiality, the consent of all parties and the rules of engagement. Indeed, Turkey's action in Cyprus in 1974, or India's in Sri Lanka in 1987 – both dubbed 'peacekeeping' by the intervening parties – offer better parallels here than do UN operations. Despite Moscow's earlier internationalist pronouncements, it has long been argued that unilateral and forcible intervention by the Russian military, disguised as 'peacemaking', was in fact an instrument of imperial restoration, or at least of a frank pursuit of the Russian national interest. Although in a category of its own, Moscow's military operation in Chechnya has cast a long shadow over Russian efforts to keep or enforce peace throughout the former Soviet Union (FSU). Thus it has been virtually agreed that no blank cheque should be issued for Russian-led peace operations on the territory of the Newly Independent States (NIS). Furthermore, Russian encroachments on the new states' still fragile sovereignty should be firmly resisted, so as to send an unambiguous message to Moscow.

The Russian government, of course, strongly disagrees with such an assessment. Its officials routinely insist that Russian peacekeepers strictly observe the UN Charter, the CSCE Final Act and other international documents which Russia has signed. Although Moscow still expresses a preference for a UN/OSCE mandate for peace operations within the CIS, in the view of both the foreign and defence ministries of the Russian Federation (RF) no additional international legitimation of Russian actions is necessary in principle, when those actions are undertaken under the auspices of the CIS as a regional arrangement. For several years before the outbreak of the war in Chechnya and the conclusion of the Dayton peace accords, Moscow was even able to claim the relative effectiveness of the Russian involvement over UN operations. It is true, of course, that since Russian peacekeepers arrived in South Ossetia and Transdniestria in mid-1992, the fighting there has not resumed, while the intervention by the Russian army in Tajikistan later in the same year led, if not to the end of the civil war, then to a dramatic lowering of the level of violence in that former Soviet republic. All of this, it was argued, should have compared favourably with the results of the UN efforts in 1992–95 in such places as Somalia or Bosnia. The essence of peacekeeping, Moscow seemed to be saying, lay in keeping the opponents' guns silent: stopping bloodshed was essential for stability, and there was no other power besides Russia, nor was there an international organization, which was capable of performing that feat.

On the more specific issues, Russian diplomats pointed out that their country – which possessed deep, and indeed unique knowledge of the conflicts in the FSU – was responding creatively to the challenges of the post-cold war era. They also noted that earlier 'traditional' peacekeeping had constituted an attempt to find a way out of the Cold War impasse which had for decades paralysed the United Nations. As to the much wider use of force by the peacekeepers, a major revision of classical UN principles was already underway and, in the light of NATO's 1995 enforcement actions in ex-Yugoslavia, the Russian attachment to 'using war as a means of protecting the peace'[1] was by no means unique.

Regarding the impartiality argument, the Russians were quick to observe that the Western Alliance forces in Bosnia were much more likely to use force to halt the Serbian offensive than they were to stop similar Croat or Moslem actions. The Russians were indeed

proud that the 'special relations' which they enjoyed with their
fellow post-Soviet republics had occasionally allowed them to turn
the warring parties themselves into 'peacekeepers', in company
with Russian forces – undoubtedly another striking novelty in the
practice of peacekeeping.

All of this, however, leaves many critics of Russian actions
unimpressed. They refuse to see how Moscow can indeed be
impartial, if not *vis-à-vis* the parties to conflict, then *vis-à-vis*
Russia's own interests. They doubt whether the consent of all
parties is always available, and genuine. And, in some cases at least,
they suspect that Russian military forces in the conflict areas are
part of the problem, rather than part of the solution.

The evolution of Russia's foreign policy from the liberal
internationalism which marked it in 1991–92 to the 'enlightened
patriotism', based on national interests, which succeeded it in
1993–94, and then on to a latter-day version of *realpolitik*,
confirmed the perception that Russia's strategy for the borderlands
was to regain a substantial degree of politico-military control over
them. Even hollow political demonstrations, such as the Russian
Duma vote in March 1996 to annul the earlier parliamentary
resolution ratifying the dismantling of the USSR, are seen as a
prelude to an imperial backlash.

For their part, most members of the Russian political elite
believe that the real issue between them and the West (which in the
context of this chapter is used to denote the United States and the
nations of the European Union; Turkey – because of its geopolitical
position, interests and role – has to be analysed separately) is not so
much the observance of a set of agreed principles or the existence
of an international mandate (here they complain of 'double
standards'),[2] but a struggle for influence in the emerging
geopolitical regions of the new Eastern Europe, the Caucasus and
Central Asia.[3] They see the West as being strongly opposed to any
new integration between the NIS and Russia – an integration
which, in the view of most Russians, is natural and historically
inevitable. The policies of the leading Western nations are believed
to be aimed at restraining Russia's efforts to assume its rightful
place as a great power. Traditional geopolitics has recently made a
striking comeback in Russia, shaping the post-communist
mentality of its elite.

In this context, the internationalization of peacekeeping in the
area of the FSU is frequently viewed as a useful tool for limiting

Russia's influence in the countries deemed vitally important to her. The underlying assumption is simple: those who play the role of peacemakers (and, the name of the relevant international organization notwithstanding, it has to be great powers, in most cases including the United States) are likely to assume political control over the conflict area – a control which they will consolidate, rather than relinquish, in the process of post-conflict settlement. Thus Russia, which feels itself extremely weak, will de facto be excluded and its sphere of influence rolled back. If deployed on the territory of the former USSR, a military unit from a NATO country – even one wearing a blue UN helmet – would be perceived almost as a symbol of 'foreign occupation'. In reality, of course, there has been great reluctance on the part of international organizations like the UN or the OSCE, as well as individual Western countries, to get involved in post-Soviet peacekeeping. The low profile of the UN observer missions in Abkhazia and Tajikistan, and that – even lower – of the OSCE efforts in Nagorno-Karabakh, South Ossetia and Moldova, have quelled some, but not all, Russian fears.

Any internationalization has thus been rather superficial if not altogether absent. Virtually without any serious aid or competition, Russia has continued to play the part of sole peacekeeper in the FSU, using the CIS as a surrogate for an international organization. Meanwhile, criticism of Moscow's actions has also continued, and has led to a long delay in Russia's admission to the Council of Europe, which only occurred in early 1996. To be sure, the brutal war in Chechnya has thrown into sharp relief the enormous differences in practice, if not in theory, between the Russian government's actions and accepted international norms. But, values and principles notwithstanding, are Russian and Western 'hard' interests really so far apart, where conflict resolution in the FSU is concerned? It is the purpose of this chapter to examine the national security interests behind both Russian peacekeeping and the Western countries' attitudes to it. The chapter seeks to establish if, and to what extent, a commonality of such interests actually exists; and how the remaining differences can be managed, if at all, so that the former Soviet republics do not become a functional equivalent of Central Europe in the immediate aftermath of the Second World War.

Primus inter Pares

Nations usually put their soldiers at risk when their perceived national interests are believed to be at stake. Moscow despatched one civilian policeman to Somalia and one to Haiti, but in the last two years it has deployed some 16,000 peacekeepers in the various parts of the former USSR (compared with about 1,200 in ex-Yugoslavia). When Moscow decided that the unity of the Federation was at stake in Chechnya, the Russian leaders felt no price was too high to defend it. In the future, Russian military activities aimed at 'stabilizing' the periphery of the Russian Federation are likely to grow, despite the inevitable human losses and financial burden.

Since the break-up of the USSR, Russians have routinely been referring to the other former constituent republics as 'near abroad'. Ostensibly an attempt to come to grips with the new and sudden reality, this term almost immediately became suspect in the West for its perceived neo-imperialist connotations. In fact, more than anything else, Moscow was initially oblivious of its near neighbours. Only slowly did it come to realize that the 25 million ethnic Russians (roughly one-sixth of the RF's own population) who, virtually overnight, became minorities in the newly-formed states, would have considerable influence on any foreign policy pursued by Moscow. No government in Moscow can afford to appear insensitive to the situation of the Russian diaspora.[4] Actually, this figure is symbolic of many things, including the incompleteness of the post-Soviet division, the difficulties of the nation- and state-building processes, the need for Russia's new self-identification, etc. Open borders between the Russian Federation and the newly independent states facilitate the spill-over of conflicts into Russia proper (for example from Transcaucasia). In the three years since the end of the USSR, Russia has had to accept over two million forced migrants and refugees from the NIS.[5] Actual (as in the case of Estonia and Latvia) or potential border disputes between Russia and some of the NIS complicate the picture still further.

'Aggressive nationalism' in the former Soviet Union, Russian leaders are telling their Western counterparts, is a security challenge to Russia and the West alike. While this is generally true, the actual risks and dangers involved for either side are different. North America and Western Europe have problems no less serious, and much closer to home, than Abkhazia or Tajikistan. More importantly, Russia itself, and the direction its transition takes, are a major problem for the West. In other words, 'aggressive nationalism' in faraway corners of the ex-USSR may be bad; Russian neo-imperialism is far worse. It is unfair to suggest that mainstream Western political opinion ignores Russian interests in the former republics altogether. Rather, it clearly prefers to see Russia's role limited in such a way as to prevent any re-establishment of an 'empire'. So Russia can certainly aspire to be 'primus inter pares', but any attempt by Moscow to 'carve out a sphere of influence' to the exclusion of others would have to be resisted. This is an interesting new development as, prior to the collapse of the USSR – which came as a surprise to nearly everybody in the West – Western countries had not had any recognizable interests in the various Soviet republics which, for several decades, had been considered totally out of bounds for outsiders. The conflicts which accompanied the end of the Soviet Union, and the weakening of Moscow's control and influence in the former republics, inevitably led to the progressive involvement of both Russia and outside powers and institutions in the affairs of the NIS – all in the name of combatting instability.

A comprehensive concept of stability-building (of which peacekeeping *per se* is but one of several instruments) includes the prevention, management and settlement of conflicts. In the passages that follow, the present chapter seeks to examine the West's and Russia's interests underlying their attempts to prevent, manage or settle the various conflicts in the post-Soviet space.

Averting Nuclear Proliferation

From the Western – and especially American – perspective, most disturbing was the type of conflict which would let loose the former Soviet nuclear arsenal. Until the end of 1991, this was a compelling reason for wishing the Soviet Union to remain united. One danger was that Soviet strategic and tactical nuclear weapons, deployed on the territory of the former republics, would be taken over by them, wrecking the non-proliferation regime; another, even more frightening, was that these successor states would themselves disintegrate, creating havoc. For Russia, the need to prevent nuclear proliferation in the ex-USSR and to keep nuclear weapons and materials under control was no less urgent. The Russian Federation, which proclaimed itself the sole successor of the Soviet nuclear power, took steps to withdraw all nuclear weapons from the areas of actual or potential conflict; it never relinquished the unity of command and control over strategic nuclear forces.

Thus, from the beginning, Western and Russian positions were fundamentally identical: proliferation of nuclear weapons in the FSU had to be averted; the entire Soviet nuclear arsenal was to be taken over by Russia. Due to the position of the three NIS which had strategic arms deployed on their territory (especially Ukraine), and which attempted to use these as bargaining chips in their dealings with both Russia and the West, this was not an easy task. The Lisbon protocol to the START I Treaty, of 23 April 1992, and the Budapest agreements of 5 December 1994 solved the issue legally, but more time and effort will be required to eliminate fully the potential danger brought about by the first-ever disintegration of a nuclear superpower.

While trilateral (RF–US–NIS) co-operation has been successful so far in securing the adherence of Belarus, Kazakstan and Ukraine to the Nuclear Non-Proliferation Treaty (NPT) as non-nuclear states, the Russians may regret that, as a result, the United States has emerged as an established third partner in nearly all strategic discussions between Moscow and Kyiv and (albeit to a much lesser extent) between Moscow and Almaty. Only Minsk has finally gravitated towards Moscow. Russia is ambivalent, as US and British security assurances are both helpful – in making the NIS more amenable to getting rid of nuclear weapons from their territory – and irritating, as they imply some sort of counterweight to Russian power.

As for the widespread concern in the West that, in Russia and other CIS states, internal controls of nuclear materials are lax, this has led both to co-operation between Russia and the West and to some friction between them. While the West does not fully trust Russia's current ability to keep its fissionable materials under control, Moscow fears attempts to put the whole of the Russian nuclear complex – the heart of its national security arsenal – under international, mainly US, supervision. The fact that the G7 nations held a joint summit with Russia on nuclear safety, in April 1996 in Moscow, shows, however, that the stimuli for co-operation in that field may be stronger than those favouring confrontation.

Thus, as a result of the commonality in Russian and Western approaches to the nuclear issue, the non-proliferation principle was upheld just in time for the April 1995 NPT Review Conference, and the transfer of the remaining Soviet nuclear arsenal to the Russian Federation is well under way. Strengthening nuclear safety has become part of the agenda for a continued G7-Russia top-level dialogue. Still, despite the broad areas of agreement, constant attention needs to be paid to these issues in the future to ensure that the process is not derailed.

The Western wariness of a Russo-Ukrainian collision, which was the subject of much discussion in 1992, stemmed, in the first place, from the clear realization that if conflict prevention were to fail in this instance, the 'nuclear dimension' of any resulting crisis virtually guaranteed that no amount of subsequent crisis management would avert the danger to Europe and North America. US mediation attempts between the FSU's two largest successor states, however, also had another aspect, which had more to do with general geopolitical considerations.

Preserving the Geopolitical *Status Quo*

After the disintegration of the Soviet Union had become a fact, the West saw its interest in consolidating the new pluralist geopolitical set-up in the 'post-Soviet space'. This is a new element, for, even at the peak of the cold war, the actual dismantling of the USSR was never regarded as a political objective. Now, the preservation of the new *status quo* – that is, the prevention of the (especially forcible) re-incorporation of the former Soviet republics (or parts of them) into a greater Russia – is an important foreign policy goal. In this context, Ukraine's continued independence is seen as absolutely essential. At the other extreme, there is perhaps the more frightening prospect of Russia, Ukraine or Kazakstan breaking up under pressure from economy-driven regional separatism.

In Russia, the earlier tendency to abandon the former republics to their fate has been succeeded by a new-found interest in mainly bilateral or selective integration with its 'near neighbours', partly with a view to pacifying them. Since 1993, Moscow has been trying hard to win international recognition for the CIS. Upgrading the still dormant Collective Security Treaty (CST), signed in Tashkent in May 1992, is traditionally seen as the best way to prevent conflicts between these states (including territorial and border disputes). The treaty pledged its signatories (that is, Russia, Kazakstan, Kyrgyzstan, Uzbekistan, Tajikistan and Armenia, later joined by Belarus) to co-operate closely in the field of security, but it falls far short of a full-blooded defence alliance. No integrated forces or command structures have been established under the CST, except for the largely symbolic Collective Peacekeeping Force in Tajikistan, which brought together a Russian division, an Uzbek battalion and a Kyrgyz company. Outside Central Asia, the treaty's role is minimal. Armenia tried, unsuccessfully, to use the Treaty in the conflict over Karabakh; in Belarus, there is great reluctance to commit troops to operations beyond the country's borders. Most importantly, however, it is Russia that has found it more effective, and far less costly, to deal with the newly independent states individually.

With NATO's process of eastward enlargement obscuring and poisoning Russo-NATO relations, an upgraded CST is often cited among the 'countermeasures' Moscow might take in response to the admission of Poland and other Central European countries to the Western Alliance. For the West, however, a new (and largely symbolic) edition of a Moscow-led alliance, to succeed the Warsaw Treaty, would be seen as confirmation of the strength of the Russian imperial instinct.

For Russia, success in nation-building in the NIS should be of undoubted value. The dismantling of the USSR was a product of the Russian elite's desire to rid itself of what has been described as the burden of so many ailing economies. Near-failures in any new state, even ones as small as Tajikistan or Georgia, had severe and almost immediate consequences for Russia. Through huge subsidies (to the tune of $17 billion in 1993 alone, according to the then Finance Minister, Boris Fedorov), Russia has been contributing heavily to the success of these states, including Ukraine, in the form of energy supplies. Nothing would be more detrimental to Russian security than a disintegrating Ukraine.

Incorporating any CIS state – or even a breakaway province, like Abkhazia or Transdniestria, – into the Russian Federation is prohibitively costly. For the time being, Belarus, which in May 1997 signed a 'union charter' with Russia, may be the only exception. All this new state-building, however, can only be considered positive by Moscow if the NIS remain friendly and respect Russian interests. Throughout the CIS, Moscow is committed to preserving its 'traditional and direct influence'.

On the one hand, the West cannot overlook the stabilizing potential of the CIS, especially in regions on its far periphery such as the Caucasus and Central Asia. On the other, it is worried by Russia's perceived determination to use the Commonwealth as a cover for regaining control of the NIS and turning the Collective Security Treaty into a Warsaw Pact Mark II. To the extent that peacemaking is regarded as a tool for reaching that goal, it remains an issue between Russia and the West.

The Baltic States and Kaliningrad

Western interests in the NIS are of unequal importance and level. As one moves eastwards, away from Europe, the West's interests in the NIS generally decrease. The admission of Estonia, Latvia and Lithuania to the Council of Europe has put a stamp of approval on these countries' yearning to be recognized as part of the widening West. A conflict involving Russia and any of the Baltic States would most probably lead to a real and severe confrontation between Moscow and the West, in which the former is almost certain to be the loser. To avert this, and to ensure, finally, the independence of the three countries, no effort was spared to bring about the speedy withdrawal of Russian forces from Lithuania, Latvia and Estonia (completed in 1993 in the first state and 1994 in the other two). Implied security assurances (albeit in the rather mild form of associated membership of the Western European Union and participation in the Partnership for Peace programme, both since 1994) should quell any irredentist ambitions in Russia. Concurrently, the minority and human rights situation in the Baltic States themselves was looked into, both to keep the local Russians quiet and to allow Moscow no credible pretext for interfering in the domestic affairs of these states.

Having recognized the independence of Estonia, Latvia and Lithuania without any reservations or conditions (such as the status of the sizeable Russian minorities there), Russia eventually dropped its ineffectual attempts at linking their status to the withdrawal of forces. Actually, the presence of Russian forces, seen as an irritant by the countries concerned, was more of a liability for Moscow than a trump card. Within 30 months of the dissolution of the USSR (and not six or seven years, as initially proposed), the Russian forces evacuated the Baltic States. To sweeten the pill, the United States allocated some $100 million for a housing programme for the returning officers. Another important Russian condition was also met: the early warning radar station at Skrunda in Latvia was leased to Russia for five years. Moscow, for its part, did nothing to encourage ethnic Russian separatism: despite many similarities, no 'Trans-Narvia' appeared in north-eastern Estonia. In a display of enlightened internationalism, Moscow decided to take the case of the Russian minorities in the area to the UN, CSCE/OSCE and Council of Europe. Also, the Scandinavians' moderating influence on their neighbours across the sea has been responsible for the success (so far) of conflict prevention.

Kaliningrad, Russia's first-ever enclave, deserves no less attention, but of a different kind. The problem appears to be, not that the former North-East Prussia is becoming a functional analogue to cold war West Berlin, but rather that Russia's inability to restructure the area's economy quickly enough might lead to the internal socio-political destabilization of Kaliningrad, and consequently to a rise in regional separatism, which would have dangerous international repercussions.

Conflict prevention in the Baltic region owes its initial success to the restraint and moderation shown by the potential antagonists. Clearly, the stakes are too high for all sides. The seeds of potential conflicts, however, have not been wholly destroyed. Pro-active policies are therefore required to arrest their growth.

Ukraine

While protection of the Balts' sovereignty is politically and emotionally important, it is Ukraine's independence which is seen as the essential guarantee of the non-restoration of the Russian empire in Europe. For that purpose, Kyiv has been given assurances that Ukraine's sovereignty and territorial integrity (Crimea/ Sevastopol implied) will be respected. While these are not security guarantees, they have a certain deterrence value. Building on its earlier success in the nuclear area, Washington is seeking the role of mediator in the issues of the status of the Crimea and the future of the Black Sea Fleet, to the growing irritation of Moscow.

For Russia, Ukraine is second in importance to no other country. A conflict between the largest successor states of the USSR, or even a major internal conflict in Ukraine, would spell disaster for Russia. Since most of Ukraine's present woes have economic roots, Russia has no choice but to continue virtually to subsidize its neighbour, while looking for ways of strengthening economic interaction. Western economic assistance to Ukraine is helpful; on the other hand, building up 'the bulwark on the Dnieper' as the first line of Europe's defences against Russia is seriously destabilizing.

Belarus

The West's view of Belarus, in contrast to that country's southern neighbour, is markedly more relaxed. For most Western governments, it appears, Belarus is little more than a Russian satellite which will eventually find its way back to Moscow. The Russo-Belarussian relationship, codified in the 1996 treaty, is often cited as exemplary in the CIS. Rather, it should be cited as unique. Even an eventual political union between Minsk and Moscow – provided it is voluntary – is viewed as no cause for concern. Strategically, Belarus, and not Ukraine, is the most important country to Moscow, for it lies on the main route between Russia and the rest of Europe.

Moldova

Moldova, which has been experiencing a Moscow-brokered truce since mid 1992, is seen as a test case of wider Russian intentions, especially *vis-à-vis* the Balkans. The withdrawal of the Russian force (until 1995, called the 14th army) from Transdniestria is considered – notably by the United States – to be a necessary element of conflict settlement. Otherwise, Moldova belongs to crisis management. Seen from Russia, an attempt to unite Moldova with Romania (which for the time being seems unlikely, but was widely discussed in 1992–93) would provoke a major crisis, if Transdniestria is not allowed to opt out of such a union. Although Moscow agreed in 1994 to withdraw its forces within a three-year period of the document's ratification, in the meantime it continues to view the Russian military force as a stabilizing factor.

The Caucasus

The Caucasus generally calls for crisis management, rather than prevention. While Moscow has been trying, in the wake of Chechnya, to prevent a general rebellion in the whole of the Northern Caucasus, Transcaucasia has become a buffer zone between Russia and Turkey/Iran. Other cases of prevention include

Ajaria (capital: Batumi), which remains the only part of Georgia that was spared violent clashes. The relationship between the Batumi authorities and the local Russian garrison is said to be close and stable. Two of the five Russian military bases to be given formal status in Georgia – one in Batumi and the other at Akhalkalaki, in the Armenian-populated district – may indeed fulfill this role of prevention. Historical Lezgistan, which straddles the Russo-Azeri border, is another example. While it is seen in the more nationalist quarters in Moscow as an instrument for putting pressure on Baku, the Russian government has been acting with considerable restraint, fearful of destabilizing Dagestan, a republic within Russia bordering on both Azerbaijan and Chechnya.

Russia sees her position in the Caucasus as fundamentally threatened and will entrench rather than withdraw. Moscow's attitude to the issue of flank limitations under the Conventional Forces in Europe (CFE) Treaty is a case in point. It is interesting to note here the fundamental difference between Washington and most West European capitals, on the one hand, and Ankara on the other, regarding the response to the Russian demand for revising flank limitations upwards. The West, whose security interests are barely affected by the southern flank limitations, has shown understanding and was prepared to lean on the Turks, its allies, in order to accommodate the Russians. Internal developments in Turkey, especially since the 1995 parliamentary elections, have heightened apprehensions in the West that Turkey, rather than joining Europe, might instead turn to Islamic fundamentalism, and leave NATO. Should this happen, the whole relationship between the United States, Russia and Turkey may change beyond recognition.

Central Asia

Due to its demographic situation, Kazakstan faces a potentially very serious challenge. A conflict between Russia and Kazakstan over the northern areas, where the Russians outnumber the Kazaks by 3:1, would bear the hallmark of a Christian–Muslim confrontation. Territorial and citizenship issues are thus all-important. So far, Moscow and Almaty have reaffirmed their respect for the existing border and reached a compromise on the problem of citizenship, avoiding dual allegiance but setting up a quick and simple procedure for exchanging Kazakstani for Russian citizenship, and vice versa. While Kazakstan's President Nursultan Nazarbaev remained a strong supporter of a Eurasian Union, which he proposed as far back as 1994, as a loosely confederal and decentralized replacement for the CIS, the two countries have moved closer to a strategic alliance. In March 1996 Kazakstan signed a treaty on closer co-operation and integration with Russia, Belarus and Kyrgyzstan.

To the south of Kazakstan, the rest of Central Asia – important strategically as a region where Russia, China and the Moslem world meet, but above all rich in energy resources like gas and oil – remains potentially the most serious conflict area within the FSU, a real powder keg. Border disputes and minority problems, clan warfare and social unrest, religious and democratic challenges to the prevailing authoritarianism, disagreements over land and water rights form a highly explosive mixture. Not all of the states which currently exist in the region may survive in the medium or long term. The fate of Afghanistan should be a serious warning to them.

Russia is obviously concerned about the fate and welfare of the six million ethnic Russians living south of the Urals and Siberia. Moscow, however, lacks the resources to integrate them into Russian society, should a large number of these Russians decide to come to the land of their forefathers in any one year. Thus, in order to prevent waves of refugees which could overwhelm her social security system, Russia has – for the sake of stability – been relying on the post/neo-communist regimes in place in the region. The West has made a similar choice, if for different reasons.

Conflict Management

By mid-1992 it became clear that no group of nations, under any mandate, which would be considered genuinely impartial, would be willing to get involved in a serious way in crisis management in the FSU. By contrast, Russia – which was hardly impartial – was both willing and able. In early 1993, Russia officially and repeatedly asked to be recognized as peacekeeper-in-chief in the CIS area. Specifically, Moscow sought a UN/CSCE mandate for its missions, and the accompanying financial contribution.

It is usually pointed out that the Russian interest in managing conflicts in the FSU stems from the neighbouring states' inability to contain violence within their borders. Frequently mentioned are the lack of barriers between the former Soviet republics, which facilitates the spill-over of armed struggle; concern for the ethnic Russian population in the areas of conflict and the desire to avoid an enormous influx of refugees, and so on. It is true that borders between the conflict-torn CIS states are more transparent than is good for national security. Turning the former administrative borders into fortified state frontiers, complete with all the required infrastructure, is considered prohibitively costly: official Russian estimates give the figure of approx. $500,000 per 1 km. Also, the demarcation of borders could lead to new conflicts where an ethnic community thus becomes physically divided (for example, the Lezgins between Russia and Azerbaijan and the Russians in southern Siberia and northern Kazakstan).[6] Still, Russia has seen no alternative to upgrading its borders with the Baltic and Caucasian states. This is hardly a credible option for Central Asia, however. Russia's 6,000 km-long border with Kazakstan is the longest in Eurasia. Moscow has been trying to find a way to seal the outer, rather than inner borders of the CIS. While this 'marks out' Russia's geostrategic space, it is difficult to overlook the stabilizing role which the Russian border troops perform in Armenia, Georgia, Turkmenistan, Tajikistan and Kyrgyzstan.

As to the internal – that is intra-CIS – borders, preventing their forcible change is a concern that Russia and the West generally share. While unrecognized, the entities which have unilaterally proclaimed their independence – Abkhazia, Nagorno-Karabakh, South Ossetia and Transdniestria – attempt to make common cause with Crimea, Tatarstan and Bashkortostan, which remain sensitive areas. Any successful secession in any NIS has serious implications for Russia, which has had to fight a war to keep Chechnya within the Federation. In the last instance, the West has agreed with the principle of territorial integrity, although it has denounced the methods used by Moscow to enforce it. Generally, since the break-up of the Soviet Union, the West is not interested in further disintegration. Questioning the inviolability of borders in the OSCE area would further undercut stability and lead, ultimately, to the Balkanization of Europe.

Stopping the spread of Islamic extremism, like in Tajikistan, appears to be another interest shared between Russia and the West. On the other hand, while the West (and especially the United States) promotes a more important role for Turkey in both Central Asia and the Caucasus as a counterweight to Iran, Russia has been doing exactly the opposite. In order to balance off Ankara, Moscow has reached an understanding with Iran, which has also become a major customer of the Russian arms industry and nuclear energy complex. While some Russians talk of turning Iran into an ally against the West, Russia's core interests require it to restrain Tehran, making sure that it does not involve itself too heavily in the Caucasus and Central Asia, and that it provokes no new regional crisis in the Gulf.

Fighting terrorism and countering illicit arms and drugs trafficking is commonly described as one of the key missions of Russian peacemakers. In principle, this coincides with Western interests. In reality, until mid-1995 conflict-related terrorism in the FSU remained localized. Since the massive taking of hostages by the Chechen terrorists, however, it has become an important factor. The spill-over of Chechen terrorist activity into Turkey has given the issue an international dimension. In principle at least, since the 1996 Anti-Terrorist Summit at Sharm-el-Sheikh, Russia and the West have been making louder noises about co-ordinating their efforts in the struggle against terrorism.

As for arms, most of them are being transferred within the FSU, with Russia being responsible for lax controls and large-scale dispersal of the Soviet weapons arsenal, especially in the Caucasus. Turmoil at the collapse of the USSR led to a number of secret deals, and outright takeovers of weapons depots, most of which were tolerated (and some are likely to have been sanctioned) by Russian officials. Supplying weapons and ammunition to the warring sides (as in Abkhazia and Karabakh, or Chechnya, for that matter) is another problem in Russia's post-Soviet conduct. Russia, however, can hardly be saddled with the blame for all of this. Ukraine and the Baltic States are often mentioned as the countries responsible for illegal arms trafficking. Drug trafficking is assisted by the Tajik conflict, but the frontier forces in Tajikistan and Russian/CIS peacemakers are scarcely capable of stopping the flow of drugs from Afghanistan to Moscow and St. Petersburg via the uncontrolled Badakhshan province. There have even been allegations that transport aircraft belonging to the Collective Peacekeeping Force (CPKF) and Russian border troops are routinely used for shipping opium to Central Russia.[7]

The need for peacemaking in the CIS has led the Russians to try to use the Tashkent Treaty as a basis for joint operations. Initially unsuccessful, in the autumn of 1993 they were able to mount the first – and still only – CIS peacemaking operation in Tajikistan. A

UN mandate for this force was claimed, but not received. The West has seen no point in rewarding Moscow for the muscular defence of Russia's own interests. On the other hand, it was claimed that 'it [was] not in Russia's interests to allow the presence of military contingents from third countries on the territory of post-Soviet states', even as peacekeepers.[8] Although this stand was later softened, most notably with respect to Nagorno-Karabakh, this was only a change in degree, not in kind.

Russian peacemaking is essentially concerned with managing new regional balances, especially in Transcaucasia and Central Asia. In the words of former Foreign Minister Andrei Kozyrev, 'any plans to create spheres of influence for anybody by means of "easing Russia out" of the post-Soviet space are both hopeless and dangerous'.[9] No power vacuum is to be tolerated, Russian officials warn, for such a vacuum 'would inevitably complicate Russia's military-strategic position and would inevitably be filled by the forces unfriendly to Russia'.[10] Meanwhile, the distinction between peacemakers and regular Russian forces is often blurred. This may be disturbing for Western observers, but in the eyes of the Russian military, actions such as sending forces to Nagorno-Karabakh in 1988, putting down interethnic clashes in Central Asia in 1989–90 and the Chechen operation of 1994–95 can all be described as 'peacemaking'.[11] This honestly-held view underlines the fundamental difference which exists between Russia and the West regarding methods of policymaking.

Peacemaking, emphasizing the 'special role' of the Russian army as the only force capable of bringing a measure of order to the conflict areas, has helped to secure a legal basis for the continued presence of Russian armed forces on the territory of the NIS. In 1992, South Ossetia became the first territory in the FSU to see a return of the Russian forces, this time as peacekeepers. In 1993, the RF Defence Ministry made public its intention to establish 27 or 28 military bases in the new states. In September of the same year, the 201st motor rifle division in Tajikistan became the bulk of the CIS Collective Peacekeeping Force. By virtue of a February 1994 protocol with Georgia, later turned into a treaty, Russia received what it had been seeking since the break-up of the USSR, that is, basing rights in Vaziani, Akhalkalaki and Batumi.[12] Russian forces in Abkhazia will continue to be based in Sukhumi and Gudauta. The treaty's ratification by the Georgian parliament, however, has been made conditional on Russia's applying pressure on the Abkhazian leadership to become part of a federal Georgian state. In Moldova, too, Moscow's proposal to Chişinău to turn the 14th army into a permanent Russian base, and later a peacekeeping force, were turned down. Fearing that, once they arrive as sole peacekeepers, Russian forces will not leave, Azerbaijan has been insisting that the Russians should be part of an international force. The West has been generally sympathetic to those who, like Moldova and Azerbaijan, want no Russian forces on their territory.

Ever since 1992, Western governments have been concerned that Russian forces in the various conflict zones should not be totally controlled by Moscow. The initial phase of the Chechen war added to this concern. The military, however, are not wholly to blame: while the Russian authorities should be more concerned about the cases of independent action and insubordination, fault lines in Moscow itself make the central government dangerously impotent. More importantly, the military's unconstrained involvement in conflicts strengthens the very tendencies and elements in Russia which the West finds most dangerous to its interests. An authoritarian Russian state, especially if it finally manages to bestride a thriving economy, may be the least welcome scenario to many in the West.

Little has been achieved towards a final settlement of disputes. In the spring of 1995, Gagauzia, a Turkic-populated area in southern Moldova, arrived at a constitutional settlement within the Moldovan state. Other crises have proven more difficult to handle. As the peace process in Nagorno-Karabakh has demonstrated, a settlement in itself appears to be less important than the roles of would-be peacekeepers, above all Russia, the United States and Turkey. Competition for control of the oil and gas resources of the Caspian Sea basin has become one of the more prominent factors in the new version of the 'Great Game'.

Conclusion

Thus a parallel analysis of Russian peacekeeping in the NIS and the interests driving Russian and Western policies *vis-à-vis* the conflicts there reveals Russia's deep-seated conviction that her national security depends on the success or failure of her efforts to re-establish strategic and, to some extent, also political control over the zones of conflict, in particular in the Caucasus and Central Asia. The trends in Russia's foreign policy clearly point towards gradual concentration on relations with the CIS states. Symbolically, Yevgeni Primakov, who replaced Andrei Kozyrev as Foreign Minister in January 1996, made a point of visiting the newly independent states before going to the 'far abroad' countries.

The West, more concerned about the conflict potential in the new Eastern Europe, is generally satisfied with Russia's apparently long-term engagement to the south of its borders. Criticism of Moscow's methods does not detract from a willingness to let Russia do what it wants in the replay of the games of the nineteenth century – this time mostly against the non-Western players in the region. While Russia can perhaps afford to ignore this criticism, it can expect no help or assistance from the West. The interests of both sides are often parallel, but there is no common cause. Concurrent interests, rather than shared ideas, are now the sole basis for interaction. Thus an internationalization of peacekeeping is a much more preferable option – though also more difficult one. Despite the failure of initial expectations, it can and should be pursued. The UN Security Council's endorsement of the CIS operation in Abkhazia (1994), and the presence of UN observers in Tajikistan, set certain standards and help to build trust. In a telling example, while the Russian government allowed OSCE missions into Chechnya in 1995, it denied access to a team from the Council of Europe, which had suspended Russian accession to that organization. OSCE peacekeeping, however, should not be confined in principle to the FSU alone. Finally, Russo-NATO collaboration in Bosnia-Herzegovina offers a chance to build the fundamentals of a partnership around a practical joint mission.

On the other hand, a new division of Europe along the western border of the CIS states, if it becomes a reality, could well lead to the establishment of two 'peacekeeping regimes': NATO-centred to the west of this border, and Russian/CIS-led to the east. Although to some this may appear stabilizing, because of the isolationist nature of such an arrangement it will serve the interests of the conservative or isolationist sections of the ruling elites, rather than the core security interests of either Russia or the West.

In a situation where national security interests are again becoming more prominent than bloc or ideological interests, peacekeeping should not be left to individual powers or closely-knit alliances. Russia as a major national player in Eurasia is likely to revert to its traditional role, and as such will occasionally have conflicts with other powers. The United States and the European

Union countries will, despite all their common values and principles, increasingly pursue their own agendas. Unlike in the period of the cold war, however, there is no zero-sum game in this new environment; these conflicts of interests are manageable.

NOTES

1. Kozyrev, Andrei, 'S mechom mirotvortsa', *Moskovskie novosti*, No.36, pp.4–11 Sept. 1994.
2. 'On the Effectiveness of State Power in Russia. Annual Message of the President of Russia', *Rossiyskaya gazeta*, 17 Feb. 1995, p.5.
3. See, for example, 'Rossiya – SNG: nuzhdaetsya li v korrektirovke pozitsiya Zapada?, *Krasnaya zvezda*, 28 Sept. 1994, p.3.
4. See, for example, President Yeltsin's UN address in *Krasnaya zvezda*, 28 Sept. 1994, p.3.
5. Regent, Tatyana (Head of the Federal Migration Service), in an interview with *Krasnaya zvezda*, 7 Feb. 1995, p.2.
6. FIS report in *Krasnaya zvezda*, 28 Sept. 1994, p.3.
7. Maj.General Gennadi Blinov, deputy Interior Minister of Tajikistan, in an interview with *Segodnya*, 2 Sept. 1994, p.9.
8. Vyacheslav Yelagin, 'Rossiiskoe voiennoye prisutstvie: pravovoi status', *Segodnya*, 2 March 1994, p.3.
9. Kozyrev, op. cit.
10. Yelagin, op. cit.
11. Interview with Col. General Yevgeni Podkolzin, commander of Airborne Forces, in *Sovetskaya Rossiya*, 23 Feb. 1995.
12. This protocol has since been superseded by a formal treaty signed in September 1995. Georgia's ratification of this document, however, depends on Russia's exercising pressure on Abhazia to drop its self-proclaimed independence and accept federation with Georgia.

10

Conclusions: The Failure of Regionalism in Eurasia and the Western Ascendancy over Russia's Near Abroad

BRUNO COPPIETERS

The 1960s witnessed a world-wide spate of regionalist initiatives. Attempts to create common markets and free-trade associations were proliferating in the Middle East, Africa, the Pacific, Western Europe and the Americas. Most of these projects failed. Except in Western Europe and South-East Asia,[1] regionalist policies did not lead to major progress.[2] Regionalism remained on the international agenda during the entire later period of the cold war, but with a much more limited scope. Regionalist rhetoric reappeared in the late 1980s in many parts of the world and this time, unlike in the previous period, it did not fail to be translated into political reality. Cohesive and effectively institutionalized regionalist experiences are no longer confined to Western Europe.[3] In his analysis of the successful new formation of interstate groupings on the basis of regions, Andrew Wyatt-Walter has taken several factors into account: the end of the cold war which had subordinated all regional arrangements; the need to deal with foreign security concerns at a regional rather than a global level; outward-orientated policies in the developing world; the rise of new trading blocs in the developed world; the decline of broad coalitions of third world countries, which were replaced by more viable regional coalitions; Western support for regional arrangements in the third world.[4]

More specific historical factors have to be taken into account when analysing Soviet regionalist policies in the period 1986–91.

Bruno Coppieters would like to thank Emil Adelkhanov, Ghia Nodia, Dmitri Trenin and Alexei Zverev for their comments on this chapter.

Regionalism was part of a broad programme of restructuring Soviet domestic and foreign affairs. Gorbachev made pathetic calls at the four corners of the Soviet Union to create regional homes together with neighbouring states.[5] He launched an appeal in Vladivostok in July 1986 for a common Asian and Pacific home. On a visit to New Delhi in the same year, he spoke about the common Indian Ocean home that India shared with the Soviet Union. In his book 'Perestroika: New Thinking for Our Country and the World',[6] which was first published in 1987, he devoted a whole chapter to the European common home. He called for a common Arctic home with Canadians and Scandinavians during a visit to Murmansk in October 1987.

This late Soviet-era regionalism was motivated by different objectives in different areas. The 'common European home' was aimed at diluting US preponderance on the continent, while the Asia-Pacific initiatives were designed to give the USSR a toehold in the world's largest trade area. Ideological motives remained subordinated to the power interests of the Soviet Union. In this respect, Gorbachev's 'new thinking' remained quite traditional. The Gorbachevian leadership, however, embedded these foreign and security policy interests in a radically new vision of socialism and civilization. Here, on the contrary, Gorbachev's 'new thinking' represented a break with traditional Soviet ideology. The vision of a Soviet Union with multiple regional identities, peacefully sharing many homes with all its neighbours, was very far removed from the isolationist policies the Soviet leadership had pursued since its accession to power. Lenin set up a foreign-trade monopoly and, at the end of the 1920s, Stalin enforced these economic barriers through the establishment of the planned economy.[7] After the failure of all revolutionary movements in Western and Central Europe, socialism was declared to have been achieved in one country. The Soviet leadership had also increasingly perceived the outside world as a political threat to its internal stability.[8] Cultural influences on the Soviet Muslim world from neighbouring Iran and Turkey were barred by the introduction of the Cyrillic alphabet. A frontier of previously unknown salience was designed to protect the political status quo and to prevent disturbances to the planned economy. The Soviet public remained uninformed about any left-wing or right-wing alternative to the Communist Party's policies.

The opening up of the country to the wider world had far-reaching consequences for political debates on domestic policies.

Regionalism as a policy for reintegrating Soviet society into the world community was accompanied by a solid dose of *glasnost*, but this did not facilitate the internal reform of the Soviet political structure. On the contrary, it accelerated the dismantling of the federal structures. The Communist Party had constituted a cement that had held the bricks of the Soviet construction together for more than seventy years – now the cement crumbled away through democratization and the opening of the country's external boundaries, leading to the collapse of the whole building.

The failure of the Communist Party leadership to find a solution to the political crisis was largely due to the lack of consensus between the different national elites, their opposition to the centre and the division within Moscow's political establishment itself between those taking a 'Soviet' and a 'Russian' view of the course of reforms.[9] The transition to a free-market economy, the further development of economic ties with neighbouring countries and integration into the main Western economic institutions were perceived in the Union's republics as being more easily achievable through the attainment of sovereignty and independence. Nationalist opposition movements in all the Union's republics propagated the thesis that national sovereignty would lead to the re-establishment of cultural, economic and political ties with the outside world. For the nationalist movements in the three Baltic states, Ukraine, Moldova, Georgia and Armenia, the outside world meant primarily the West. For Azerbaijan and Central Asia, it also included countries such as Turkey or Iran.[10] The nationalist Rukh party considered that Ukraine's economic potential was no less than that of Italy, France, Germany or Britain, and would flourish once it was freed from all ties to Moscow. The quasi-colonial status of Ukraine had allegedly prevented the country from enjoying the same standard of living as Western countries.[11] As early as 1990, Azerbaijan started negotiations with Western oil companies on developing its oil resources.[12]

The Soviet Union failed to be perceived by the 25 million ethnic Russians outside the Russian Soviet Federated Socialist Republic as an effective guarantee of their civic rights. Even the Russian or Russianized minorities in the Baltics and Ukraine were ready to support the demands for independence put forward by these republics. The Ukraine is particularly important in this respect. The Soviet Union could perhaps have survived the secession of several smaller republics in the Baltics, the Caucasus or Central Asia, but not the independence of Ukraine. Well over half the large Russian and Russianized minority of the Ukraine voted in favour of national independence in the referendum of 1 December 1991 which confirmed the previous declaration of independence. According to some political observers, Russian and Russianized voters saw the alternatives in political rather than in ethnic terms. Their vote for independence was motivated by their opposition to the old bureaucratic centre,[13] by their greater dependence on local authorities than on those in the Kremlin and by their refusal to pay for the burdens of imperial policies. This example illustrates the failure of Soviet policies to integrate even the Slavic republics of Eurasia. The deep-seated objections of the political establishment, both in Russia and in the other Union republics, to any federal rearrangement or opening up to the wider world within a Soviet structure became fully apparent after the defeat of the conservative coup in August 1991.

The Failure of the Commonwealth of Independent States

The chances of the Commonwealth of Independent States of providing a foundation for the successful integration of Eurasia, and of linking the process of nation-building in Russia with that in the other former Union republics, on the basis of equality and sovereignty, have never been rated very highly. The CIS has survived, for lack of alternatives. During the first five years since its creation, some 750 documents were adopted, but only roughly a third of these are claimed to have been implemented. The political structures of the CIS have not provided for the real integration of its members. Not all member states have attended its meetings, and not all participants in the meetings have signed the final documents.[14] The only far-reaching attempt to integrate two former Soviet republics – the creation of a Union between Belarus and Russia in May 1997 – took place outside the framework of the CIS.

The CIS was formed in a period when Russia's priorities did not include a strongly integrated Eurasian commonwealth. Russia's Western orientation led at first to the complete neglect of Central Asia and the Caucasus by its Foreign Ministry. Russian Foreign Minister Andrei Kozyrev first visited Central Asia in April 1992, by which time US Secretary of State James Baker had already been there three times on official visits. Russian embassies in Central

Asia were established after those of Turkey, Iran, China and the US,[15] and it was only in late 1992 and early 1993 that Russian diplomats established their presence in the Transcaucasus. The Russian military, however, played a prominent role both in the Caucasus and in Central Asia – they were actively involved in the civil wars and ethnic conflicts in Georgia and Tajikistan.

In his analysis of the general conditions conducive to regional arrangements, Andrew Hurrell observes that a declining hegemony may press the hegemon 'towards the creation of common institutions to pursue its interests, to share burdens, to solve common problems, and to generate international support and legitimacy for its policies'.[16] This observation may be confirmed by the shift in Russia's policies in 1993. In the heated debates on Russia's national identity in 1992, most of the participants agreed to dismiss as unrealistic the hope of being quickly and fully integrated into Western structures. In 1993 a more assertive attitude was adopted towards what was now called 'Russia's Near Abroad'. Russia's government, confronted with the country's declining power, considered a leading position among the former Union republics more necessary than ever. According to President Yeltsin's September 1995 decree 'On The Establishment of the Strategic Course of the Russian Federation with Member States of the Commonwealth of Independent States', Russia's leading role in the CIS was regarded as an indispensable condition for its recognition as a global power by the world community.[17]

Russia failed to be further recognized as a global power. It was unable to halt NATO's eastward expansion or to mobilize opposition to this project among the CIS members. With the sole exception of Belarus, no member of the CIS accepted Russia's 'counter-block' rhetoric in 1995. The creation of a new security environment at Russia's western borders did not have any direct consequences for the security interests of the states in Central Asia or the Transcaucasus. Russia had apparently underestimated the extent to which the CIS members would be able to dissociate their own security perspective from that of Russia. Most CIS leaders, through their opposition to Russia, were eager to enhance their prestige on both the international and the domestic scenes. This lack of Russian leadership does not mean, however, that the governments of Central Asia and the Transcaucasus could follow the example of the Baltic states and break away from the CIS. They have to recognize that their independence of Russia consists primarily in finding the most appropriate form of dependence.[18] Georgia and Azerbaijan, which, in the first few years after independence, attempted to free themselves from all Russian influence, lost substantial parts of their territory to secessionist forces. This was partly due to the interference of the Russian military. They then had to acknowledge that their integration into the CIS and their acceptance of Russia as principal mediator were preconditions for recovering their territorial integrity. In this respect, the CIS did not have any alternative.

In the opinion of most of its member states, the CIS should remain a regional organization, not a supranational authority or a hierarchy of powers which would give Russia a decisive role in modelling their futures. It should constitute a channel of communication with Russia and the other former fellow-republics of the Soviet Union, enabling both bilateral and multilateral negotiations to take place. As an institutional form given to a provisional arrangement with Moscow, the CIS may provide them with a political forum in which to discuss issues linked either to their internal sovereignty – Georgia pressurizing Russia, for instance, to take a harder stand against Abkhazia – or to their external sovereignty – military or economic co-operation first and foremost with Russia.

The CIS is seen by most of its members as a provisional form of integration. Its transitory nature and its failure to create a scheme whose benefits are perceived to be higher than its costs were clearly expressed by most CIS leaders – except for the countries poor in resources, Belarus and Kyrgyzstan – at a CIS meeting in March 1997. Asked, on his arrival in Moscow for this CIS summit, what would happen if the CIS ceased to exist, Georgian president Eduard Shevardnadze answered that nothing would happen, as the CIS could in any case show no positive results.[19] The proposed Concept of Integrationist Economic Development was assessed by Georgia as contravening its national legislation and international commitments. The setting up of a customs union within the framework of the CIS would preclude Georgia's membership of the World Trade Organization. The Turkmen president Saparmurat Niyazov also came out against any form of supranationalism in the CIS. Uzbek president Islam Karimov asserted that his country would 'never agree to build supra-state structures on economic ties'. The CIS was just 'a commonwealth, and one must not demand anything more from it'. Kazak leader Nursultan Nazarbaev stressed during a press interview on the eve of the summit that two levels of integration should be distinguished: at the 'global level', Kazakstan had close relations with Russia, but on the 'regional level' co-operation outside the CIS with Uzbekistan and Kyrgyzstan should be regarded as more effective.

The Failure of the Caucasian Home and of the Black Sea–Baltic Union

The assessment that integration may be more effective on the regional level than on the more global level of the CIS is problematic, to say the least. The material on the Caucasus, Central Asia, Ukraine and Russia collected for this book confirms that unifying projects like the Commonwealth of Independent States, the Caucasian Home and the Black Sea–Baltic Union, like all other institutional co-operative arrangements that have been modelled in the post-Soviet space, are commonly considered to have a positive content – the creation of political stability, the development of economic relations and communication links – or are even seen as expressions of 'an objective need', but all have failed utterly to create cohesive institutions whose efficiency may be compared to present-day regional experiences in Western Europe, South-East Asia or the Americas.

The authors of this book depict in detail how the national elites in the independent republics have conceived their regional policies. Hrant Avetisian, Rafig Aliev and Alexander Kukhianidze write of the difficulties of establishing nationhood and an integrated regional security community in and among the deeply divided multi-ethnic societies of the Caucasus. In this region, the sense of a regional community is not sufficiently developed for differences to be settled without going to war.[20] Yet a strong sense of regional identity does exist, and is expressed in the idea of a Caucasian home.

The concept of a 'cognitive region' is most appropriate in the context of the Caucasus[21] in order to analyse the strong mobilizing effect of the idea of a 'Caucasian home' in the twentieth century. The cognitive dimension of Caucasian regionalism should be seen as part of a political ideology, serving various political ends. In his historical analysis of the policies of the Ottoman empire in the Caucasus region at the beginning of this century, Hrant Avetisian examines the plan to unify the peoples of the Caucasus as an ideological tool of Pan-Turkism. The call for all the peoples of the region to join together as a single family, united in their opposition to Russia, is assessed as having been a divisive element in the attempt to settle the violent regional conflicts in the region, in so far as it was used to try to establish the hegemony of the Ottoman empire.

Rafig Aliev meanwhile analyses the different interests the idea of a Caucasian home may serve in the post-Soviet world. It may serve religious interests, being associated with the religious unity of the Muslim peoples of the region. It may also serve state interests or those of particular political groupings. The Assembly of Mountain Peoples of the Caucasus (AGNK), created in 1989 – later to become the Confederation of Mountain Peoples of the Caucasus (KGNK), and still later the Confederation of Peoples of the Caucasus (KNK) – was a concrete expression of the political interests of smaller ethnic groups and nations of the Northern Caucasus, aiming to unite them but failing to represent all the groups. The leading role of Chechen politicians, who strove to extend the influence of their republic over the whole of the Caucasus, before the outbreak of open war with Russia in December 1994, was another expression of the contradiction between the unifying idea of a Caucasian home and particular political interests.

The idea of a 'Caucasian home' may also serve economic interests, as a tool for co-operation between states which cannot live in isolation from one other. This idea, sometimes known in Western literature as 'soft regionalism', refers to a situation in which the often informal processes of social interaction, and of trade and investment, flow between the different units of a region, and are the driving forces behind a regional integration process in which state policies retain their decisive power to influence economic events.[22]

The concept of a Caucasian home does not necessarily exclude Russia. At their meeting in Kislovodsk on 3 June 1996, the presidents of Russia, Armenia, Azerbaijan and Georgia officially endorsed this concept. From the perspective of the four Caucasian governments, the Caucasian home should be based on a comprehensive settlement of the ongoing conflicts and on the formation of a common economic area. The four heads of state declared their full support for the Russian President in achieving a definitive settlement in Chechnya.

Some of the factors which explain the failure of Caucasian integration projects are also described by Sergei Vlasov in his analysis of the failure of the Ukrainian plan to create a Black Sea–Baltic Union. The main aim of this project – to counterbalance Russian influence through a tripartite model of European security – did not conform to the views prevailing in 1992 among the other possible participants, who regarded the bipolar Russia–NATO framework as more appropriate for their own foreign policy. Some critics even depicted this form of regional integration as the creation of an arc of instability, squeezed between NATO and Russia. As is the case with all plans for Caucasian integration, the Ukrainian proposal for a Black Sea–Baltic Union has been criticized as an attempt to establish Ukraine's leadership in the region. Nor would it offer a solution to the minority and territorial issues that divide the region.

The Russian Factor

The problems involved in the creation of 'imagined' national, regional or world communities are analysed in all chapters of this book as being closely linked to specific interpretations of state interests. Dmitri Trenin writes that Russia points out that it strictly observes the UN Charter, the CSCE Final Act and all the other documents that are considered to constitute the legal basis of peaceful relations in the world arena, rejecting all Western criticism in this respect. Both Russia and the West, when involved in ethnic conflicts in the post-Soviet space, appeal to the interests of the world community – an imaginary world community – in pursuing their *realpolitik* and in criticizing each other's mediating or peacekeeping efforts.

Cultural affinities do not necessarily lead to integration. No pan-Slav nationalism links Ukraine to Russia. Their mutual relations are primarily determined by state interests. Arkadi Moshes considers that Russia and Ukraine, the two main Union republics in the Soviet Union, have been unable to constitute a stabilizing factor throughout the whole post-Soviet space, due to the Ukrainian fear of Russian imperialist ambitions and an escalation of sharply-worded accusations from both sides. The nation-building process in Ukraine is threatened from both inside and outside by the Russian factor. From the inside, there is serious potential for destabilization and even secession in Crimea and in the eastern and southern regions of Ukraine with their ethnic Russian and Russian-speaking majorities. From the outside, Ukraine perceives the Commonwealth of Independent States (CIS) as a potentially dangerous Russian tool for limiting Ukraine's sovereignty.

The growing distance between Central Asia and Russia may be explained by both economic and political factors. The Central Asian governments fear that too close a relationship with Russia may lead to a reproduction of the centre–periphery relations characteristic of former Soviet times. For Alexei Malashenko, the opposition between their civilizational allegiances is, however, even more important in explaining the reorientation of Central Asia. He refers to Huntington's analysis, but avoids using the term 'clash of civilizations' to describe future relations between Russia and Central Asia. The formula 'estrangement of civilizations' would be more appropriate to express his idea that Russia and Central Asia share some common economic and political interests, but that deep differences exist in their perceptions of their civilizational identity and of their cultural environment, making it impossible for both parts of Eurasia to be reunited.

All republics in Russia's Near Abroad understand independence as, first and foremost, independence from Russia. Georgia's and Ukraine's conceptions of external sovereignty are the best examples of the fear of a Russian hegemon. The complete failure to set up supranational institutions in the post-Soviet space may easily be explained, therefore, by the perception of Russia's participation in such an attempt as a threat to their national sovereignty. Many unifying projects proposed by Moscow have divisive consequences. The Russian factor does not, however, explain why other regional arrangements – for instance in the Transcaucasus, in Central Asia or those proposed by Ukraine – in which Russia does not take part, have not, in more than five years of independence, led to an integration process, and have only resulted in vague projects for effective co-operation. The fact that the governments in these two regions consider projects embracing the whole of the region popular and are constantly taking new co-operation initiatives (the Tajik incapacity to participate in regional co-operation initiatives and the Turkmen unwillingness to do so may count as the major exceptions) makes an explanation of this failure even more urgent. This book offers some keys to understanding.

Internal Sovereignty

One of the factors negatively influencing the creation of new institutional arrangements is the lack of internal sovereignty – the constitution of political and legal authority and legitimacy within a state – in the Newly Independent Republics. This seriously hinders the establishment of their authority in relation to other players in the international arena. Moldova, Azerbaijan, Georgia and Russia are confronted with secessionist movements, Tajikistan with a civil war, and Kazakstan and Ukraine with serious secessionist threats in which neighbouring states (not necessarily governments) are directly involved. Unlike in regionalist experiments in other parts of the world, governments in Eurasia perceive regional integration as a limitation on their external sovereignty and, due to their lack of internal sovereignty, they have great difficulty in putting forward far-reaching regional initiatives.

Alexander Kukhianidze's contribution to this book is illustrative in this respect. He highlights the impact of the conditions of the Armenian and Azeri minorities in Georgia on that country's foreign policies *vis-à-vis* Armenia and Azerbaijan. The lack of formal political status within the Soviet federal framework for the Azeri- and Armenian-populated districts in the east and south of Georgia – unlike Abkhazia, South Ossetia or Nagorno-Karabakh – may help to explain the absence of secessionist movements in these regions in the first few years after independence. The close links between these communities and their respective 'mother country' at the borders of Georgia also help to explain why the Georgian government has great difficulty in taking high-profile initiatives to contribute to Caucasian integration. Georgia has to be careful not be perceived as taking a partisan approach in its foreign policies on Armenia and Azerbaijan, so as to avoid being threatened by protest movements from its own minorities.

The Georgian political establishment has, however, far more political affinity with the Azeri than with the Armenian cause in the Nagorno-Karabakh conflict. The support of the Armenian population of Abkhazia for Abkhaz claims, and popular support in Armenia for the principle of self-determination, help to explain the tensions between Armenians and Georgians. Georgia favours close co-operation with Azerbaijan. It is claimed that a so-called axis between Baku, Tbilisi and Kyiv would solve energy transportation problems for those three countries independently of Russia. Both the limits and the risks involved in such a regional policy are explained in the chapter by Kukhianidze. A Georgian foreign policy that fails to keep the right balance between the two warring parties in the Nagorno-Karabakh conflict may jeopardize not only state relations between Georgia and Armenia, but also relations between Georgians and Armenians within Georgia itself.

The Western Factor

Several authors have pointed out that no 'Great Game' between Russia and any Western power is today being played out in Central Asia. The hyperbolic formula of a 'great game', expressing the romantic feelings of nineteenth-century writers, is not appropriate for describing present-day competition between various state or oil and gas company interests in the Caspian Sea region. Any comparison with Russian expansionism and Western imperialism in the nineteenth century also has to take into account the fact that, unlike in the past, the countries in Russia's Near Abroad have to be counted as sovereign players in the international arena.[23] Their foreign policies are aimed at strengthening their positions in their region by the attainment of a certain balance between Russian and Western interests. The failure of the CIS does not mean that it may be in the Western interest to marginalize Russia in its own Near Abroad. From the perspective of the powers which are involved in a competition for influence in the region, mutual exclusion is not realistic. This search for a balance of interests, both on the part of the smaller states in the region and by external regional powers, is very different from nineteenth-century imperialism.

The Russian government seems, however, to fear the consequences for its regionalist policies of its own lack of leadership and of the high expectations of Western policies shared by the CIS members. At the CIS meeting of March 1997, President Yeltsin criticized both Kazakstan and Uzbekistan when he said that CIS countries which were turning nearly all their industrial resources over to 'foreign' partners could not speak of co-operation with Russia.[24] Such a statement may be out of touch with economic reality, as it does not present an alternative to Western capital investment, but it is based on the realistic assessment that the expectation of economic co-operation with the West – coupled with co-operation in other fields – is radically altering relations between the CIS countries to Russia's disadvantage. The challenge to

Russia's declining hegemony does not come from regional or subregional arrangements between Central Asian or other CIS members that would like to exclude Russia – it comes from the Western ascendancy over Russia's Near Abroad.

Russian political leaders are not alone in their criticism of the high expectations of Western policies which exist in Central Asia and the Caucasus. Iran, which has made some unsuccessful attempts to influence policies in its former provinces in the Caucasus and Central Asia, has repeatedly criticized the pro-Western policies of its northern neighbours. On an official visit to Moscow in April 1997, the chair of the Iranian parliament, Ali Akbar Nateq-Noori, criticized the blossoming relations between Azerbaijan and the United States. Azerbaijani president Geidar Aliev's senior adviser, Vafa Guluzade, rejected these criticisms, stating that the pro-Western policy of Azerbaijan was the 'only possible and proper strategy'. Azerbaijan had been isolated from the West for two centuries and, according to Guluzade, this has harmed both his country and the Caucasus region as a whole.[25]

The Western factor, far more neglected in the academic literature on Eurasia than the Russian factor,[26] may constitute a further explanation of the relative failure of all existing regionalist experiments aimed at institutionalizing a co-operation framework. This thesis may at first sight appear to contradict the observation that Western policies generally favour regional co-operation projects. Since the birth of the new independent republics, the European Union has projected its own conception of regional integration on Eurasia, linking its technical assistance policies to an integrative regional approach. The Transcaucasus and Central Asia (including Mongolia) are seen as two regions which may gradually transform themselves into some kind of regional units. Co-operation with the already existing regional co-operation initiatives set up by neighbouring countries – such as, for instance, the Economic Co-operation Organization of which Iran and Turkey are members – is seen as a solution to the transport and other economic problems in the Transcaucasus.[27] The establishment of new communication links along the old Silk Road – for instance, the Transport Corridor Europe-Caucasus-Asia (TRACECA) – belongs to the same set of policies. The United States supports regional co-operation at a military level in Central Asia – for instance, the creation of a peacekeeping battalion with the participation of Uzbekistan, Kyrgyzstan and Kazakstan – but has failed to find a

balanced approach to the Transcaucasus. Its subsidies to Armenia
have exceeded its support for any other state in Russia's Near
Abroad, whereas the US Congress refused similar aid for
Azerbaijan. In contrast to the European Union, the United States
tries to marginalize Iran in its pipeline policies, but it follows an
overall integrationist line similar to that of the European Union.

Western integrative policies are far from sufficient to make
regionalism work. As with Russia's regionalist unifying policies,
intentions are at odds with consequences. In the following, I will
focus on the consequences for regionalism that follow from the
declining Russian hegemony and from the expectations in Central
Asia and the Transcaucasus of greater involvement by the West – or
even a leading Western role – in their regions. 'Globalization' and
'hegemony' are used as guiding concepts in this analysis.

The Consequences of Globalization for Regionalism in Eurasia

Since the cold war, the metaphor of 'globalization' has largely
dominated discussions on international relations. This points to
universal processes at work in the interconnections between states
and societies, the decreasing importance of territorial boundaries,
and the decreasing monopoly powers of the state. Unlike the
metaphor of regionalization, it stresses the predominance of
'rational' economics, of markets and capital investment over 'old-
fashioned' power politics, geopolitics, statists' views of integration
and the dynamics of state competition.[28] Globalism may work in
favour of or against regionalism.[29] Security, for instance – whether
narrowly or broadly defined – may be guaranteed both by regional
international institutions and by issue-specific ones that are not
regionally based. Economic development may favour regionalization, but the financial and productive forces that are the basis of
such development cut across those regions and are generally far too
powerful to be constrained by any regional arrangement. As
Western interests largely dominate these specialized institutions,
globalization processes tend to favour a 'Western' rather than a
specifically regional cohesion.[30] According to Wyatt-Walter, it is,
however, difficult to judge which metaphor – regionalization or
globalization – is more likely to be confirmed on a world scale by
empirical data.[31]

In Central Asia and the Caucasus, 'Western'-orientated
globalization processes are coming up against Moscow-centred

forms of regional integration. The contradictions between regionalist tendencies under Russian hegemony and globalization tendencies under Western hegemony are clearly illustrated by the difficulties Central Asian states have had in finding outlets in foreign markets by joining regional and international trade organizations. The discussions in Uzbekistan and Kyrgyzstan in 1995–96 on entering the Customs Union with Russia, Belarus and Kazakstan demonstrate their mutual economic dependence (favouring Russia's domination of the region), and the new challenges posed by international economic institutions dominated by Western interests. Russia seemed at first to be able to impose costs on those who refused to join the union, by increasing the customs duties on goods transiting its territory.[32] Central Asian countries take different options when faced with this problem. The Uzbek government managed to make the country less dependent on Russia for grain and energy, but it has not solved the problem of transport to world markets. As a 'double-locked' country, it needed to avoid paying high transit fees through Kazakstan, Russia and Ukraine. It hoped, nevertheless, that foreign investments would strengthen its economic sovereignty sufficiently for it to remain outside the Moscow-controlled union, thereby avoiding the high political costs that this would entail. Kyrgyzstan, needing the Russian market as an outlet for its substandard processed goods, having to export its mineral ores to international markets through Russia[33] and heavily indebted to Moscow, did not have this freedom of movement and entered the union. Only Turkmenistan, with the completion in 1996 of a railway connection through Iran to the Persian Gulf, and thanks to the construction of a gas pipeline with Iranian help, has found a partial solution to its transport problems.

These factors may explain the motives prompting the Kazak and the Kyrgyz to join – and the Turkmen and Uzbek governments not to join – the Customs Union, established in March 1996.[34] Kazakstan's membership of this Union was the main issue in the negotiations on the country's admission to membership of the World Trade Organization in 1997. WTO membership has the advantage of improving market access to the OECD and newly industrialized countries. The trade organization's emphasis on multilateral trade is not, however, consistent with the privileges that Customs Union members extend to each other's exports. Kazakstan was put under pressure to leave the Customs Union in order to have its application to the WTO accepted.

Shared Western Hegemony and Regionalism in Eurasia

The concept of 'hegemony' may be of more interest than that of globalization in analysing the factors which favour or impede regional integration. The notion of 'hegemony' is to be found in both Russian and Western academic literature on post-cold war Eurasia, being generally associated with the political force of the United States as the sole world power. In the following, this concept will be used to analyse the effects of declining Russian power and Western ascendancy – including the ascendancy of both European Union countries and the United States – over Russia and over Russia's Near Abroad. According to Trenin, the US and the European Union countries are increasingly pursuing their own political agendas, despite all their declarations on their shared civilizational values and democratic principles. Such differences between the strategic interests of the US and the EU in Central Asia and the Caucasus should not be neglected, but may be regarded as secondary in the pursuance, partly through international security organizations, of a shared Western hegemony of this part of the world. Unlike the vast majority of authors dealing with the problem of hegemony, I do not identify hegemony with a 'one-superpower world' or with the dominance of a single political authority or state.

In order to be considered a hegemon, a power needs to fulfil several conditions.[35] A hegemonic power should first be regarded as legitimate by its subordinate powers. Here, the concept of 'benevolent domination' may be used: this expresses the idea that the leadership of the dominant, hegemonic power is perpetuated by constructive behaviour and the acquiescence of the dominated members, and not exclusively by force or military might.[36] This meaning of hegemony is quite close to the Gramscian use of the term, according to which leadership is attained through the active consent of the subordinated.[37] Second, hegemony may be defined as a preponderance of resources. In the economic context, this means a preponderance of material resources and in the military context, a preponderance of military might. Third, in a more general context, a hegemon should be able to provide public goods, for example by providing collective security or monetary stability, or to compel the recipients of these benefits to contribute to them.[38] The function of hegemons in the international arena is reminiscent in this respect of the role of any government on the domestic scene. According to the theory of hegemonic stability,

> the hegemon plays a leading role in establishing an institutional environment which is favourable to its own interests (free trade, informal empire) but also accepts costs in being the mainstay of the system providing financial services, a source of capital, and a pattern of military support. According to this conception, the hegemon is the main beneficiary of the system but also the main provider of externalities to the other members: it receives disproportionate benefits but accepts disproportionate burdens.[39]

The hegemon ensures the provision of the public goods, in so far as it can capture the largest share of their benefits.[40] The hegemon is therefore more interested than others in providing these goods, even when this means that smaller and subordinated players may enjoy them largely for free. The hegemonic stability theory predicts that the absence of a hegemon will impede the procurement of those public goods.[41]

The material in this volume provides ample evidence of the fact that Russia's capacity to act as a hegemon in the Eurasian region is declining. First, its leading role, its regionalist policies and even its military presence are encountering severe opposition from the other CIS members. Unlike when central authority was exercised by the Soviet leadership, relations between the CIS members have to be based on freely-given consent. Uzbekistan and Azerbaijan have refused to acquiesce in the stationing of Russian border guards at the former Soviet borders. The Georgian president, Eduard Shevardnadze, claims that in 1993 he was forced to accept Russian military bases on Georgian territory in exchange for the withdrawal of Russian military support to secessionist and rebel forces. In this case, the concept of 'freely-given consent' refers to a lack of choice.

Secondly, Russia does not have sufficient preponderance in economic or even military power to establish its role as a hegemon. Its economic decline since independence, its falling trade figures with Central Asia and the Transcaucasus and its military defeat in Chechnya are sufficient to illustrate this point. Thirdly, Russia is at present unable to provide its CIS partners with the public goods they are requesting. Ghia Nodia describes how Western-dominated institutions such as the International Monetary Fund and the World Bank are supporting Georgia in its attempt to achieve monetary stability, a role that Russia is unable to perform. Russian peacekeeping forces stopped bloodshed in Transdniestria and South Ossetia, and enforced a provisional agreement on Transdniestria, but seemed generally unable to go beyond the freezing of conflicts, falling short of the kind of peace settlements requested by the other CIS members, in particular Georgia and Azerbaijan. At the CIS summit of March 1997, the Kazak President Nursultan Nazarbaev proposed to establish a CIS Committee on Conflict Situations. This committee, composed of the prime ministers and/or ministers for foreign affairs of all member states, would study the internal and international conflicts in the CIS and submit recommendations for their resolution to the Council of Heads of State. In making this proposal, Nazarbaev warned that failure in this effort 'would render the CIS irrelevant'. Moldovan president Petru Lucinschi, likewise describing conflict resolution as essential to the viability of the CIS, rejected the proposal that such a Committee should have the military function of leading CIS peacekeeping forces, as Russia had suggested.[42] These contradictory interests and expectations illustrate the difficulties inherent in pursuing an integration process in a situation where those with pretensions to leadership cannot count on acquiescence.

The material in this book attests to the fact that countries such as Georgia and Ukraine have expected greater involvement by Western countries since their independence. What Nodia describes as Georgia's search for a new patron after the collapse of the Soviet Union may very well be described as the search for a new hegemon. The authors of the various contributions also bear out that this expectation has not been met. Russia's hegemony is waning without being replaced by a Western hegemony over Eurasia. The West may count on acquiescence in its economic involvement and also – as demonstrated by Partnership for Peace – its military policies in the region. There are not such high expectations of other world or regional powers, such as Turkey, Iran, Japan or China. Western countries also have an absolute preponderance of economic and military resources over all the Eurasian countries, including Russia – this was described above as a second condition for the establishment of hegemonic relations.

In his introduction to this volume, Trenin considers that, as a consequence of its competition with the United States, Western Europe may in the future strive to incorporate Russia's economic potential, particularly its natural resources. This would lead to the subordination of Russia in the competition between the two main rival Western powers. Western institutions are actively involved in the procurement for the Eurasian countries of some public goods such as monetary stability or loans, but at present, however, they seem unable to provide the kind of public good that is required in order to settle the ethnic and regional conflicts that are now threatening the regional stability of Central Asia and the Transcaucasus. The discussions on NATO's eastward expansion and the still marginal interest of Central Asia and the Caucasus for Western security have not left much room for such an active form of involvement. NATO's support for the creation of peacekeeping battalions in Central Asia and – as proposed by Georgia in May 1997 – in the Black Sea region had deep symbolic meaning, but it fell short of creating military forces that might be sufficient to halt ethnic or regional conflicts or to enforce a peace settlement. The deployment of Western peacekeeping forces in co-operation with CIS troops, through the OSCE in Nagorno-Karabakh or through the UN in Abkhazia, still remains a remote possibility. Trenin stresses the great reluctance of these organizations to become involved in post-Soviet peacekeeping. Military co-operation policies as provided through Partnership for Peace are insufficiently developed for the Western hegemony over Russia's Near Abroad to be considered a reality at present.

Georgia's Aspiration to Western Hegemony

The chapters by Nodia and Coppieters deal with the problem of belonging to 'imagined' communities which transcend not only national but also regional boundaries. The authors write of the Georgian public's sense of belonging to the West, and of the Western European attitude towards an independent Georgia. Both chapters are concerned with the failed attempt by Georgia, a small republic at the periphery of the Soviet Union, to be recognized as part of the Western world. The Georgian intelligentsia identified civilization with European civilization before the Soviet invasion in 1921 and with Western civilization since the struggle for national independence. To Georgians, the West is first and foremost a historical and cultural category. The Georgian view of the West may also be likened to a mental map where the lines express the hope of an historical alternative to Georgia's geographical location.[43] Georgia's tragic fate has been seen as a consequence of its geographical location, as it is surrounded by former empires that have suppressed Georgia's independence or by alien civilizations that are still threatening Georgia's European and Western identity.

This subjective conception of the West is far removed from the 'Western West', from the Western perception of the boundaries of its own sphere of interest. Both the US and Western European governments consider security issues in Georgia as peripheral, and dealt with the civil wars and ethnic conflicts in Georgia in the period 1991–93 almost with indifference, despite the threat of having Georgia completely dismembered. Benevolence is a positive form of indifference, which was exemplified by humanitarian aid to the Georgian population and by diplomatic support for the position of Georgia in its negotiations with the governments of Sukhumi and Tskhinvali. Both forms of support for Georgia are largely indifferent to the Georgians' own view of their national identity as being European and Western.

The Western European governments' awareness of their own Western and European identity is far more differentiated than the Georgian map of Europe and the West. This differentiation is objectively determined by the great variety of institutions which have European security as one of their objectives. According to the European Union, Georgia is situated at the outer periphery of Europe, in the borderland between Europe and Asia, and not in Europe proper, at least not in that part of the periphery of the European Union that may in the foreseeable future be integrated into the European Union. The Council of Europe has quite a different conception of Europe, in line with its own political objective of supporting the democratization process in Eastern Europe. For the Council of Europe, Georgia's and the two other Transcaucasian states' awareness of themselves as European states is a substantial element of their European identity.

The asymmetric relationship between Russia and the West, which has been accentuated since 1992, increases Georgia's pro-Western attitude, despite the profound disillusionment of Georgian public opinion and the Georgian elite at the lack of Western involvement in the Caucasus region during its civil and ethnic wars. The radical readjustment of Georgian foreign policies in autumn 1993, as expressed by Georgia's entry into the CIS and by its acceptance in principle of the stationing of Russian troops on its territory, has not led to a lessening of the hopes pinned on a pro-Western policy.

NATO's initiatives for a Partnership for Peace open to all 'able and willing' OSCE members put the Georgian attempts to be integrated into a Western security architecture into a new perspective, which would be helpful in counterbalancing Russia's influence. In this respect, Georgia's aim is very similar to that of the Central Asian governments when they agreed to co-operate militarily with the Atlantic Alliance in order to strengthen their positions in a Moscow-centred CIS.[44] The success of PfP as an institutional mechanism for military co-operation between countries with very different security perspectives and political traditions led in 1996 to a new NATO proposal. The foundation of a Euro-Atlantic Partnership Council (EAPC) in May 1997 aimed to enforce mutual political and military co-operation between PfP partners. Unlike PfP, in which co-operation was exclusively conceived of as being between NATO and NATO members on the one hand and individual OSCE members on the other, EAPC was to make mutual co-operation between non-NATO members possible.

Unlike in Western Europe, where the economic and political integration process went hand in hand with the build-up of NATO as a powerful security organization,[45] the CIS failed to complete the process of taking over the military forces of the former Soviet Union. It may be tempting for Western organizations to respond positively to the expectations of Western hegemony expressed by governments in Russia's Near Abroad. It remains to be seen if the strengthening of Western security organizations on Russia's southern flank and the aspirations of several Central Asian and Caucasian countries for greater Western involvement in their region will lead to an effective Western hegemony in Eurasia. It also remains to be seen whether such a presence could offer a new chance for the settlement of ethnic conflicts and enhance the efficiency of regionalist integration projects, or if it should be seen as a sign of Western 'imperial overstretch',[46] in which Western governments are following Russia's example by extending their imperial ambitions beyond the limits of their resources. A third possible scenario may be based on more prudent policies, in which the West would, as Trenin writes, acknowledge 'the stabilising potential of the CIS, especially in regions on its far periphery such as the Caucasus and Central Asia', but would simultaneously succeed in having Western hegemony accepted in the whole of the Former Soviet Union, Russia included. In all three scenarios, both

Russia's waning and the Western countries' rising power in Eurasia are taken for granted.

NOTES

1. Indonesia, Malaysia, the Philippines, Singapore and Thailand formed ASEAN in 1967.
2. Louise Fawcett, 'Regionalism in Historical Perspective', in Louise Fawcett and Andrew Hurrell (eds.), *Regionalism in World Politics. Regional Organization and International Order* (Oxford: Oxford University Press, 1995), p.14.
3. Louise Fawcett and Andrew Hurrell, 'Introduction', ibid., p.5.
4. Andrew Wyatt-Walter, 'Regionalism, Globalization, and World Economic Order', ibid., pp.74–121; Louise Fawcett, 'Regionalism in Historical Perspective', in ibid., pp.9–36.
5. See Ahmed Rashid, *The Resurgence of Central Asia. Islam or Nationalism?* (London and New Jersey: Oxford University Press and Zed Books, 1994), p.225.
6. M.S. Gorbachev, *Perestroika: New Thinking for Our Country and the World* (London: Collins, 1987).
7. Matthew Evangelista, 'Stalin's Revenge: Institutional Barriers to Internationalization in the Soviet Union', in Robert O. Keohane and Helen V. Milner, *Internationalization and Domestic Politics* (Cambridge: Cambridge University Press, 1996), p.165.
8. On the following see the conclusions of Michael Waller and Alexei Malashenko to Michael Waller, Bruno Coppieters and Alexei Malashenko, *Conflicting Loyalties and the State in Post-Soviet Russia and Eurasia* (London: Frank Cass, 1998).
9. See Alexei Zverev, 'Ethnic Conflicts in the Caucasus 1988–1994', in Bruno Coppieters (ed.), *Contested Borders in the Caucasus* (Brussels: VUB Press, 1996), pp.13–14.
10. On relations between Iran and the Muslim republics of the Soviet Union, see Seyed Kazem Sajjadpour, 'Iran, the Caucasus and Central Asia', in Ali Banuazizi and Myron Weiner, *The New Geopolitics of Central Asia and its Borderlands* (London and New York: I.B. Tauris, 1994), pp.197–215.
11. Paul Kolstoe, *Russians in the Former Soviet Republics* (London: Hurst, 1995), p.178.
12. Andrei Shoumikhin, 'Economics and Politics of Developing Caspian Oil Resources', *Perspectives on Central Asia*, Vol.1, No.8, (Nov. 1996), online on http://www.intr.net/cpss/casianw/novpers.html
13. Kolstoe, op. cit., pp.175–8.
14. Yuriy Kulchik, Andrey Fadin and Victor Sergeev, *Central Asia after the Empire* (London and Chicago, IL: Pluto Press, 1996), p.47.
15. Grigory Bondarevsky and Peter Ferdinand, 'Russian Foreign Policy and Central Asia', in: Peter Ferdinand (ed.), The New Central Asia and its Neighbours (London: Pinter Publishers, 1994), p.41.
16. Andrew Hurrell, 'Regionalism in Theoretical Perspective', in: Fawcett and Hurrell (eds.), op. cit., pp.52–3.
17. Bruno Coppieters, Werner Bauwens, Bruno De Cordier and Firouzeh Nahavandi, 'The Central Asian Region in a New International Environment', *NATO Review*, Vol.44, No.5, Sept. 1996, p.27.
18. Rajan Menon, 'In the Shadow of the Bear. Security in Post-Soviet Central Asia', *International Security*, Vol.20, No.1, p.174.
19. On the reactions of CIS leaders to the CIS summit in Moscow in March 1997 see *Monitor*, Vol.III, No.64 (1 April 1997) received by internet from Jamestown Foundation brdcastmx@jamestown.org
20. On stable peace as a characteristic for security communities according to Karl Deutsch, see Emmanuel Adler and Michael N. Barnett, 'Governing Anarchy: A Research Agenda for the Study of Security Communities', in: *Ethics & International Affairs* (1996), Vol.10, p.63.
21. On this concept of Emmanuel Adler see Hurrell, op. cit., p.41.
22. Ibid., p.39.
23. Roland Dannreuther, 'Creating New States in Central Asia', *Adelphi Paper 288*, IIIS, London, March 1994, p.5.

24. On the reactions of CIS leaders to the March 1997 CIS summit in Moscow see *Monitor*, Vol.III, No.64 (1 April 1997) received by internet from Jamestown Foundation brdcast@mx.jamestown.org
25. *Monitor*, Vol.III, No.74 (15 April 1997).
26. Martha Brill Olcott, *Central Asia's New States. Independence, Foreign Policy, and Regional Security* (Washington: United States Institute of Peace, 1996).
27. European Commission, Commission Communication, 'Towards a European Union Strategy for Relations with the Transcaucasian Republics', 1995.
28. Wyatt-Walter, op. cit., pp.74–5; Andrew Hurrell and Louise Fawcett, 'Conclusion: Regionalism and International Order?', in Fawcett and Hurrell, op. cit., p.324.
29. Hurrell, op. cit., pp.54–6.
30. Ibid., p.55.
31. Wyatt-Walter, op. cit., p.75.
32. On the detrimental impact of regional arrangements for outsiders, see Hurrell, op. cit., p.44.
33. *OMRI Daily Digest* I, No.38 (22 Feb. 1996); *Monitor*, Vol.2, No.9 (18 May 1996) received on internet by listserv isn (listserv@cc1.kuleuven.ac.be).
34. *OMRI Daily Digest I*, No.65 (1 April 1996).
35. The following list of criteria is deduced from Lea Brilmayer's study on the normative implications of American hegemony. Brilmayer does not list these criteria in a systematic form. Lea Brilmayer, *American Hegemony. Political Morality in a One-Superpower World* (New Haven, CT and London: Yale University Press, 1994).
36. Ibid., p.1.
37. Ibid., p.14.
38. Ibid., p.17.
39. Robert O. Keohane, *After Hegemony: Co-operation and Discord in the World Political Economy* (Princeton, NJ: Princeton University Press, 1984), p.31, quoted in Brilmayer, op. cit., p.18.
40. Brilmayer, p.115.
41. Brilmayer, pp.116–17.
42. *Monitor*, Vol.III, No.65 (2 April 1997) received online from Jamestown Foundation, brdcast@mx.jamestown.org
43. See Andrew Hurrell's analysis of regions as cognitive entities and mental maps, Andrew Hurrell, p.41.
44. Tajikistan has for obvious reasons not been participating in PfP. On Partnership for Peace with Central Asia see my chapter in Adrian Hyde-Price and Lisbeth Aggestam (eds.), *New Perspectives on Security and Identity in Europe* (London: Macmillan, forthcoming).
45. Fawcett, op. cit. , p.33.
46. On imperial overstretch as a cause for the decline of empires see Paul Kennedy, *The Rise and Fall of the Great Powers: Economic Change and Military Conflict from 1500 to 2000* (New York: Random House, 1987); Brilmayer, p.3.

Notes on Contributors

Bruno Coppieters is Lecturer in Political Philosophy and East European Politics at the Vrije Universiteit Brussel (Free University of Brussels).

Alexei Zverev is a Research Associate at the Vrije Universiteit Brussel. He lives in Moscow, and was administrative co-ordinator of the project on ethnic and regional conflicts in the Former Soviet Union from which the contributions to the present volume have been compiled.

Dmitri Trenin is Senior Research Associate at the Institute of Europe of the Russian Academy of Sciences, and Deputy Director of the Carnegie Moscow Centre.

Rafig Aliev is Director of the Irshad Centre of Islamic Studies and Deputy Director of the Institute of Oriental Studies at the Azerbaijan Academy of Sciences (Baku).

Hrant Avetisian is Professor of History at Yerevan State University and Director of the Institute of History at the Armenian Academy of Sciences.

Alexander Kukhianidze is Lecturer in Political Science at Tbilisi State University (Georgia).

Aleksei Malashenko is Head of the Islamic Studies Department at the Institute of Oriental Studies at the Russian Academy of Sciences (Moscow). He is Programme Associate at the Carnegie Moscow Centre.

Arkadi Moshes is a research associate at the Institute of Europe at the Russian Academy of Sciences (Moscow).

Ghia Nodia is Professor of Sociology at Tbilisi State University and Chairman of the Caucasian Institute for Peace, Democracy and Development (Tbilisi, Georgia).

Sergei Vlasov is Senior Researcher at the Institute of International Economics and International Relations at the Ukrainian National Academy of Sciences (Kyiv). He works as Head of the Situation Analysis and Information Committee of Ukraine's State Commission of Nationalities and Migration, and is a specialist in the Presidential Administration of Ukraine.

Index